Best Sermons 1

Best Sermons 1

James W. Cox, Editor

Kenneth M. Cox, Associate Editor

1817

Harper & Row, Publishers, San Francisco

Cambridge, Hagerstown, New York, Philadelphia, Washington
London, Mexico City, São Paulo, Singapore, Sydney

FIRST EDITION
Designed by David M. Hamamoto

Library of Congress Cataloging-in-Publication Data

Best sermons 1.

Includes indexes.
1. Sermons, American.   I. Cox, James William.   II. Cox, Kenneth Mitchell.   III. Title: Best sermons one.
BV4241.B42   1988   252   87-45696
ISBN 0-06-061611-3 .

---

88 89 90 91 92 HC 10 9 8 7 6 5 4 3 2 1

Contents

III. DOCTRINAL/THEOLOGICAL

IV. ETHICAL

V. PASTORAL

VI. DEVOTIONAL

Preface

In the last few years, preaching has been receiving an unusual, even surprising, amount of attention. Several major books on the art and craft of preaching, as well as numerous other related books, attest to that fact. Preachers seem to yearn to imbue their messages with genuine quality. At the same time, they want their sermons to be understood, believed, felt, and acted upon, because competition for the hearers' attention and commitment is keen and unrelenting. Sermons that honor Scripture, appeal to the imagination, touch the heart, and offer food for the mind are welcome everywhere.

This book is the fruit of an attempt to bring together some of the best efforts of contemporary preachers to articulate their messages for congregations. A remarkable variety is here—sermons from women and men; Protestant, Catholic, and Jew; seasoned pastor and student; professor; sermons preached in churches large and small and in university chapels.

These sermons should be useful for devotional reading, for study by seminarians and pastors, and for insight into what is being said from present-day pulpits. Twenty-eight of the sermons were commissioned by the editor from preachers of considerable visibility. In some instances, the authors were suggested by members of the board of contributing editors, though none of the authors recommended himself or herself. Twenty-four of the sermons emerged from a competition in which more than two thousand sermons from around the world were submitted. After all these sermons were read and evaluated, those receiving the highest scores were made anonymous and submitted to the panel of judges who made the final selections.

As with any competition of this nature, selecting the best of many fine entries is not easy. The evaluation of a sermon, whether that sermon is heard or read, is an inherently subjective undertaking, and certainly none of the judges could claim to have applied only objective standards. However, in the final round, each entry was evaluated by three judges, who were mindful of the most important criteria—originality, scriptural and/or Christian basis, relevance, clarity, and interest.

Judges for the contest were:

Walter J. Burghardt, S.J., *Theologian in Residence, Georgetown University*

James W. Cox, *Professor of Christian Preaching, Southern Baptist Theological Seminary*

David Allan Hubbard, *President and Professor of Old Testament, Fuller Theological Seminary*

John Killinger, *Senior Minister, First Congregational Church, Los Angeles, California*

James Earl Massey, *Dean of the Chapel and University Professor of Religion and Society, Tuskegee University*

Carolyn Weatherford, *Executive Director, Woman's Missionary Union, Southern Baptist Convention*

William H. Willimon, *Minister to the University and Professor of the Practice of Christian Ministry, Duke University*

Our thanks to the judges, who provided their talents and insights in helping choose the best sermons in this first annual competition. Moreover, our thanks especially to the many preachers who took the time to submit their work. We encourage all to renew your efforts and continue sending us your best sermons in the future.

JAMES W. COX
KENNETH M. COX

I. EVANGELISTIC

1. The Drawing Power of the Cross

Kenneth L. Chafin

"And I, if I be lifted up from the earth, will draw all men unto me."
This he said, signifying what death he should die.—John 12:32–33

WHEN I WAS a child growing up on a farm, one of my favorite toys was a magnet that came out of the magneto of a Model T Ford. Before cars had batteries, the magneto delivered the spark to the motor's cylinders. The way in which that magnet attracted different metals fascinated my small boy's mind.

Today I'm much more interested in persons who attract people than in metals that attract other metals, whether those persons are politicians, entertainers, writers, teachers, or preachers. They are called charismatic persons, and some of them have good character and some don't. What they all have in common is that they draw people.

The text for this sermon gives John's clue to what draws people to Jesus Christ, and it's a bit of a surprise. If the question "What draws people to Christ?" were asked of most Bible-study groups, the answers would mention different aspects of his life, his teachings, or his ministry. There is a good chance

Kenneth L. Chafin was born in Tahlequah, Oklahoma, in 1926. He was educated at the University of New Mexico and at Southwestern Baptist Theological Seminary, where he received his doctorate. After serving nearly thirteen years as pastor at South Main Baptist Church in Houston, Texas, Dr. Chafin currently is Carl Bates Professor of Christian Preaching at the Southern Baptist Theological Seminary in Louisville, Kentucky. He is the author of five books.

that no one would suggest "the cross." Yet John ties the draw-ing power of Christ directly to the manner of Christ's death.

Each year, during the season before Easter, I always try to read through all of the different accounts of Holy Week. I try to immerse myself in the mood and the movement and the events of that week. I never fail to be repulsed by the manipu-lation, petty religion, hatred, violence, conspiracy, and cruel-ty. I find myself asking again, "How could an event like this draw people?" The clues are found in John 12:23–33, which serve as the context of verse 32.

A New View of Life: Fulfillment Through Sacrifice

Part of the attractiveness of the cross is that through it Christ presents a completely new view of life: fulfillment through sacrifice. The announcement that "the hour is come" (v.23) must have excited the people and filled them with a vi-sion of the golden age toward which the Old Testament prophets pointed. But, like us, they tended to tie their nation-alistic and religious expectations together.

They must have been staggered at the very idea of glorifi-cation in terms of sacrifice. Yet Jesus' analogy of the grain of wheat is a reference to his own death (v.23). Just as the grain of wheat had to "die" in order to increase, so Christ must die to fulfill his mission. He made it clear that those who selfishly grasped life would ultimately lose it, and that it was only by surrendering one's life to God and to others that it was multi-plied. It may come as a surprise to people today that this con-cept was strange to those who heard Christ, but we need to remember that the Jews did not connect the passages in the prophets which dealt with the suffering servant to their messi-anic expectancy. Even the apostles were confused at the con-cept of fulfillment through suffering.

Even in our society, which has made best-sellers out of books like *Looking Out For Number One* and *Winning Through Intimidation*, this understanding of the cross is still strong medicine. In churches where a "health and wealth" message is preached as biblical faith, if the members were really to hear Christ's message they might reject it as being much too negative.

Yet in spite of all this, it is the invitation to "take up your cross and follow me" that makes the Christian religion most attractive. The call to sacrifice challenges the self-centered life that, even in the midst of our self-indulgence, we know is really empty. Those who work with people who try to find fulfillment in materialism know that what is found is a larger emptiness. There is something in "taking up a cross" that strikes a chord deep within our souls.

In one of my classes, a student said in his sermon, "If we preached the cross, it would empty our churches." I'm inclined to think that the opposite might be true. It is the loss of the call to sacrifice that lessens the attractiveness of the church. This is why so many young people are so vulnerable to the religious sects that prey upon their sense of guilt at having so much and giving so little. They have been provided with everything by churches that loved them, but which were not wise enough to see their need to be told that real life would come not from getting everything but from giving all.

Faith Sees Victory and Not Defeat

The cross draws us because it is the way in which Christ moved beyond all the tensions of his ministry to triumph. We should not judge the disciples' despair at the cross, for we look at the cross through the perspective of the empty tomb, through the reality of Resurrection. Ordinary vision would stand at the foot of the cross and say, "This is the end." Only the eyes of faith could take in that scene and say, "This is the beginning." But it helps us all to understand our natural tendency to draw back from sacrifice when we see what this text reveals of Christ's own inner conflict as he faced the cross.

The Gospel of John omits the account of Christ in the garden of Gethsemene, but records its tension here. The Bible often deals more honestly with Christ's inner conflict than we deal with our own doubts and fears. Verses 27–28 tell of Christ's thoughts when his soul began to be troubled. They were considered as both natural and real. This fact ought to rescue us from that false picture of the good Christian as one whose life has no doubts, no reluctance, or no inner conflicts.

Years ago I wrote a book entitled *Shaping a Successful Life*, and my publisher arranged a series of radio, television, and newspaper interviews in order to promote the book. One of the chapters dealt with what people should do with the "down" experiences and periods of their lives. I'm convinced that it's not a matter of "whether" troubles will come into a life, but of "when" and "in what form." To me, the clue to life is not whether or not troubles come, but how they are dealt with. To my great surprise, most of those who interviewed me wanted to discuss that chapter. They had a hard time reconciling the idea of success and any problems. One even said, "If there's going to be trouble, why should people follow Christ?"

It was as Christ saw the cross as the eternal purpose of God, and not as a miscarriage of justice, that a different picture of the cross emerged. When Christ realized that "for this cause came I unto this hour," then the cross became a mighty act of God's love and revelation and sacrifice. It was in this context that the sense of triumph developed.

What had been the symbol of death became the sign of new life. What had looked like humanity's worst mistake became God's greatest act. What seemed like Satan's triumph became God's eternal victory. What had looked like a tiny and narrow sect of Judaism became a worldwide religion with a message of hope for every human being. We are drawn to the cross because we see in it God's overruling sovereignty in our lives and in the world. The cross has become for us a symbol of triumph.

The Place Where We Meet God

First, the cross is attractive to us because God speaks to us through it. We sense in our inmost being that it was God who was there dying on the cross. Thus it becomes a place of revelation. We learn that at the core of the universe there is a God who is personal, moral, caring, and purposeful. The cross contends that we have not been abandoned in this vast universe.

It is also a place of sacrifice. The cross indicates that God takes our sins seriously. There is, even with all the different theories of atonement that our scholars have developed, a sense of mystery as to how this can be. Yet, in the midst of our inability to comprehend it all, we are comfortable with standing at the cross and saying with the early church, "Christ died for my sins."

It is also a word of hope to all who suffer. The cross shows how things will finally conclude with the Devil being judged. Thus, the cross is a constant reminder that there will come a day when love will overcome hate, truth will conquer the lie, and even life will destroy death.

Consequently, the cross draws us because in the depths of our being we sense that we were somehow involved. The Negro spiritual asks the question, "Were you there when they crucified my Lord?" and our hearts answer, "We were there." And as we stand at that place, we are laid bare with what amounts to a spiritual soul scan. Several years ago, because of some hearing and balance problems, my doctor thought that I might have a tumor in my inner ear. To test his theory, he subjected me to a series of brain scans. He assured me that "nothing could hide from the probing beams of the newer machines." Yet even as I submitted myself to the tests, I knew that years before when I stood at the cross I had been scanned in a much more powerful way. And this draws us.

At the cross, all the things that we call life are exposed for the sham that they are, and we are freed to dram of real life. While there is something in us that likes to hold on to our illusions, there is still the deep desire to know what is real and valuable and eternal. That is why the cross draws us.

We are drawn to the cross because we see operating there a power that has the potential for breaking our cycles of failure and rescuing us. In our self-centeredness we have sought freedom apart from God, and have found slavery instead. At the cross we glimpse the possibility of real freedom—spiritual freedom.

At the cross we see a love that has forgiveness written all over it. Although I have no training in the field of counseling, I have great admiration for those who do. Once, when I was having lunch with a psychologist friend, I asked if there was one thing he wished he could do for his clients that was not possible for him to do. To my surprise, he said without hesitating, "I wish I could say to them, 'Your sins are forgiven.' So many of the people whom I see could manage their problems so much easier if they could find forgiveness for their sins." At the cross people can stand and hear the words of forgiveness, and this continues to draw people to the cross.

One of the most-loved gospel songs over the years has been "The Old Rugged Cross." One of the stanzas contains the lines, "O that old rugged cross so despised by the world holds a wondrous attraction for me."

Does that cross attract you? It's the place where we learn the clue to real life. It's where we learn of life that is victorious. It's the place where we meet God and know love and forgiveness and hope that is eternal. It's the place where saving faith is born.

2. We Belong to God
David H. C. Read

Scripture: He came unto his own. . . ."—John 1:11
Readings: Genesis 1:27–31; 1 Corinthians 6:12–20; Luke 12:13–21

WHY ARE WE HERE? What brings together this mixed group of people at this time and in this place? There are so many things each of us could be doing: strolling in the park, puttering about at home, sampling the offerings on the TV screen, or just lying in bed smothered by *The News York Times.* So what brings us here? In this city and in this generation we can discount the cynical answers that used to be given—it's a sign of being a respectable citizen, your neighbors will look sideways at you if you're not a churchgoer. Today in New York there are other circles to move in if it's prestige and reputation you're after, and your neighbors (if you know who they are) don't give a damn whether you go to church or not.

For the most part, I believe, we are here because we belong, or want to belong, to a community that believes in God and tries to act on that belief. A living church stands for a *working* belief in God. After all, the polls tell us that just being an American citizen means belonging to a community that be-

---

David Haxton Carswell Read was born in 1910 in Cupar, Fife, Scotland. A Presbyterian, Dr. Read was educated at Daniel Stewart's College, the University of Edinburgh, the Universities of Montpellier, Strasbourg, Paris, and Marburg, and New College, Edinburgh. He has served as minister of Madison Avenue Presbyterian Church in New York since 1956. He has preached and lectured around the world, received numerous honorary doctorates, and is the author of more than two dozen books.

lieves in God. About 95 percent of Americans say they do.
That can mean almost anything, or nothing, and is hard to
square with the almost totally secularized society in which we
live. A working belief in God means, in the Christian and Jewish tradition, that God is a real factor in all we think and do,
that we seek a relationship with him that is as close and personal as that we have with our dearest friend. It means that in the
great circle of belonging—belonging to this nation, belonging
to a home, a circle of friends, a club, or a community—we
find, as our lodestar on this mysterious voyage through, that
the most powerful truth is that we belong to God. Such a conviction will inevitably alter the way we confront all the great
choices that come our way in life, and the ultimate question
mark of death.

Psychologists have said that the two most powerful instincts in human beings are for religion and sex. That may account for the fact that when religion loses its grip on society,
sex is apt to take over as the reigning god. Some days ago when
I was pondering this sermon, I turned on the TV at random. A
bad habit, you may say, but this time I was rewarded. There
was John Updike, the novelist, being interviewed about his latest book. When I came in he was being asked how he reconciled the strong religious themes in his novel with the candid
treatment of sex. His answer revealed that he saw no discrep-
ancy, and that for him, as a confessed Christian and churchgoer, the two great instincts are not necessarily at war but that
everything profoundly human is related to our deep sense of
belonging to God. On the spur of the moment he put the case
flippantly: "People go to church," he said, "because they want
to live forever. They go to bed because they want to feel what
it's like." As I let that remark sink in I felt I'd like to hear a
sermon by Mr. Updike enlarging on my theme this morning!
It's that working, all-inclusive sense of belonging to God that
should be the real reason for allying oneself with a community
that seeks above all else to love the Lord our God with heart
and mind and all we have, and our neighbor as ourselves.

"He came unto his own." These words are familiar to

churchgoers. They come from that perpetually stimulating, illuminating, and puzzling poem we know as the Prologue to the Gospel of St. John. I expect that if I asked one familiar with this phrase what was intended by the words "He came unto his own," the answer might be: "It means that Jesus was born a Jew," or that his message was directed to the Jewish people, or perhaps, as some modern versions actually translate, "He came to his own country." But the context of these words reveals that the author was not speaking about the historic Jesus: the climactic words—"The Word was made flesh and dwelt among us"—occur some verses later. He is speaking about the *Word*—which means God revealing himself to the human race, God communicating with his human family. He is speaking about God's call to the great human family that had wandered away from the Father's home. For him the Incarnation was the supreme act of God's parental love, but from the dawn of history to this very moment, God comes unto his own. Everyone—American, French, German, Russian, African, Chinese, prosperous or starving, cultivated or uncivilized, healthy or disabled, believer or unbeliever—belongs to him.

This is one basic belief that marks living church members off from all who, consciously or unconsciously, reject his claim; that marks off a church as a community that proposes another aim in life, another conviction about life's meaning (or lack of meaning) from those that seem to dominate the society in which we live. It is our business now to ponder the implications of such a working belief. "He came unto his own"—if you are now hearing the claim of the living God, if you are now among those who, in the words of the Prologue "receive him," then we are ready to explore "belonging to God" as a working belief.

The men and women of the Bible who as believers have left their mark on history, and those who impress and influence us today as examples of faith in action, draw one tremendous conclusion from the fact that we belong to God. For them it's not a theory lurking in the back of the mind: "Yes, of course, in the end he's the boss." For them it is a daily working belief: "Since I belong to God then *nothing*, not my worries, my pains, my fears, my sense of loneliness or depression, not the worst catastrophe that can happen to me, not death itself, can separate me from his love." The great images of the Bible come to life: He is our rock, our refuge and strength, our mighty fortress, our sure foundation. He is the ultimate Lord of all being and underneath us are his everlasting arms. Jesus descended into this hell of alienation from man and God that is our deepest fear, in the working belief that nothing could break the tie that bound him to that everlasting love. "Father, into thy hands I commend my spirit," were his last earthly words, and when he appeared again his disciples were given for all time their share in this assurance. They knew what he had meant when he said, "I give unto them eternal life; and they shall never perish, neither shall any man pluck them out of my hand. My Father who gave them to me, is greater than all, and no one is able to pluck them out of my Father's hand."

This working belief can be expressed very simply: to accept that we belong to God means that there is a point beyond which we cannot fall—the solid rock of an eternal love.

Belonging to God is, then, a belief that is lodged in the depth of the soul and begins to shape the direction of our lives. But there is more to ponder. We're not just talking of that mysterious self that we call the soul. We are not invisible angel spirits, but human beings clothed with bodies like the animals, solid, complicated bodies, from which we cannot escape, although we may rise beyond them in dreams and prayers. Yet it has become so difficult to persuade people that religion, this business of belonging to God, has to do with these bodies as well as our souls. The Bible has much more to say about the body than about the soul. A worshiping congregation is a marvelous assembly of bodies which cannot be transformed into some nebulous flotilla of invisible spirits. When I realize deep down that I belong to God, I should realize that this goes for my body, too. It's a gift from God which I hold in trust for him, and that has practical consequences as a working belief.

In the passage we heard from Paul's letter to the Corinthian church, he dealt with one aspect of our treatment of the body. Corinth was known for its total sexual license. It was one big 42nd Street. And Paul had discovered that some of the young Christians there were interpreting his gospel of the grace of God and freedom from the law to mean that, so long as their souls had been saved, they could do what they liked with their bodies. Hence his thunderous denunciation of the licentious bed-hoppers of Corinth. "What? Know ye not that your body is the temple of the Holy Ghost, which is in you, which ye have of God, *and ye are not your own?*"

Your body, he is saying, is not your own. It belongs to God, and you are responsible for it as a steward of God's gift. This has implications far beyond the point that Paul was making here. If we, including our bodies, belong to God, then we have a duty to respect those bodies. Without giving into the prevailing hypochondria, we owe these bodies of ours at least enough care to keep them in repair, as good stewards of this gift of God.

So when we talk about the Christian doctrine of stewardship, we mean much more than the use of our money. When people come to recognize that word, "stewardship," as an ecclesiastical code word for fundraising, they are tempted to switch off. Money and possessions do come into the picture, but only because they are such an integral part of the lives that belong to God. The basic belief is what Paul means when he simply said, "Ye are not your own." The power and glory of the Gospel—and the joy—lie not only in the assurance that, since we belong to God, we have a safety net through which we cannot fall; but also in the discovery that all we have—bodies, homes, talents, ambitions, bank accounts—we hold in trust for the God to whom they belong. When that becomes real belief, a new and satisfying power is at work in our lives.

"He came unto his own." What we really are: *his own*. This is the crucial decision in anyone's life: recognizing that we are "his own" and not "our own" to do what we like. That is what's meant by receiving him, this living, giving, loving God.

To as many as receive him, the One who became one of us in Jesus Christ, he gives the power to become the sons and daughters of God. To receive him means just saying, "Yes, Lord, I'm not my own. I belong to you. Take the *whole* of me."

Then it must become as clear as daylight that a community of Christians with this working belief will want to share this discovery with all our neighbors. Evangelism is for us not an attempt to brainwash others into becoming Presbyterians. It's the joyful invitation to all who are feeling lost or alone to share what Christ has given us. Rejoice with me! "He came unto his own," and "his own" are not the members of a holy club. "His own" includes the entire human family, but there are millions in our world who don't know it. Shouldn't we tell them—by what we say, what we do, and what we are?

> Lord, we are thine, help us to know it, to know
> it in the depth of our heart and to act
> accordingly, through Christ our Lord. Amen.

3. Washed

H. Stephen Shoemaker

Text: Revelation 7:9–17

IT SEEMS dreamlike, this vision, a vision of heaven's future given to John by the angel, a glimpse of "Joy, Joy beyond the walls of this world" (J. R. R. Tolkien). It was said of the great Scottish poet, Robert Burns, that he could not read this passage without tears coming to his eyes; and we can see why. It is wonderful.

I

John looked and saw a vision of heaven's final victory. He saw a great multitude, too many to number. That answers the question "Who are the few who shall be saved?" That few is a multitude too large for the human mind to count. God's love is redeeming, far more than our human hearts can even imagine. If that is not good news to you, you have not heard the good news.

And the multitude is not only large, it is also diverse. From

H. Stephen Shoemaker was born in Statesville, North Carolina, in 1948. He was educated at Stetson University, Union Theological Seminary in New York, and the Southern Baptist Theological Seminary, where he received his doctorate. Dr. Shoemaker is pastor of Crescent Hill Baptist Church in Louisville, Kentucky. He has written two books, *Re-telling the Biblical Story: The Theology & Practice of Narrative Preaching*, and *The Jekyll & Hyde Syndrome: A New Encounter with the Seven Deadly Sins*.

every nation, race, tribe, class, and tongue. There is no homogenized heaven. There will be more different kinds of folk than you would ever expect to meet. People from every corner of human life, from every school of theology, and some with no theology you could ever pass on or put in a book. If that is not good news, you have not heard the good news.

And what were they wearing? Clean, fresh, white robes. And what are they doing? Standing before the Lamb, the Lamb that taketh away the sins of the world, the Lamb slain for our sins, the one who bore our sins and bore them away. They are standing before the Lamb, and they are waving palm branches and singing,

> Salvation belongs to our God
> who sits upon the throne and
> to the Lamb.

And their songs are answered by the songs of heaven's perpetual choir singing:

> Amen! Blessing and glory and wisdom
> and thanksgiving and honor and power
> and might be to our God for ever and
> ever! Amen.

George Frideric Handel, one of the multitude in white robes, smiles and nods approval. It was pretty close to what he's written. He had heard it right.

There is joy all right, joy beyond the walls of this world, joy we on earth can only sense here and there, now and then. It is pure delight in the presence of God and his Son. If that is not good news to you, you have not glimpsed the good news.

II

Then one of the elders of heaven came to John and said, "Who are these clothed in white robes and where have they come from?" John answered as I would have: "Sir, you tell *me!*" And he said, "These are they who have come out of the great tribulation." No, that's not quite right. What he said literally was, "These are they who *are coming* out of the great tribulation."

And we look again at the people and blink and rub our eyes, for now they are changed. Disturbingly so. They no longer are wearing white robes, but are wearing earth's garb, the clothing they wore while coming through the tribulation of this life.

There's Peter crucified upside down on a Roman cross; there's Joan of Arc hearing heaven's voices, burned at the stake as a witch; there's Bonhoeffer about to die in Hitler's prison writing prayers, singing psalms; there's Sojourner Truth, black woman converted and called by Christ in Civil War times to fight for the freedom of blacks and the rights of women; there's Abraham who hung onto faith through years of unfulfilled promises and through those moments of terror as he led his son up that hill to an unthinkable death; there's Ruth, who lived out steadfast love in her mother-in-law's country and taught the Jews what their God was like; there's Luther hurling inkpots at devils, searching for faith, standing on God's word and splitting a church he was trying to purify; there's Martin Luther King, Jr., announcing God's dream that God's people were not ready for, unveiling the violence of our ways, and dying at the hands of that exposed and terrified violence.

There they are, they, and uncountable more, who have come through the tribulation. But not only them do we spy. We look more closely, and we begin to see our own faces among those who are coming through the tribulation.

There's the man who has chosen to be honest in his business and whose business has floundered. There's a woman who has had an abortion and is haunted by her decision. She did the best she knew to do, faced with tragic alternatives, but she can't shake the feeling of guilt, sorrow, or remorse. There's the widow left to walk on through life alone, her husband snatched from this life. There's the man giving every ounce of his energy to the cause of peace and watching the world ignore God's word and hurtle itself toward a fiery Armageddon. There's the sexually abused woman-child, violated, feeling stained by misshapen love, struggling with unnecessary guilt—what could I, should I, have done to stop it? And there's the man who has lost his integrity, bit by bit; he has seen it run through his fingers like water. And now he wonders who in God's name he is, and yearns to find himself again.

There they are, we are, the multitude of those who so want to love and serve God, who have been at times bested by life's demands, but who, yearning to be God's children, have never quit the faith.

We blink and rub our eyes, for what we see is not the final white-robed glory, but the terrible bloodied path of life's tribulation. And what we see on their faces is not unmixed joy, but fear and doubt and discouragement, guilt, and remorse.

How can any of us come through the tribulation?, we ask. And then the voice says, "They have washed their robes and made them white in the blood of the Lamb."

"Are you washed in the blood of the Lamb?" It is a question we Crescent Hill folk would more likely see scrawled on the side of a barn along some back road than printed in the worship service bulletin. It seems so gory, so literal, so low-class, so what-we-once-were-and-never-have-to-be-again-thank God. "Red neck, white socks, and Blue Ribbon beer" and "Are you washed in the blood of the Lamb?" To be sure, somewhere along the line the music of those "blood hymns" became a parody of itself, and we feel more comfortable singing, "When I Survey the Wondrous Cross" or "O Sacred Head Now Wounded."

But we dare not trade in biblical metaphors for psychological ones: unconditional positive regard cannot replace the blood of the Lamb. When you are going through life's tribulation, "I'm O.K., You're O.K." will not get you through to the other side.

The blood of the Lamb is our human poetry pointing to the ineffable self-emptying love of God acted out on the cross.

It points to the truth of grace: what we cannot do for our-selves, God has done for us. Jesus Christ bore our sins and bore them away. He was broken on a cross, and from his breaking at our hands has come our healing. We cannot wash away the stain of our sins, nor can we rid the world of its tired and terrible sins, but he is the Lamb which taketh away the sins of the world. You may think you don't need that, but the world is filled with tragic victims of the truth: if you don't ac-cept the atonement, you are doomed to repeat it. We all, dying of Adam's blood, are cleansed by the only truly finally cleans-ing flood, the blood of the Lamb that taketh away the sins of the world.

You see, the cross if far more than the *revealing* of the love of God. On the cross, somehow, some way, Christ bore my sins, took my place, died for me.

Those who have made it through life's tribulation know why they made it, why their robes are white. So they are not ashamed to sing these words to us:

> Have you been to Jesus for the cleansing
> power? Are you washed in the blood of the
> Lamb?
> Are you finally trusting in his grace this hour?
> Are you washed in the blood of the Lamb?
> When the Bridegroom cometh will your robes
> be white? Are you washed in the blood of the
> Lamb?
> Will your soul be ready for the mansions
> bright? And be washed in the blood of the
> Lamb?
> Lay aside the garments that are stained in sin,
> and be washed in the blood of the Lamb.
> There's a fountain flowing for the soul
> unclean, O be washed in the blood of the
> Lamb.

Will you make it through life's tribulation? The word *tribu-lation* means literally a *grinding*. What happens in the grinding of life is a testing; it is no less than the revealing of the sons and daughters of God, as the wheat is separated from the chaff.

Those who are given white robes are those who no longer trust in themselves for their salvation, for their wholeness, for their victory, but rather in Jesus Christ. They have undergone persecution in the name of Christ and for the sake of his way of love. Somehow they have kept the faith.

That word *persecution* may seem oddly out of place in our easy American existence, but the testing of persecution always surrounds the church. It only changes faces. In bad times the followers of Christ are persecuted by the enemies of Christ. In good times the followers of Christ are persecuted, tested, by those who would call themselves his friends. In bad times the tests are big and dramatic; in good times the tests are small and subtle. In bad times we are tempted to renounce Christ's name. In good times we are allowed to keep Christ's name, but we are tempted to betray his way, in neglect of the poor, in dishonesty, in personal cruelty, and a hundred other ways. The tribulation's grinding never stops.

How can any of us make it? Who can get to heaven with robes clean and white? None of us! We are they who have washed our robes in the blood of the Lamb?

Scrawled on the inner walls of one of the Nazi concentration camps was a prayer. The unknown author prayed it while washing his or her robe in the blood of the Lamb.

> O Lord, when I shall come with glory in your
> kingdom, do not remember only the men of
> good will; remember also the men of evil. May
> they be remembered not only for their acts of
> cruelty in this camp, the evil they have done to
> us prisoners, but balance against their cruelty
> the fruits we have reaped under the stress and
> in the pain; the comradeship, the courage, the
> greatness of heart, the humility and patience
> which have been born in us and become part of
> our lives, because we have suffered at their
> hands.

> May the memory of us not be a nightmare to
> them when they stand in judgment. May all
> that we have suffered be acceptable to you as a
> ransom for them.

And then the prayer concluded, "Unless a grain of what falls into the ground and die. . . ."[1] Whoever that was who wrote that had seen the vision of the Lamb.

Conclusion

Flannery O'Connor wrote a short story inspired by this text from Revelation. The main character, Mrs. Turpin, goes into a doctor's office and finds herself thrust into the company of people she despises. Mrs. Turpin is a good, respectable Christian woman and she silently thanks Jesus that he didn't make her like the other people in the room, in her words, "white trash" or "nigger" or "lunatic" or "ugly." Her prayers are silent, but her attitude comes out clearly in her conversation. Suddenly, the ugly young woman across the room attacks her and calls her a warthog from hell. Mrs. Turpin feels the words driven into her heart; they tear into her as a conviction of the Spirit. She goes out into her backyard, and as she gazes into the pigpen, she sees a vision. From the ground a brilliant, swinging, fiery bridge is raised from earth to heaven and along that bridge "a vast horde of souls were rumbling toward heaven":

> There were whole companies of white-trash,
> clean for the first time in their lives, and bands
> of black niggers in white robes, and battalions
> of freaks and lunatics shouting and clapping
> and leaping like frogs. And bringing up the end
> of the procession was a tribe of people whom
> she recognized at once as those who, like
> herself . . . had always had a little of everything
> and the God-given wit to use it right. She
> leaned forward to observe them closer. They

were marching behind the others with great
dignity, accountable as they had always been
for good order and common sense and respectable behavior. They alone were on key. Yet she
could see by their shocked and altered faces
that even their virtues were being burned
away.[2]

Mrs. Turpin had been given vision as had John on the Isle
of Patmos. And so have we.

We blink and look and the vision is again changed. All
those people battered and bruised, wearing the bloodied garments of life's tribulation, guilt-ridden, discouraged, uncertain; there they are wearing white robes, fresh-scrubbed in the
blood of the Lamb, smelling clean with the rays of eternal sun-
shine; there they are singing and shouting hallelujah.

And we look at them and see our own "shocked and altered faces," for we, too, have been invited to the heavenly
banquet. Hear the invitation: You who are coming through
the tribulation, who trust in the Lord and love him, the white
robes are ready for you; come, come, put them on, there's one
made just for you. Christ is holding it for you now; put down
what's in your hands, put one arm in and then the other.
That's right. Don't you look good!

NOTES

1. Cited in James W. Fowler, *Becoming Adult, Becoming Christian* (San
Francisco: Harper & Row, 1984), pp. 121–2.

2. Flannery O'Connor, "Revelation," *The Complete Stories* (New
York: Farrar, Straus and Giroux, 1982), p. 509.

4. Something for the Yuppies to Consider

C. Neil Strait

Scripture: Matthew 4:18–20

TWO WORDS become the focus of our thoughts: "Follow me." Jesus, walking by the sea of Galilee, saw some fishermen. He said to them, "Follow me." They did . . . and their lives were changed.

These are not spectacular words. If we were phrasing an invitation, we would want it to be more appealing, more Madison Avenueish, more flamboyant. But Jesus spoke words to a cluster of fishermen. They followed, and their lives were changed.

These are not good recruiting words. Certainly a person could not get people to follow him with a simple invitation like this. It is too bland, has little promise, does not have the ring of excitement to it. But Jesus spoke these words to a group of fishermen. They left their nets, followed Jesus, and their lives were changed.

These are not challenging words. Just "follow me"? These words did not tell where he was going, nor what the followers would do after they arrived. The words raise questions, but

C. Neil Strait was born in New Lexington, Ohio, in 1934. He has received degrees from Olivet Nazarene University and the Nazarene Theological Seminary, and, following several pastorates, currently serves as district superintendent, Michigan District, Church of the Nazarene. He is the author of several books.

give no answers. If we are going to give our lives, do we not want to know what the bottom line is? Sure we do. But Jesus gave this invitation to some fishermen. They obeyed, and their lives were changed.

For some of us, somewhere, someone, or something has called to our life. Maybe it was spectacular, challenging, appealing. And we have followed! All out, totally, with deep resolve. Today, we are on a journey. But, in our honest moments, the secret sorting-out times, we know it has not changed us, made us better, given life meaning. It has not led us anywhere and we are still at square one. The void, the vacancy, the directionlessness has traveled with us.

Others of us have heard his call: "Follow me." Those simple words invited us to a journey, and today we are on a pilgrimage with Jesus. We know who our leader is, we know where we're headed, and we know who is taking care of us along the way. We are being changed, daily, and life has a richness about it that can only be explained by grace and truth. We are feeling the challenge of mission, of service and life in the arena of faith. We followed him, and life has never been the same.

Some are still waiting, analyzing the voices, the invitations. They are still trying to decide which one to follow. They try to justify the waiting and indecision by their attempts to sort things out. But the consequences are loaded and the uncertainty is risky. Too many, as all of us know, have been caught in the waiting patterns of life. Because you do not follow him—or anyone—life is not going anywhere. Oh, there are activities, places, and people. But when the door closes and you have to contemplate your thoughts alone, the void looms large, and you realize that square one has become home base.

The Jesus of the New Testament, the man of Galilee, the Savior of the cross, issues his invitation—"Follow me"—for just such people hung up on ground zero. The problem is, too many times his invitation is discounted without fair analysis and disregarded without just consideration. What is behind the invitation . . . or who is behind it? Where does he lead us?

Just what is the bottom line? All of these are good questions. What are some answers?

I. Jesus Is the Only One Who Can Call to Life with Authority to Be Its Leader

His very walk along the seaside has been endorsed in heaven by his Father, who sent him to be among us to liberate us and make us whole. His first words in the synagogue underline this: "The Spirit of the Lord is upon me; therefore he has anointed me to preach good news to the poor. He has sent me to proclaim freedom for the prisoners and recovery of sight for the blind, to release the oppressed, to proclaim the year of the Lord's favor" (Luke 4:18–19 NIV).

Throughout the New Testament, there is the recurring theme of God's love for his creation. Jesus characterizes his mission with these words: "For the Son of Man came to seek and to save what was lost" (Luke 19:10).

Let's look at this thought more closely. Jesus is the only one who can call to life with authority to be life's leader. What does all this mean?

First, many qualify to be leaders, but they would not be servants. Jesus is both leader and servant. The New Testament writer, Paul, spelled out this servant's role in this manner:

> Your attitude should be the same as that of
> Christ Jesus: Who being in very nature God,
> did not consider equality with God something
> to be grasped, but made himself nothing,
> taking the very nature of a servant. . . .
>
> (Phil. 2:5–6a)

Others are qualified to be leaders and may be even a bit servantlike, but could never be saviors. Jesus is leader, servant, and savior. Paul declares this fact in these words: "You see, at just the right time, when we were still powerless, Christ died for the ungodly. Very rarely will anyone die for a righteous man, though for a good man someone might possibly dare to die. But God demonstrates his own love for us in this: while we were still sinners, Christ died for us" (Rom. 5:6–8).

Anyone else would, somewhere along the line, insist on being a master and making you the slave. The big difference with Jesus is that while he is master, he is a master with a servant's heart and a master with love as his motive, and he makes us his own! When you sort out the meaning of all this, then you know why he is the only one with authority to invite life to follow him.

Consider this a bit further. Jesus has authority to give life something better because he is the Creator. He who has made us knows what life needs in the heart to be at peace. Famous Amos, of chocolate-chip-cookie fame, said, "Life is an inside job." He is right. And no one is so qualified to give life what it really needs as Jesus. Others who put forth their ideas and their promises must, somewhere in the process, control life in order to change. Our world has witnessed this in the Jim Joneses and the self-proclaimed messiahs. Their claims and calamities clutter the pages of history. C. S. Lewis said somewhere that "Because man is fallen he needs an authority to lift him to the right." I submit both from the testimony of the Word and from the samplings of contemporary man's pilgrimage in darkness, that Jesus is the only authority that speaks to life with an answer. Thus, he says to all of us, "Follow me."

II. Jesus Is the Only Leader Who Can Be Light (Hope and Assurance) When It Is Dark

Jesus said, "I have come into the world as a light, so that no one who believes in me should stay in darkness" (John 12:46). Elsewhere he said, "I am the light of the world. Whoever follows me will never walk in darkness, but will have the light of life" (John 8:12).

The question is not so much whether this is true, as it is "Is there anyone else, or anything else, who makes this claim and has backed it up?" The darkness and disappointments from a thousand roads traveled give testimony that a lot of ways do not give light, or hope, or help. A self-professed yuppie said to his mother, "I know all the dead-end streets. What I am looking for is one road that leads somewhere."

The "light" of which Jesus speaks is not a physical light. It is the light of truth, of love, of guidance; the light of hope, assurance, meaning. It is the light which all seek, but which no one finds until he follows Jesus and finds it in him. There is a chorus that contains this truth: "Find it in Him, Find it in Him, Lose everything, just to find it in Him."

All of us walk, sooner or later, along the avenues of life where the "lights go out." Tragedy comes uninvited, and suddenly. Sorry invades. Failure comes. Relationships crumble. Bad news enters the picture. Despair and disappointment hang their drapes of darkness. Who speaks to life in these moments with the words that ignite hope and give promise? Who takes the ugly threads of ruin and begins weaving meaning back into life? Who comes in the midst of darkness and shares light? No one but Jesus. I like the little girl who asked the question, "What was God doing last night during the storm?" Then she answered her own question by saying, "Oh, I know, he was making the morning!"

Do you know anyone else who makes mornings? Who gives hope? Who is there when the lights go out? Do you know anything equal to the light and truth and hope that Jesus gives? The Christian who has heard the invitation, "Follow me," and has obeyed the invitation, believes the words of an old hymn:

> When I am burdened, or weary and sad,
> Jesus is all I need.
> Never He fails to uplift and make glad.
> Jesus is all I need.

So I submit that Jesus is the only one who can give light in the midst of darkness.

III. *Jesus Is the Only Leader Who Commits Himself to Us for the Entire Journey*

Listen to his promises. "And surely I will be with you always, to the very end of the age" (Matt. 28:20). Again, "Never will I leave you; never will I forsake you" (Heb. 13:5). Do you know anyone who will make a promise like this, and keep it?

Jesus left the event and the memory of a cross to prove his commitment. Those who leave a cross as a symbol of their commitment are good candidates for integrity and dependability. Do you know any crosses that underscore such promise and commitment?

I read of a cult group that awakened one morning to find its leader gone. Where did he go? Why did he leave? What made him leave? Would he return? Such questions never need to be asked of Jesus. He will never leave us, so the questions stop right there.

Here, then, are three reasons to consider Jesus. Consider him against the backdrop of your experiences, your dead ends, your disappointments and failed promises.

There comes a time in the lives of us all when we need to assess life, look at its priorities, view where it is going, and evaluate its meaning.

Jesus still gives his invitation: "Follow me!" And those who do follow him find change and challenge. They walk with one who loves and cares, understands and forgives. They walk with one who can ignite hope and put meaning back into life. They walk with one who goes with them everywhere and will walk with them all the way home.

5. Who Is Jesus Christ?

Kathleen J. Crane

Scripture: Matthew 16:13; Mark 8:27; Luke 9:18

A FEW YEARS AGO I flew out to Madison, Wisconsin, to see our oldest son wrestle in a college tournament. On my way back, two Sikhs, men from northern India, with their heads in turbans, sat down beside me. We had a pleasant conversation, but I didn't force my beliefs on them. I helped the older man next to me with his dinner tray, and I told him about a friend I had from India. I told him the bishop of South India had visited the Princeton campus. Our professor had asked us to befriend him, because his wife had died a tragic death, and he was very lonely. I baked him some cake and took it to him, and he invited my husband and me to his home for an Indian meal. As I told my neighbor on the plane this story, he seemed to have tears in his eyes. Then he went to sleep. As we neared Newark Airport, he opened his eyes and turned to me and said, "Tell me about Jesus Christ." What would you have said? Who is Jesus Christ?

Kathleen J. Crane is director of Christian education at First Presbyterian Church in Cranbury, New Jersey. She graduated from Drake University and was awarded an M.A. from Princeton Theological Seminary in 1982. She is currently president of the Association of Presbyterian Church Educators, Eastern Region, and is an ordained deacon and elder in the Presbyterian Church (U.S.A.). She is a frequent speaker and leader of workshops on faith sharing, prayer, and Christian education.

I'd like to suggest that there are three ways we can answer this question: a general answer to the question "Who do people say Jesus is?"; a specific, personal answer to the question "Who do you say Jesus is?"; and a corporate answer to the question "Who does the church say Jesus Christ is?"

Who do people say Jesus is? A prophet, along with Mohammed and others, a Jewish leader in his time, someone who did good deeds, a great teacher, the greatest man who ever lived. Some people see a man of action, a mystic, a revolutionary, a liberator, or a great moral leader.

A few years ago Alexander Solzhenitsyn received the Templeton Award—religion's equivalent of the Nobel Peace Prize. He warned that people have forgotten God. He said, "In the Soviet bloc, hatred of religion is the driving force of Communism, and the West is in decline because the meaning of life is reduced to the pursuit of happiness." He is saying that under Marxist philosophy, Jesus is someone to hate and oppose. By contrast, in the West, Jesus is someone to deny or ignore.

When Jesus asked this question his time was short. Was there anyone who recognized him for who he was? Would there be anyone to carry on his work after he was gone? This problem involved the survival of the Christian faith. He wanted to know before he set out for Jerusalem whether anyone understood. He didn't ask the question directly, he led up to it. He first asked, Who do people say that I am? They replied: some say John the Baptist, others say Elijah, and others, Jeremiah or one of the prophets. John the Baptist was a great figure—Herod Antipas feared that he might even return from the dead. Elijah and Jeremiah were among the greatest of the prophets. They thought they were putting him in the highest categories they could find. The Jews believed that the voice of prophecy had been silent for 400 years; they were saying that in Jesus, people heard again the direct and authentic voice of God. These were high tributes, but not high enough. Human categories, even the highest, are inadequate to describe him.

Jesus wasn't content with the people's answers of John, Elijah, or Jeremiah. Those answers implied that there were precedents and parallels. Jesus claimed to be unique. A Roman emperor had a statue of Jesus and a statue of Plato side by side in his pantheon. He thought he was paying Jesus a noble tribute. He was, but that was not the gospel.

Jesus asked right away, Who do you say that I am? He moved the impersonal discussion to a personal challenge. History forces this question upon us. Jesus has affected people in a far greater sense than Julius Caesar or Alexander or Napoleon ever did—who can he be? The Bible forces it upon is: a carpenter apprentice made claims such as "I am the way, the truth, and the life; no one comes to the Father, but by me." Who can he be? Conscience forces it upon us. This Jesus of Nazareth, whose words still pierce us like a sword, whose eyes still haunt us, whose loving, accepting way is so attractive—who can he be?

This question is for all of us, children, youth, and adults. Who is Jesus Christ? It is the most important question any of us will ever answer. It is also a question we need to answer more than once. We need to respond to it as children, as youth, and many times as adults. For we want our faith (and our relationship to Christ) to be a dynamic, living reality, not just a memory.

Maybe you've heard the expression "God had no grandchildren—there are only children of God." Christianity is always one generation from extinction. This points up the importance of Christian education. Every time you agree to teach a class, or pray as a family before a meal, or at bedtime with your children, you help keep the Christian faith alive. We don't become Christians automatically because our parents are Christians. God calls each generation to say yes—to respond to his gift of grace.

Would you describe Jesus as a person of the past, or as someone in the present? On Easter I said, "The Lord is risen!" and you replied, "He is risen indeed!" Is that a general statement, or a personal answer? Is he alive to you?

This passage of scripture teaches that our discovery of Jesus Christ must be a personal discovery. You could know all about the life and teachings of Christ, even know what all great thinkers and theologians have said about Christ, and still not be a Christian. Being a Christian is more than knowing about Jesus; it involves knowing Jesus.

This question should be on the wall of every church: "Who do you say that I am?" This question and answer are the most important conversation in Matthew's Gospel.

Jesus was dissatisfied with the general answers, so he asked his disciples: "Who do you say that I am?" This question had never been asked before. Through all the months of training and fellowship with these men, Jesus had been leading up to this question. The future of his work depended upon their answer. As the question was asked, there must have been a moment of silence. These men faced the question about the ultimate mystery of the being of God. Suddenly, Peter responded, in his impetuous, loving way—you are the Christ, the son of the living God! This answer by Peter affirms two great truths about Jesus: his sonship and his Messiahship.

The Resurrection helped many people to believe that Jesus was the Son of God. In all four Gospels, Jesus is called the Son of God. But Peter made this statement before the Resurrection!

To say that Jesus is the Christ is to say that he was the promised Messiah, the suffering servant described in the Isaiah passage. *Messiah* is the Hebrew word for *anointed*. The word *Christos* in the Greek, from which we get the word *Christ,* also means *anointed.* It is more accurate to say, Jesus, the Christ, the anointed one, the promised Messiah.

Is the idea of a Messiah relevant today? Was it just a Jewish idea for those times? What does *Messiah* mean to us? To them, it meant that someone was coming who would be the hope of the world, the fulfillment of every promise, and the answer to every prayer: one who would straighten out all human troubles, right all earthly wrongs, and bring in the Kingdom of God. That was the idea, and it hasn't lost its meaning—it has more meaning now than ever!

You are the Christ, the Son of the living God! How could Peter say that? Something had happened to Peter that he hadn't dare put into words until now. He began to feel toward Jesus the way he felt toward God. When Jesus asked Peter to follow him, Peter didn't realize at first who he was following. He just knew Jesus was someone he wanted to follow, and Jesus accepted him at that very elementary level of faith. It was enough for a beginning. Jesus accepted people where they were, not demanding full belief at once, but allowing faith to grow and mature. Peter watched Jesus speak with authority. He saw how he touched people's lives and changed them. Peter also noticed how Jesus was affecting him: he was being changed. Jesus did for him what only God could do. He had to confess it—"You are the Christ, the promised Messiah, the Son of the living God!"

In the last resort, however, Peter's knowledge of Jesus (and ours) comes as a revelation from God. Jesus said, "Flesh and blood has not revealed this to you, but my father who is in heaven." Peter could say with conviction: "I know." Only God can make us finally sure of God.

Jesus gives us a focus for understanding who God is; it is hard to visualize or understand a Spirit. In the confirmation class, we viewed part of the movie *Jesus of Nazareth,* and we were helped in our understanding. Jesus gives us a human vision of God.

Who does the church say Jesus Christ is? What or who is the church? I believe the church is an extension of the Incarnation. We usually understand Incarnation to describe Jesus as God in human form. The church is often defined as the "body of Christ." We represent Jesus to the world through this body, the church. How well do we represent Jesus Christ?

Let me share a story I once heard. Some people came up to God and said, "Who are you, how can we know who you are?" God pointed to his church and said, "This is who I am."

Who is it we represent? In viewing the movie *Jesus of Nazareth,* three things impressed me about Jesus. First, how accepting he was of all people. He didn't condemn the woman caught in adultery; he forgave her. Second, he showed compassion for people in need, and just one example was his healing of a blind man. Third, he was willing to follow God's will. Those would be good guides for any church: be accepting, show compassion, and seek to follow God's will.

You may know the song, "I am the church, you are the church, we are the church together." The church is people. I heard Willard Heckel speak a couple of years ago. He was Dean of the Rutgers Law School and a former moderator of our national church. He said he was complaining about the problems in the world and the church, and his whole life was changed when a woman challenged him with this question: "What are you doing about it?" God wants to use us, his people, to change the world.

Because Jesus is God and is alive, he has the power to change the lives of people like you and like me. When I was in the Kendall Park Presbyterian Church, I made many calls on new residents to welcome them to the community and invite them to church. I'd like to share one story with you. One time I called on a woman who was Roman Catholic; her husband had no church affiliation. I asked her if she worshiped anywhere. She said she didn't, and the Catholic faith wasn't meaningful to her anymore, and she wanted to go to church again. I invited her to come to our church. She and her husband and their children all came and they became active members of the church. A few years ago, her husband, Richard Bennett, was killed in a car accident. It was hard on all of us in the church— he was in his forties, and he left a wife and three daughters. At the funeral, the pastor said, "Richard Bennett grew up in the Bronx, and he had a tough early life. He soon learned to use his fists in the streets, and he had some ability in this area, which he developed into an amateur boxing career of thirty-plus fights. At that time, his relationship to God and the church was virtually nil. Four years ago, he and his family came to Kendall Park, and they began coming to our church. Rick never had one moment when he suddenly believed, but he had a gradual awareness of the love of God for him, and he began to invite others to come to church. He was denied a quantity of life in years, but he found a quality in the few years he had with us." The next day I went to see his widow, Maria. I took her a white mum plant, and I told her I chose white because of the Resurrection. She said, "Oh, that's my hope!" I said, "It's a sure hope, because it's a promise we have from the risen Christ." Just then she looked at me and said, "Because of you, he found Christ!" We hugged each other and cried, and I'll never forget it!

The story doesn't end there. A seminary student from Kenya named Wilson Lang'at came to our church. One of his needs was to have his wife and child join him while he was studying. Maria Bennett agreed to give part of the memorial fund to Wilson, to bring his family over. One day I had lunch with Wilson, and I said we were connected in a way, and I shared this story with him. He was happy to hear it, and said that when he finished school and went back to Kenya, he would tell the people there this story.

We are part of the church, and God really can work through each one of us to make a difference.

Finally, I can't answer for you; I just raise the question. I will say that my faith, my relationship with Jesus Christ, is the most important thing in my life. Who is Jesus Christ . . . to you?

6. The Question of All Ages
Robert A. Penney

And when he was come into Jerusalem, all the city was moved saying, "Who is this"?—Matthew 21:10

ONE OF THE THINGS a reader of the New Testament will notice at once is how the question of the identity of Jesus often arose. Even his own disciples often wondered who he was. Although other men had arisen, presenting some unique claim or manifesting some special quality or ability, these were soon classified by their fellow men and their true worth assessed. Some gifted rabbi would arise and teach in the synagogue of one town, but men would soon grasp his teaching and the rabbi would move on to another town. Unique individuals were always appearing on Mars Hill among the cultured Greek philosophers, and whilst these ancient scholars were always delighted to hear some new thing, they soon had the worth of a man and he would move into new territories to make the best of his limited powers of rhetoric, or debate, or whatever his particular ability may have been. With Jesus it was different. From the beginning of his earthly life and ministry to the end, he was always arousing curiosity and intense interest. He always made people ask questions about him and the most com-

---

Robert A. Penney is a probation and parole officer for the city of Birmingham, England. A member of the Free Evangelical Baptist Church, he has also served as a pastor and welfare officer. Penney's roots are in Scotland, where he attended Lenzie Academy and the Bible Training Institute in Glasgow. He has written many articles for religious journals in Great Britain.

mon of these was: "Who is this?" This identity was a puzzle to them. He was a man like themselves and yet somehow he was different. He couldn't be classified. And if any did think that he was another Judas of Galilee, to whom Gamaliel referred— a one-day wonder—then they found they were mistaken, for this man could confound the wisest and most intellectual among them and at his death he still had men wondering as to his true identity.

"Who is this?" Both friends and foes alike asked this question. The question was asked by the scribes and Pharisees, the exponents of law, ethics and morality: "Who is this that forgiveth sins?"; by the representative of royalty, King Herod: "Who is this of whom I hear such things?"; by the representative of politics, Pontius Pilate: "Who art thou? Art thou the king of the Jews?"; by the leaders of religion at the religious trial of Jesus: "Art thou the Son of the Blessed?"

It is the same today. When the teaching of Christ is applied to the immorality and loose living going on today, the question is asked, "Who is this?" When the ethical teaching of Christ— such as the Sermon on the Mount—is applied to the present-day corruption of government and local politics, the question comes, "Who is this?" When the spiritual teaching of Jesus is brought to bear upon the nominal, official leaders of established institutional religion, the cry again goes up, "Who is this?"

Jesus knew that this question of his identity was always on people's lips and he became curious about the various conclusions they were arriving at, so one day he asked his apostles, "Whom do men say that I am?" and they replied, "Some say that thou art John the Baptist risen from the dead, others say Elias and others say one of the prophets." But Jesus turned the question back to them: "But whom say ye that I am?" and Peter confessed, "Thou art the Christ, the Son of the living God"; and Jesus told Peter that this truth had not been revealed unto him by his own human wisdom and insight, but by God himself.

Note that the revelation of the truth wasn't found in the sphere of religion, law, politics, ethics, or in the king's palace, but in the heart of a simple fisherman from Galilee. The great question of the day—"Who is this?"—doesn't find its answer in the mighty glory of the Roman Empire nor in the shining splendor of Greece nor in the great elaborate and honorable religion of the Jews, but on the lips of an ignorant fisherman. "God hath chosen the foolish things of the world to confound the things which are mighty." If you are in the same position as so many who wondered who Jesus was in the days of his flesh, the answer for you is not, "This is the Prophet from Galilee," but is found in Peter's great reply, "Thou art the Christ, the Son of the living God." If you seek the answer to your question from those who have never been enlightened as to the true nature of Christ's person, whose eyes have never been opened to observe Christ as the Redeemer of men, who have never seen the glory of God in the face of Jesus Christ, whose hearts have never been regenerated by the Spirit of God, then you will be disappointed and you must turn sorrowfully away. The answer as to who this is can only be given by those whose hearts have been set on fire by the warmth of his love, by those who have been changed by his matchless grace, by those who have thrilled to the music of his name, by those who know his risen power pulsating in their veins. This man whom we preach is not merely a prophet of God. He is the Son of God, the Savior of mankind, the Savior of your soul. This man is the answer to your great quest in life. This man, in his person, is the very essence of the Christian gospel. This man, who rides down the long corridors of time and across our path to where we are in history, is the way, the truth and the life and he wants to turn our question, "Who is this?" into the glorious and triumphant answer, "Thou are the Christ!"

Christianity has never sought nor claimed to give men cast-iron, mathematically demonstrated proof of its claim. What it does do is offer men and women evidence and I have three pieces of evidence to offer you now.

I

First, I believe that Jesus Christ is the Son of God and the Savior of mankind because of *the miracle of the Bible.*

The miracle of the Bible? Isn't the Bible on the same level as other great religious books? Haven't the modern critics explained the processes by which our Bible was composed and how it came to us? Modern criticism may have explained certain problems, but it has also done a great deal of harm, and the extreme critics, of course, have robbed the Bible of many of its miraculous elements and of its verbal inspiration. But the results of modern critical research are incomplete, and whilst we welcome anything that is going to clarify some of the so-called problems of the Scriptures, we cannot accept the contention that the Bible can be explained adequately in human terms. One cannot escape the miraculous elements of the Bible. The Scriptures themselves declare that they are given by inspiration of God and that this inspiration came as holy men spake by the Holy Ghost.

Thousands of years before Christ, men like David, Isaiah, Jeremiah, and Ezekiel prophesied about the coming Messiah, gave some details of his life and gave exact details of his death. Joel, the prophet, prophesied concerning the Pentecostal outpouring of the Holy Spirit recorded in Acts 2 hundreds of years before the event. And is it not miraculous that there are events recorded in the Old Testament concerning the Jewish nation which are taking place at the present time? How do you explain all this in human terms? How do you explain, in human terms, the fact that the Bible has been preserved all down the long centuries? It has been preserved from the wrath of ungodly men, from the fury of hell, from the flames to which it has been committed time and time again. Manuscripts and fragments carried by early Christian scribes have been preserved from extinction on the high seas; others have been preserved from the effects of long journeys by early pilgrims across desert sands and from long dusty roads throughout Asia and Syria. Many others have endured the devastating effects of the dampness and dirt of old Roman dungeons. At a later time, a succession of scholars worked laboriously translating New Testament manuscripts, which had miraculously come together to form one complete whole, and many of these men, just prior to the Reformation, suffered great persecution and even death. John Wycliffe was severely persecuted for his part in the translation of the Bible into English. William Tyndale was strangled as an old man and then burned for his part. When the Reformation dawned, the Reformers built the new faith upon what Gladstone called the "infallible Rock of Holy Scripture," and they said, in effect, "This book is the one which reveals the Christ who is the answer to every man's need"; and John Knox took the pulpit from the side of the church in St. Gile's Cathedral in Edinburgh and placed it in the center, symbolic of the centrality of the Word of God, the central message of the written Word being the Christ, the living Word.

The Bible is a miracle! It was banned and burned, and many of its translators suffered death, but it has emerged as the world's best seller and the most influential of all books. Men thought so highly of this book and were so convinced of its miraculous nature, so convinced that it was the Word of God to man, that many of them were prepared to die for it. Men don't die for something fake, for an invention, for a book of fairy tales, myth, or legend. Men don't die for the works of Homer, Milton, Shakespeare, or Shaw. Yet men died for the preservation and promotion of the Bible as the Word of God. This, then, is my first piece of evidence: the miracle of the Bible.

II

The second piece of evidence I wish to offer is the *miracle of the church.*

Here again, as in the case of the Bible, the fury and onslaught of hell has lashed against the bulwarks of the faith. Jesus foretold it would, and it wasn't long before the ferocious forces were unleashed. Satan, through the agency of evil men, sought to strangle the church in her infancy. Herod killed James with the sword. The leaders of religion stoned Stephen, the first Christian martyr, urging them on with fury and hatred. Soon there was wholesale slaughter. Christians were flung to lions in the Roman sporting arenas. Some were wrapped in the skins of wild animals so that they would be more savagely attached by dogs. Some were crucified, others were smeared with pitch and set on fire, and these living torches were used by the Emperor Nero to illuminate his gardens. You don't die like that for a fable, a fabrication, a fallacy. The attempt was made to stamp out the church at her birth.

The attempt was made to stamp out the church at the dawn of the Reformation. Hundreds died at the stake, from loyal archbishops to lowly peasants. Who is this? Go and ask the question of Stephen and he will reply, as the stones are breaking every bone in his body: "I see Jesus standing at the right hand of God." Who is this? Address your question to the early Christian martyrs as they are enduring unspeakable agonies under Nero and they will reply: "This is Jesus, the Redeemer of our souls," or take your question to sixteen-year-old Mary Wilson, who was drowned on the shores of the Solway Firth in Scotland, and she will sing to you "The Lord's my Shepherd" as the waters rise to overwhelm her. Who is this? Take your question to Archbishop Latimer and you will hear him say to Archbishop Ridley as they are both about to be burned at the stake, "Be of good cheer Master Ridley: we shall this day by God's grace, light such a torch in England as will never be put out." Or take your question to the members of the underground church in China, Russia, Hungary; and they will reply: "This is Jesus, the Son of the living God!"

The triumph of the Christian church! The miracle of the Christian church! Is the miracle of the church's survival after almost twenty centuries of such scorn, criticism, and persecution not a substantial piece of evidence?

III

My third piece of evidence is the *miracle of changed and transformed lives.*

This is undeniable evidence for Christ and his religion. You may argue about the trustworthiness of the Bible if you so wish; you may find some justifiable criticism of the church and its organization, but you can never deny the evidence of a godly life. No one can explain *that* away.

The multitudes were amazed when they saw the disciples of Christ, who previously were timid and afraid, speaking with a power and a boldness that were supernatural. The pagans of the first century could hardly believe that so many could give up their pagan and immoral practices to suffer and die so courageously for this Jesus. Indeed it was the changed lives of men and women that won the greatest amount of converts to Christianity in those days. The ancient world was shattered when Saul of Tarsus—one of the greatest intellectuals of his day—was transformed from a blasphemer and a proud, haughty Pharisee and persecutor, into a follower and disciple of the despised Jesus. When Christ confronted Saul on the road to Damascus, Saul naturally asked, "Who art thou Lord?" but toward the close of his life many years afterward, he expressed his years of proven experience concerning Jesus in these words: "The Son of God who loved me and gave himself for me."

All down through the centuries Christ has been transforming human lives, not only the lives of intellectuals but the lives of thousands of ordinary men and women. Alan Redpath, John Stott, Billy Graham, and others tell us in their books of the most despicable characters in every country of the world, apparently beyond all human aid, who have been completely transformed by the reception of Christ into their lives. This is the miracle of changed and transformed lives.

Perhaps you are a more "respectable" person. You have planned your own future and at present you are enjoying life to the full, but Christ has come across your path sometime in the past or perhaps even at this moment, and you are confronted with the challenge of his message and his claims. Perhaps you see him as a threat to the settled course of your life and you are crying out with a note of apprehension: "Who is this?" Many have been in your position. Those who have yielded to his claims have been changed from selfish aspiration and ambition to unselfish and fruitful service for the one who is the Christ, the Son of the living God.

"Who is this?" We have considered, briefly, some of the evidence. Has it been in any way convincing? Have you reached your verdict? Are you satisfied with such evidence? If not, what kind of evidence are you looking for?

7. I Can't Believe It!

Richard P. Hansen

Scripture: Luke 24:13–43

AS I WAS growing up, I would occasionally have the opportunity to go and see the University of Nebraska play football in Lincoln. When the visiting team ran out into that huge coliseum, filled with at least a hundred thousand red-covered fanatics, I often imagined how the Christians must have felt coming out into the Roman Coliseum to face the lions. And just as in Rome, the football score often paralleled the old joke: "Lions, 45—Christians, 0."

When I went off to college, I went to Iowa State, not exactly a football power in the Big Eight. Whenever Nebraska came to town, I'd slink over to the stadium, which was like a high school field compared to the great coliseum in Lincoln, and prepare myself for the inevitable. Except for one year. Iowa State played inspired football. We were only six points behind in the closing minutes, which was a victory in itself! And in those two minutes, Iowa State drove all the way down the field. Our quarterback threw the best pass of his life, threading the ball through four or five defenders for a touchdown. The crowd erupted for joy! I remember dancing around, hugging my fraternity buddies and yelling, "I can't believe it! I can't believe it!" It was too good to be true.

Richard P. Hansen is senior pastor of the First Presbyterian Church in Visalia, California. He attended Iowa State University, was awarded a Master of Divinity degree from Bethel Theological Seminary, and earned a Master of Theology degree from Princeton Theological Seminary. Hansen is married and has two children.

When Jesus appeared among his disciples, they must have had the same kind of experience. "I can't believe it!" They "disbelieved for joy," the Scripture says. Seeing Jesus alive again was simply too good to be true. *The power of the Resurrection for them, as it is for us, is the journey of "I can't believe it" to another.*

About twelve hours earlier that day, two of those disciples walked along the road to Emmaus. Perhaps they felt the same stunned shock of disbelief that many of us felt when we heard that John Kennedy had been shot. Or more recently, when we heard that the space shuttle had blown up, killing all aboard. Their minds were numb; they couldn't take in what had happened. All they could do was walk with their heads down, watch their sandals biting into the dust, and mutter to themselves, "I can't believe it!" They didn't even notice the stranger who walked up alongside until he asked, "What can't you believe?" Then the whole tragic story came spilling out about how they had expected Jesus to be the one who would finally conquer their enemies, the hated Romans, and redeem Israel out of bondage to the Roman Empire. But instead of being crowned as king, he was crucified on a cross. The stranger must have smiled to himself. How often had he told them: *his* enemies were sin and death, and the only way to conquer them was through the cross. "Foolish men," he chided them, "you 'can't believe it' because you've misunderstood the Christ."

Perhaps some of us have misunderstood. Perhaps it's our very misunderstanding, like that of those disciples on the road, that keeps us from meeting the risen Christ. There are two common misunderstandings. One is that Jesus came to be a great ethical teacher. The other is that Jesus came to show us how to live, to give us a moral example that we could follow. Jesus' enemies knew better. Jesus' enemies knew that he wasn't simply a rabbi looking for students or a virtuous man trying to give a good example to the world, he was a *king* looking for subjects. You see, if you know you're a king then the first thing you need is subjects, people who give you authority over their lives. That's why Jesus was such a threat to the chief priests and the Pharisees and the scribes. And that's why he is a threat to you and me.

Teachers we can ignore. Good examples we can take or leave. But when someone asks the total commitment of our lives, eventually we either have to give it or feel threatened by him.

Do you know what the placard said that they put above Jesus' head on the cross? It had nothing to do with wrong teaching or a bad example. It read, "The King of the Jews." Jesus was crucified because he claimed to be a king.

What does all this have to do with Easter? Simply that the one who was crucified as a king was resurrected as a king. Have you ever noticed that he only appeared to those who believed in him as their king? Now I admit they had the style of his kingship wrong. They expected a coronation, not a cross. But if the disciples didn't know the score, at least they were in the right ballpark. They believed he was a king. They'd staked their lives on it.

Do you know how a changed life happens? It happens when we realize that Jesus Christ was crucified and resurrected to be our king, and when we put our lives in his hands. Jesus' resurrection means we can say, "*I* am risen! My past has no power over me. I can begin life new this day."

Let me tell you about Chuck, a man in his early forties that I knew at a former church. Chuck was a big barrel of a man who worked in an auto parts store. He thought religion was for weaklings. Although his wife, Sandy, attended church faithfully, he only came once or twice a year. He was an enjoyable guy, but he had a drinking problem that was slowly eroding his marriage and his family.

The first time I met Chuck was at a gathering at our home. Chuck came to that gathering slightly inebriated. His wife was mortified. About three months later, Chuck and Sandy went to a marriage encounter weekend. About a month after that, I couldn't believe it when I heard that Chuck had joined one of the discipleship groups that our church sponsored. In fact, I couldn't believe it so much that the next time the group met, I went and peeked in the window of the room in the church where they were meeting. There was Chuck, studying the Bible with five other men.

The practice in that church was to invite those who had been involved in the program to share with the congregation what this experience of discipleship had meant in their lives. Guess who volunteered a few months later? One year after I first met him in our home, Chuck stood in the pulpit and unashamedly told hundreds of people the difference that Jesus Christ had made in his life. He even quoted one of the Bible verses he'd memorized. And as I looked out over the congregation, my eye caught Sandy's. I saw tears coming down her face. She sought me out after the service and said, "Chuck is a different person than he was a year ago. I can't believe it!" But I could believe it, because he'd met the risen Christ.

Audrey's story was quite different. Audrey was a woman in her mid-forties who had spent her whole adult life in the church. She'd married into a "pillar-of-the-church"-type family, and so she was expected to be very involved in the life of the church. Whenever the church doors were open, Audrey was there. Seventeen years after she was married, her husband came to her one evening and said that he no longer loved her; he had found someone else. His prominent family in this small town took his side through the long, painful divorce. She was left isolated, devastated.

During that painful process, Audrey began to realize that most of what she had done up to that point in her life, particularly her heavy church involvement, had been to please the expectations of others. It was simply "the right thing to do." Now she had to sift through her life to see if there was any faith there of her own. One evening during a Lenten service the pastor was preaching upon Jesus' last words from the cross, "It is finished." She sat for a long time in the darkened sanctuary after everyone else had left, thinking back over her life and how far away she had been from God, even at the same time as she was fulfilling all the expectations of being a good church member. And over and over she said to herself in the darkened sanctuary, "It is finished. It is finished."

A short while later, she joined a study group that I was leading. Even though she had sat through hundreds of sermons and taught for years in the Sunday school, she began reading the Bible as though she'd never read it before. You see, now her heart burned within her. She knew that Jesus was real. And a few months later, she told the whole group in words that I'll never forget, "Two years ago, I thought I was being a good Christian but I was so far away from God; I look at my life and the change that has happened since then. . . . I just can't believe it!"

You see, *the risen Christ doesn't come in to change the lives of deserving people or pious people or religious people. He comes to change the lives of willing people.* Even after that long talk on the way to Emmaus, he was prepared to walk on. He doesn't barge his way into our lives; he only comes if he's invited in. And when those disciples invited him to stay with them—when he was invited in—*then* they realized who he was.

It was as though the reservoir of joy that had been building as their hearts "burned within them" along the road suddenly split wide open. That's the truest testimony of a real encounter with Christ—we can't keep it to ourselves. They walked back to Jerusalem in total darkness. When they returned to the other disciples, it was an incendiary fellowship—the joy that each had to share ignited more joy in the others.

If I could get that way over a football game, imagine how they must have hugged each other and clapped each other on the back, saying, "I can't believe it! It's too good to be true!" The risen Christ does change lives. He changed the disciples. He changed Chuck and Audrey. He's changed me. I hope he's changed you.

And so on this Easter Sunday, let's sing, "He is risen." But let's shout inside ourselves, "*I* am risen. *My past* has no power over me; I can begin life new this day. *Death* has no power over me; I will live forever. Hallelujah!"

Can you believe it?

Our Father, I pray that You would take the despairing "I can't believe it" of people resigned to a life that has them boxed in, captive to a situation in life, or other people, or even things in their own lives that they can't stand about themselves. That you would take that "I can't believe what's happened to me" and transform it into the "I can't believe it" of those who have encountered the risen Christ, and have broken through to joy. It all depends upon whether we will take him as our king; if we will give as much of ourselves as we know to as much of him as we understand at this moment. Help us to do that, if we so choose, for Christ's sake and for our sake. Amen.

8.   How to Enjoy God
Neil Babcox

Text: Psalm 139:7–12; Ephesians 3:14–21

ONE OF THE truly great statements about the relationship between God and humanity is found in *The Westminster Shorter Catechism:*

> Q.   What is the chief end of man?
> A.   Man's chief end is to glorify
>   God and enjoy him forever.

Not bad, for a group of stodgy Calvinists! Our ultimate purpose for living? To glorify and enjoy God forever.

But I wonder . . . how many people really enjoy God? Do you? Not just Do you believe in God?, but Do you enjoy God? It's a searching question!

You'd think we Christians would be among the most joyful people on the face of the earth. We do have something to celebrate, you know. After all, Jesus did not say, "I have come to bring you gloom, and believe me, I have plenty to share." He did not say, "I have come to make you miserable, even more miserable than you already are." He said, "I have come that you may have life, and have it abundantly."

Neil Babcox is pastor of the Alexandria First Presbyterian Church of Mount Pleasant near Milford, New Jersey. After receiving a B.A. in philosophy at Southern Illinois University, Babcox attended Princeton Theological Seminary and was awarded a Master of Divinity in 1986. He has also been a pastor in Illinois and is the author of *A Search for Charismatic Reality: One Man's Pilgrimage.*

And yet, for many people, religion is more a burden than a blessing. Too often, God's presence is about as welcome as a state trooper's when you're doing seventy-five on the interstate. The Bible is a heavenly rendition of "Rules for the Road," and the church is traffic court, where guilty offenders gather to be sentenced and pay their fines.

We get a hint of this kind of feeling in Psalm 139 (Good News Bible):

Where could I go to escape from you?
Where could I get away from your presence?
If I went up to heaven, you would be there;
If I lay down in the world of the dead, you would be there.

It sounds as if the psalmist would like to get away from God. The problem is, there's no place to go. He certainly can't escape God's presence in heaven, but neither can he escape it in the world of the dead. Everything in between is pretty well covered too! Is there no place where a self-respecting man or woman can go to get away from God?

Sometimes we feel the same way. We may not like to admit it, but this business of religion can become a dreadful bore and, worse yet, an intolerable burden.

One reason people do not enjoy God's presence is because of the prevalence of "oatmeal theology." Johnny and his mother were having a dispute about oatmeal. Johnny's mother was trying her best to persuade the boy to eat his oatmeal, but he wouldn't budge. Finally, in desperation, she said, "Johnny, if you don't eat your oatmeal, God will punish you." Still, Johnny refused, and his mother sent him to bed. Before long, a great storm arose. Lightning flashed like a strobe light and the wind whipped the rain against the house. Johnny's mother rushed upstairs to comfort her son. "Johnny, are you okay?" she asked. "I guess so," he replied, "but this sure is an awful fuss to make about a little oatmeal."

We all have our "oatmeal," and we're just as certain as sin God is going to punish us for not eating it, even if he has to send a thunderstorm to do it!

God thunders "thou shalt not" from Mount Sinai, Moses hurls the tablets of the law at our feet, and the prophets, like heavenly district attorneys, prosecute us. Our first inclination is to run and hide, like fugitives, from divine justice. But before long, we hear the hounds of heaven baying in the distance, and once again we realize there is no place to hide.

The only alternative, then, is plea bargaining. Hoping for a lighter sentence, we cop a plea with the judge. The problem is, the bargaining process inevitably turns sour, and we wind up feeling guilty and oppressed by our religion. We come to church because we want to make a good showing before God—at least occasionally—and we stay away from church because, after all, we can only tolerate so much of this bondage.

And so the question remains: Is it possible to enjoy God's presence, or must we continually seek ways to hide from our Creator like guilty fugitives?

I think it is possible, as the authors of *The Westminster Shorter Catechism* have suggested, to enjoy God, given the proper orientation.

First, to enjoy God, we need a new perspective; that is, we need to see God as revealed to us in the person of Jesus Christ. As we read in the Gospel of John, "No one has ever seen God; the only begotten Son, who is in the bosom of the Father, he has made him known."

Outside of Jesus Christ, God can be an unknown factor, or worse yet, a terrifying reality. Sometimes on a starry night, I find myself struck with the awesome reality of God. When I look at the billions of stars, galaxies, and solar systems above me, I cannot help but think, "What manner of being is it that created all this? And how is it that such an infinite, incomprehensible power can be interested in my life?" I tell you it sends a chill down my spine, until I think of Jesus Christ, and then I realize that the great being who created all of this is none other than the God and Father of our Lord Jesus Christ, who sent his Son into the world, not to condemn us, but to bring us salvation.

The way to know the mind and heart of the Creator, then, is through the lens of our Lord's incarnation. As Jesus said to Philip, "If you've seen me, you've seen the Father."

Do you really want to know what God is like? Then open your New Testament and behold the Savior. Behold his words, for his words are God's words. Behold his acts, for his acts are God's acts. Behold his sufferings, for his sufferings are God's sufferings.

See him as the friend of sinners. See him filled with compassion, healing the multitudes. See him weep. See him pray. See him like the good shepherd, seeking and saving the lost. See him suffering on the cross. See him bear the pain, the sorrow, and the humiliation, and ask yourself:

> Alas! and did my savior bleed, and did my sovereign die!
> Would he devote that sacred head for sinners such as I?
> Was it for sins that I have done he suffered on the tree?
> Amazing pity! Grace unknown!
> And love beyond degree!

When you are tempted to doubt God's love, go to Calvary. There you can see Jesus Christ and, in seeing him, God. There you will see love beyond degree, love that melts "religion" and recasts it in the mold of a joyous and loving devotion.

Second, to enjoy God, we need a new approach; that is, we must come to God on the basis of grace. Grace means that God loved us first, long before we were aware of it. Grace means God loves us freely, not because of who we are or what we've done, but because we are created in the divine image. Grace means that God loves us always, no matter how far we stray, or how deep we fall. As God said through the prophet Isaiah, "Can a woman forget her own baby and not love the child she bore? Even if a mother should forget her child, I will never forget you."

When will we realize that we cannot impress God with our righteousness? When will we realize that we need not and cannot merit God's favor? When will we realize that salvation is a gift to be received in the empty hands of faith alone? God did not give us the Law so we could dream up schemes to work our way to heaven. The law was given to show how far we have strayed from God's righteousness, and thus to drive us into the arms of grace.

We will never be able to enjoy God so long as we think we must earn his love. Let us, therefore, abandon all self-righteousness and learn what it means to be saved by God's amazing grace. When the meaning of grace begins to unfold before you, you will not be able to contain the joy.

Third, to enjoy God, we need a new relationship. The way to get rid of that nagging feeling, that God is always on your back, is to get God into your heart. There is no joy in religion when all we have are external ceremonies and rules. There is no joy in religion when we attend church, but inwardly are empty. The good news of the gospel is that our hearts can be temples of God, indwelt by the Holy Spirit. This is the greatest of all the gifts God has to give: the Spirit of Christ dwelling in our hearts by faith. God is not just a reality above us and around us. God can be reality within us.

As we read in Paul's letter to the Ephesians:

> For this reason, I bow my knees before the
> Father, from whom every family in heaven and
> on earth is named, that according to the riches
> of his glory he may grant you to be
> strengthened with might through his Spirit in
> the inner man, and that Christ may dwell in
> your hearts through faith; that you, being
> rooted and grounded in love, may have the
> power to comprehend with all the saints what is
> the breadth and length and height and depth,
> and to know the love of Christ which surpasses
> knowledge, that you may be filled with all the
> fullness of God.

Our religion, then, doesn't have to be either boring or burdensome. On the contrary, with a new perspective, a new approach, and a new relationship, it can be a source of the profoundest joy. Seek God in Christ. Approach God on the basis of grace. Accept God into your heart by faith. Then go out and glorify and enjoy God forever.

II. EXPOSITORY

9. Seed Bearing Seed

John R. Archer

Scripture: Matthew 13:1–9, 18–23

THIS GENERATION has witnessed a transition—some would say a revolution—in America's farm country. *Agriculture* has become agri*business*. The farmer who was once responsible for feeding seven people now stretches the resources of the land to feed as many as three hundred, some of them ex-farmers. From our stomach's point of view, we are still deeply connected to the land and its fruit. Yet the distance widens between the tilling of the soil and the consumption of food, and increasingly the intervening space is filled with supermarkets, urban and suburban development, and not a few wistful faces of those whose former occupation kept their hands and hearts close to the earth.

Almost despite that, the Gospel reading for this morning is Jesus' parable of the weeds among the wheat. It is part of a series of related stories about sowing and growing and reaping. They have been called "peasant parables," stories of the kingdom directed to a crowd assembled from the Galilean countryside. These people knew that the separation of weeds and wheat was a tedious but necessary business after a summer

---

John Richard Archer was born in 1945 in Buffalo, New York. He was educated at the State University of New York, Buffalo, the General Theological Seminary, and the Graduate Theological Union in Berkeley, California, where he received his doctorate. An Episcopalian, Dr. Archer currently is director of academic affairs at the College of Preachers, Washington Cathedral, Washington, D.C.

harvest. But also listening to this parable, so the Gospel says, is a group of disciples for whom the images require some explanation.

When we hear the word "disciples," we automatically think of Peter and Matthew and James and John. But the Gospel does not name these disciples, except to say that they were gathered in a house—a real contrast to the followers who were content to hear Jesus in the open air and then return home. These house-disciples ask for and receive a theological translation of this parable. And it is this that the church has chosen to embrace virtually ever since.

Maybe these house-disciples *were* Peter and Matthew and James and John. Maybe fishermen and tax collectors didn't know much about farming either, and couldn't hear the parable with the "ear of the heart." That ear is sensitive to non-verbal expression. It would know the sinking feeling that the householder experienced when he discovered that someone—an enemy—had sabotaged his crop. It would feel the frustration from evil intent, wondering how badly the wheat harvest had been compromised. It would understand the vital connection between "seed for sowing" and "bread for eating" of which the prophet had spoken. Perhaps Jesus spoke to some who had heard the cry of a child going hungry because the wheat didn't grow. They were attuned to the "groaning of creation" in a personal way long before Paul wrote about it. They could identify with God's remorse and Jesus' tears over the assaults of the devil upon the fields of God's ripening kingdom.

How much easier it has been—and still is—to respond to the explanation that Jesus offers to his housebound audience. It seems very clear. The sower is the Son of Man, the field is the world, the good seed the kingdom's children, the weeds or tares the children of evil, the enemy the devil. You can almost hear the whirring of the wheels in the intellect of selected disciples, as they disengage from the earthy metaphors of soil and plants and the anticipation of harvest, and construct a pattern of judgment that concentrates on the sorting of tares from grain. The Lord cautions that the harvest is the close of the age, and that the reapers are angels. But, historically, the church has often chosen to accelerate the date of that harvest and weed the field before its appointed time.

Scholars agree that the weed sown in the field was quite probably the darnel weed. It's a vinelike plant that intertwines itself with the wheat stalks, and its crown looks quite a bit like wheat itself. In the Middle Ages, the darnel weed was often used as a biblical symbol for heresy: thought and practice that appeared Christian, but threatened to sap the life of the harvest field that had come to be understood not as the world, but the church. In England, the symbol had a special poignancy, because the darnel weed had sneaked into English wheat fields with shipments of seed-corn from France, a country whose faith England viewed with suspicion. The English church, like others of its time, was not content to wait for the angels. It seemed urgent to rid the field of such weeds, which personified evil by practices such as reading the Bible in English, or listening to sermons that spoke out against the value of the Crusades, or questioned the traditional authority of the pope, or suggested that a penitent Christian might confess his or her sins to God without benefit of auricular confession to a priest. In 1391, one of these weedy heretics, Walter Brute, even went so far as to say that the Eucharist might be celebrated by a woman!

I bring this up because history has a tendency to repeat itself. We are at least as quick to spot the weeds today, in our own field. Evangelicals on the right have thundered for years against the moral laxity of mainline Protestant churches, and lately many mainline Christians have had a field day at the discovery of a similar species of weed growing in the Fundamentalist garden. Ecumenical dialogue has long been hindered by a residual feeling that one denomination or another has been subtly infected with the evil seed of mistaken beliefs. Voices which are led to preach peace are accused of having been strangulated to that high pitch by the insidious vine of Communism. Christians who argue for defense are in their turn accused of having grown up in the fields of Mars, the god of war.

So this parable raises an important question for this and every generation of Christians who are tempted to content themselves with the easy explanation. The question is this: How can be return to the parable itself, and having returned, recover an ear to hear it?

First of all, we need an image, a picture for the parable that will supplant the need to extract retributive doctrine from the story. I used to think that the pictures of serfs tilling the fields, found in books of hours and medieval manuscripts, served such a purpose. But these were produced for people who stayed as far away from fields as possible, and they betray a certain distance from their subject.

There are closer images than these. For example, I have come to know a series of paintings from the Gospels, primitive yet compelling pieces of art painted by peasants from the islands of Solentiname, located in Lake Nicaragua. Ninety families live there, some of them farmers. These are paintings produced in response to the gospel at work in their lives. Without exceptions, they are brimming with the energy of faith.

One of them was painted in 1981, by Rodolfo Arellano. The subject is Matthew's first parable of the sower, but the central figure is still the Son of Man. The painting shows Jesus as a *campesino* in broad-brimmed sombrero and blue jeans, broadcasting seed in a field half full of budding plants, ringed by trees and flowers, with mountains in the distance. The sky is a deep purple; dusk is falling. As you look at the painting—even in your mind's eye—you can tell that it was done by someone who is in touch with the life of such parables.

In response to a similar picture in her mind, we hear Natalia, a midwife in that same community, say, "We are all seeds. Seeds bearing more seeds." We hear Oscar say that "Christ rose from the dead because he was a healthy seed. In the harvest, we have seen that not every seed is born . . . but if we're going to rise from the dead like Christ, we must be the same kind of seed he was." Finally, Julio adds his voice, saying, "I see one thing. The seed alone, without the land, doesn't do anything. So this doctrine without us is of no use. Without us there is no kingdom of heaven."

What do the art and observations of the peasants of Solentiname say to us—this field, this world, this people—about Jesus' parable, to us, who, ourselves, growing and grafted to the source of life by baptism, live with the certain knowledge that evil flourishes in our midst, who know that distortions of God's promise do prevail within sight and earshot, even as we strive to turn ourselves toward the sun of righteousness?

They say many things, I believe, among them these: Jesus is in this our field, sowing good seed. And insofar as Christ dwells in us, we are sowers, too. Until the harvest, the close of the age, the tares of evil will persist and grow in that same field. We cannot help but see them. Their presence is signalled not so much by wrong thinking—by doctrines or ideologies that seem strange to our ears, or by opinions that differ from our own—as by action: action that perpetuates injustice and oppression, action that promotes violence at the expense of peace, action that exploits other human beings, denying their right to grow in order that other people might flourish more conspicuously. It is not enough to condemn such action. We must work to transform it, even as the Sower gave his life on the cross to hold out the possibility of life, transfigured and reclaimed.

Centuries ago, a eucharistic prayer expressed that hope in a way that still has deep meaning. It has come down to us in the form of a hymn, which many of you may have sung, and which runs in part: "Father, we thank thee who hast planted thy holy name within our hearts. Knowledge and faith and life immortal, Jesus thy son to us imparts . . . As grain, once scattered on the hillsides, was in this broken bread made one, so from all lands thy church be gathered into thy kingdom by thy Son."

We are not reapers. In anticipation of the harvest, we are sowers and tillers. Yet we are also seeds—seeds who bear more seed, in fruit that shows us to be children of God's kingdom. This parable is intended to prepare us to accept that revelation. We are sown by God's Son, in the field of God's choosing. We grow by the grace of God's spirit, seed bearing seed. We yield our fruit to the working of God's purpose, until the final harvest, when all things which have matured by God's grace will find and receive eternal life, in a kingdom without end. Amen.

10. On Being Pentecostal
Fred B. Craddock

Scripture: Acts 2:2–21

PENTECOST is a noun. It is a good noun, strong and clear, confident of its identity, able to stand up in any room and say what it is. That's what nouns are; that's what nouns do. If you want definitions, nouns can give you definitions. *Pentecost:* An early harvest festival celebrated in the ancient Near East, among many peoples, including the Jews. *Pentecost:* An early harvest festival transformed into a celebration of the revelation of the law given at Sinai. *Pentecost:* The birthday of the church. *Pentecost:* A festival celebrated fifty days after Easter or, in Judaism, seven weeks and one day after Passover. *Pentecost:* The last day of the liturgical year and the beginning of ordinary time. *Pentecost:* The last Sunday of Easter. Pentecost is a noun: clear-eyed, level-gazed, certain of its identity.

But when you make Pentecost into an adjective, it grows anxious, nervous, and uncertain, standing first on one foot, then on the other. It wants to be a good adjective, as it runs around looking for a noun to modify, but doesn't know which

Fred B. Craddock, a native of Humboldt, Tennessee, was born in 1928. His graduate studies include degrees from Vanderbilt University and Phillips University, where he received his doctorate. Dr. Craddock, an ordained minister in the Christian Church (Disciples of Christ), currently holds the Bandy Distinguished Chair in New Testament and Preaching at the Candler School of Theology at Emory University in Atlanta, Georgia. His seven books include the text *Preaching.*

noun and doesn't know what we are talking about. The adjective is "Pentecostal." We don't admit we don't know; we use the word and assume we know.

"Did you know that my roommate is Pentecostal?" she asked.

"Really?" ("Really?" is a way of responding as though you understand.)

"Well, I know, at least I've heard, that she's Pentecostal, but she's doing well in her classes."

"Really?"

"How is your church doing?"

"Well, I'm not sure. I've only been there a year, and we have a fairly heavy Pentecostal element."

"Really?"

"Our church is growing. On Sunday morning, we have a regular, formal, traditional service, but on Sunday evening some have a Pentecostal service."

"Really?"

What are we talking about?

A few years ago, when I was on the West Coast to speak at a seminary, just before the first lecture, one of the students stood up and said, "Before you speak, I need to know if you are Pentecostal." The room grew silent. I don't know where the dean was! The student quizzed me in front of everybody. I was taken aback, and so I said, "Do you mean do I belong to the Pentecostal Church?" He said, "No, I mean are you Pentecostal?" I said, "Are you asking if I am charismatic?" He said, "I am asking you if you are Pentecostal." I said, "Do you want to know if I speak in tongues?" He said, "I want to know if you are Pentecostal." I said, "I don't know what your question is." He said, "Obviously, you are not Pentecostal." He left.

What are we talking about?

In spite of the fact that the church doesn't know what the adjective means, the church insists that the word remain in our vocabulary as an adjective. The church is unwilling for the word simply to be a noun, to represent a date, a place, an event in the history of the church, refuses for it to be simply a memory, an item, something back there somewhere. The church insists the word is an adjective; it describes the church. The word, then, is "Pentecostal."

Now this word has been embarrassing sometimes, because different groups in the church have, with sincere motives in most cases, I am sure, sought to implement that term by saying, "Let us reproduce, let us imitate the events and experiences of Acts 2." In other words, the way to be Pentecostal is to reproduce the first Pentecost. Now that's embarrassing and tragic, because one cannot actually imitate an event from another time and place. Events that are meaningful are geared to the time and place and people and needs and circumstance in which they occur, and to take that uncritically to another time and place and people is confusing and fruitless, however sincere the motive. Sometimes it has been embarrassing because some have tried, again quite sincerely, to manufacture the enthusiasm and achievement of the Pentecost which Luke describes. But one does not manufacture enthusiasm and achievement. You know and I know, we all know that Pentecost was a gift of God. It was not generated by those present, neither leaders nor observers. It was at the initiative of the Holy Spirit that there was a Pentecost.

In spite of these misguided efforts, the church still insists that somehow "Pentecostal" is an appropriate adjective for describing the church. In the renewal of its life and witness, especially in times of faltering evangelism, the church seeks to reclaim, to recover that quality, perhaps reading, praying, asking, thinking, reflecting again on Pentecost. Perhaps that day will not be just a memory, but also a hope, something that will occur again.

And that's what I'd like for us to do; think again about Acts 2 and Pentecost.

After a rather chaste and brief—surprisingly brief—description of the unusual, extraordinary phenomena of that day when the believers were all gathered together, Luke provides a rather detailed presentation of the audience. The crowd is very large. Jews have come from every nation under heaven.

In addition, there are converts to Judaism and other visitors. From every nation they have come, and they have come to Jerusalem! And they have come for the festival that celebrates the revelation of God to Israel. Now that, too, is very important, because no festivals or celebrations live very long if they are nothing but recollections of the past. What keeps them alive is that in the bosom of every good memory lives some hope that maybe it will all be true again. And so they come—with a yearning, with a seeking, with an asking—to Jerusalem.

Do you not find it striking that Luke describes the listeners before he presents the preacher or the sermon? Luke starts the story at the ear of the listener, but at the mouth of the preacher. Luke begins with the appetite and then gives the bread. He does not take the bread and throw it at the heads of the people in the audience. He does proceed as if to say, "First of all, this is what is to be said; now let's figure some clever strategies by which we can get them to hear it." In fact, there is no sermon until the people say, "What does this mean?" There is no call to be Christians until the people say, "What does this mean?" There is no call to be Christians until the people say, "What must we do?" Let's think about what it means to begin with the listeners. We are talking about timing. We are talking about appropriateness. How often has the door been closed to the gospel because of someone's poor timing or inappropriate comments, even about Jesus Christ? Luke begins with the listener, with listening to the listener. The world is full of good speeches that failed because they were given at the wrong time to the wrong people.

Notice also that Luke says this audience is made up of folk from every nation under heaven. He gives a partial list of the known nations of that time. "Every nation under heaven" consisted primarily of the world around the Mediterranean, including sub-nations and islands in the sea. Asia is represented, Europe is represented, North Africa is represented, and peoples from those places are all present on the occasion of the first presentation of the gospel of God concerning the dead and risen Christ.

Now what does that mean? Obviously, the first thought is that the gospel is universal, it's for everybody in the world, and that is true, stated not only by Luke but by all the writers in the New Testament. To the Jews first, but also to the Greeks, says Paul. To every creature, says Matthew. From Jerusalem to Judea to Samaria, and to the ends of the earth, says Luke. We know that the gospel is for the whole universe, but what is vital in this story is that these nations—all nations of the earth—are present when the gospel begins. Think what this means! All nations of the earth are not just the destination of the gospel; they are the point of origin of the Gospel. Where did it all start? And the Asians said, "With us." Where did it all start? The Europeans said, "With us. We were there when it started." The Africans said, "We were there when it started." From every nation under heaven, the people said, "We were there when it started."

To understand Luke's Pentecost it is necessary to understand that the gospel doesn't just go to the ends of the earth; the ends of the earth are present from the very first day. There is no secondhand, third-hand or fourth-hand faith. There is no church or nation that can say, "It belonged to us and now we are going to give it to you through our benevolence, evangelism, and mission work." No, No, No! Our listeners rise up and say, "We were there that same opening day you were there." For any church that would be Pentecostal, Pentecost removes all ground for any sense of triumphalism, for that ugly sense of arrogance and superiority that takes over the church sometimes simply because we get the notion that the salvation of other people in the world depends upon our behavior. Luke says it started in all the world at the same time. Now you can take that literally, symbolically, figuratively, or whatever, but his point is very clear. And if we miss it in Luke, we can get the figures from 475 Riverside Drive. The information that comes to me indicates that when China was closed to the United States and to the West in 1959 there were six hundred thousand Protestant Christians and about one million Roman Catholic Christians in China. When China was re-opened to America and to the West twenty years later, in 1979, there were more than three million Protestant Christians and more than three million Catholic Christians, and we weren't over there doing the converting. How did that happen? Pentecost says that the beginning point as well as the destination of the gospel is the whole world.

Luke says that in this audience the people heard each in his or her own tongue. This is admittedly a complex expression, difficult to understand. What does it mean? Does it mean that we are to make sure that we translate the Christian faith into every language and dialect and idiom of the world so that everybody can hear in his or her own tongue? Of course, it means that anything less is disobedience. But in Luke's description, the reference is not to the duty of the evangelist, but to the condition of the listener. The listener heard in his or her own language. Luke is referring to the capacity of the listener to hear the gospel. Now this is a tedious subject.

Over fifty years ago in Germany there was a running debate between Karl Barth and Emil Brunner over what was called "the point of contact." What is the "point of contact" of the gospel upon the ear of an unbeliever? Professor Barth said, "There is no point of contact. The image of God in the listener has been totally erased by sin." He said to his students, "Don't prepare introductions to your sermons. What are you trying to do, get them interested? Don't get involved in the idolatry of preaching, trying to be interesting. Just present the gospel. God prepares the ear, God gives the message; trust totally in God for all of it; that's it." Professor Brunner said, "No, no, no, no. . . . There is something very important in the way you craft the sermon. Many a preacher will, on account of what is said, go to heaven, but on account of how it is said, go to hell. We have responsibility for attracting listeners and for being clear because there is some capacity in the listener, however you may describe it, to hear the gospel." Later Paul Tillich rephrased the issue and responded to it with his method of correlation between the life questions asked by a culture and the responses given by the Christian faith. The assumption is that anyone who can ask an ultimate question is also capable of hearing an answer. Rudolf Bultmann shifted the meaning of "contact" between message and hearer. "Let's not talk of point of contact; let's talk of point of conflict. There is disturbance and resistance whenever the gospel is preached, because sinful persons encounter the power and the grace of God." Whether you call it contact or conflict, *something* occurs because the listener is not totally dead spiritually. Luke has no term for it. He doesn't refer to natural theology nor to the listener's "image of God." He doesn't say there is in everyone a faint recollection of Eden, nor does he have a term like "prevenient grace." What Luke says is, "People who listen to the gospel for the first time can hear it; people who hear the gospel for the first time *recognize* it."

You would expect such a view when Luke is describing the movement of the gospel among the Jews in Jerusalem. When Peter preaches in Jerusalem, he can say to his audience, "Jesus' way of life you all know. You know the prophets, you know the writings. Of course they knew and could *recognize* in Jesus some of their own tradition. But when the gospel moved out beyond the reach of Moses and the Law and the Prophets, beyond any knowledge of the Bible or of the life of Jesus Christ, what did the preacher say? When the preachers arrived in Lystra (Acts 14), they faced an audience that didn't know Moses or Jesus or Scripture. To them the preachers said, "Listen, folk, we come to you as people of a common nature, created from a common God, the beneficiaries of a common providence, to talk to you about a God who has never been without witness in the world, seeing that God gives to everyone everywhere goodness and rain and fruitful seasons and makes glad the human heart." Please do not misunderstand: the preachers are not saying, "What you already know is all we came to say." They came to preach Jesus Christ, but in doing so they said, "What we came to preach to you about redemption concerns the same God you know through creation. There is a continuity with what you already have discerned."

When Paul arrived in Athens, Greece (Acts 17), he stood

on the Areopagus, looked around and said, "This unknown God of yours if the subject of my sermon." Of course he could not make Old Testament references or refer to Jesus' life. Paul simply said, "There is one God who created all of us, a God who gave us life in appointed places and times for us to live. This is a God who created every one of us with a certain reaching, longing, seeking in our hearts. This is a God who has stirred even your own poets to say, 'In God we live and move and have our being.' This is a God who stirred even your own philosophers to say, 'We are all the offspring of God.' " And so he continued his message.

Point of *conflict,* point of *contact,* I don't know. I do know that Luke began the story of the church insisting that there was something in the listener that recognized the truth of the gospel, call it what we will.

Now I do not mean this as some kind of preacher ploy on the part of Luke or on my own part. Not at all. It may sound that way: "Ah, this is really beautiful; match up the appetite with the food and say, 'How symmetrically it worked out.' " That is not what Luke is doing, nor am I. It is not a case of putting a magnet in every human breast in order to say, "Notice how people are attracted to the gospel." What Luke is saying and what I am saying is exactly what the whole world knows: there is a hunger for what the gospel offers. Even the systems of tyranny in the world are but perversions of this same longing, seeking capacity of the human spirit. When Adolf Hitler sold his program to the German people, he didn't sell prisons and ovens and genocide. You know what he sold? He spoke of a way to peace and joy, of every home a quiet place, of children happy and well. Did Germany want that? Of course! Then came the means, the painful, necessary steps. Holocaust! I do not seek to excuse anyone, but rather to say the German people didn't vote for holocaust. They voted for something for which people everywhere search, search, search.

When Karl Marx sold the Russian people on a system of communism, he didn't sell them on the idea "Let's get rid of forty million Ukrainians; let's put microphones in every public building; let's suspect, watch, imprison, exile." He didn't sell that. What he sold was, "From each according to ability, to each according to need, so that all may. . . ." "So that all may"; what a wonderful thing! The most terrible systems of the human race are distortions of a longing for peace, quiet, love. The depths to which people sink are but another register of the heights to which they are capable of rising, because God has never been without witness in the world. Never. Anywhere. That is why upon hearing the gospel for the first time, listeners experience déjà vu; they have a sense of familiarity when offered a new experience.

Actually it does not really matter whether one is an old liberal who says, "I think the image of God is still there in all of us." It does not really matter if one is Barthian and says, " 'Twas grace that taught my heart to fear, and grace my fear relieved." It does not matter whether one prefers Tillich's or Bultmann's construction of the human situation. Nor does it matter whether one thinks of the human spirit as having a *memory* of Eden or a *hope* of Eden. Rather, Luke's word for us is simply this: "Do you want to be Pentecostal in a good, healthy, lively, renewing sense? Do you want the church to be Pentecostal? Then spend some thoughtful, careful, prayerful, listening time—listening to the listeners, in their concrete, historical circumstances." And if we listen to the listeners, carefully, prayerfully, thoughtfully, then we will notice, and will stand among them and say, "I think I speak for every person here, Parthians, Medes, Elamites, Europeans, Asians, Americans, Chinese, Africans, South Americans . . . I think I speak for every person here when I ask, 'Show us God and we'll be satisfied.' "

11. What's in a Nickname?

John N. Gladstone

Scripture: Mark 3:17; John 1:42; Acts 4:36

I WILL NEVER FORGET the day when I ceased to be known only by my name and I acquired a number. For eighteen years I had been just "John Gladstone." Then, on my first day as a raw recruit in the Royal Air Force, I became 5845326. It was a humbling experience. Our names are important to us. They are more than distinguishing labels; they are hallmarks of individuality, symbols of our worth as persons. Paul Tournier, the distinguished Swiss doctor and writer, says: "The proper name is the symbol of the person. If I forget my patient's name, if I say to myself, 'Ah! there's that gallbladder type, or that consumptive I saw the other day,' I am interesting myself more in their gallbladders or their lungs than in themselves as persons. And the relationship between doctor and patient goes wrong. The personal touch is gone, the patient ceases to be a person and becomes a bit of a mechanism to be put right—and knows it." We are pleased when people remember our names and annoyed when they get them wrong. Donald Fleming, in volume two of his memoirs, *So Very Near,* tells of the first meeting between President Kennedy and Prime Min-

---

John Norris Gladstone was born in 1921 in London, England. He was educated at Manchester Baptist College, Manchester University, in England, and has served as senior minister at Yorkminster Park Baptist Church in Toronto, Canada, since 1965. Dr. Gladstone has written several books, most recently *Living with Style.* This sermon is from that volume.

ister Diefenbaker in Washington. Unfortunately, the President publicly mispronounced the Prime Minister's name as "Diefenbawker." John Diefenbaker took some offense at this, and it was the beginning of a number of irritations that later soured the relations between these two men.

Many of us acquire not a number but a nickname. This is the *eke-name*, the added name of Old English. These added names are given for a variety of reasons: in fun, in affection, in derision. They can usually tell us a great deal about the person in question, providing a penetrating comment on that person's appearance, character, or career. A notable exception to this was the nickname of Canada's most internationally recognized prime minister, Lester B. Pearson. He was usually known as "Mike" Pearson, and he entitled the first volume of his memoirs "Mike." He explains how this nickname was given to him when he was in training as a pilot with the Royal Flying Corps in World War I: "My squadron commander decided that Lester was no name for an aspiring fighter pilot. He thereby immediately called me Mike. The name has stuck." Here was a nickname given without rhyme or reason, merely on the whim of a commanding officer who sounds as if he had too big an opinion of himself. Most nicknames are much more significant and descriptive than that. If someone is known as "Smiler," that tells you a lot. He either smiles frequently or never at all. "Old Misery" admits of only one interpretation. So too does "Skinflint." It was once given to a man who owned a chain of restaurants. It is said that when he was dying, his family gathered around the bedside and heard his last words. He was muttering, "Slice the ham thin, slice the ham thin."

The New Testament is rich in nicknames, as Dr. Gordon Robinson has pointed out. Sometimes they tell of a trade, sometimes they are diminutives, sometimes they describe the geographic origins of the holders. Some are contemptuous and some are affectionate. There were Alexander the Coppersmith of Cyrene, who found his added name in the place he came from; James the Less, who was presumably a very short man; Simeon Niger, who came from North Africa;

Thomas the Apostle, known as Didymus, which means the Twin; and Simon the Zealot, a member of a fanatical political party dedicated to throwing off the yoke of Rome. More interesting still is the fact that Jesus was obviously adept at giving nicknames to people. He called the crafty and cruel Herod "that fox," and the young daughter of Jairus "Tabitha," which means "Lambkin." Did he have nicknames for all the disciples who formed his inner circle? We can well imagine that he did.

I want us to look at three significant nicknames found in the New Testament, two of them given by Jesus himself and the other by the early church at Jerusalem to one of its outstanding members.

I

The first significant nickname is *the Thunderer.* It was given by Jesus to John the son of Zebedee, and to his brother James. Mark 3:17 records, "James the son of Zebedee and John his brother, whom he surnamed Boanerges, that is, sons of thunder." The thunder boys! It sounds like a modern motorcycle gang of leather-coated ruffians. James' life was cut short, for he was martyred early, but John went on to achieve distinction and prominence. So we will call John *the man who mastered the implication of his nickname.*

Suppose I were to ask you what your image is of John the disciple? I suspect it is a very pleasing one. We think of him as the beloved disciple, the one who meditated so profoundly on the life, death, and resurrection of Jesus that the Gospel that bears his name, the fourth Gospel, is always known as the spiritual Gospel. It leads us to the heights of devotion and is an inexhaustible source of comfort, faith, hope, and love. J. M. Barrie said that his mother's Bible opened automatically at John 14, so often did she turn to that passage of glorious assurance: "Let not your hearts be troubled; believe in God, believe also in me. In my Father's house are many rooms; if it were not so, would I have told you that I go to prepare a place for you?"

No funeral service would be complete without a reading of these words, and they always convey the comfort of God to bereaved people. This is the disciple John we know—quiet, loving, thoughtful, gracious—a man close to his Lord. And yet—his nickname at the beginning, given by Jesus, was "the Thunderer"!

Now this raises two questions. The first is: Why was John given the nickname? One suggestion is that John and his brother James were men with the gift of thunderous eloquence who knew how to declaim and how to stir emotions. This is sheer speculation, for there is no evidence at all to support it. Certainly the church throughout the centuries has had preachers with this kind of gift, however out of fashion and favor it may be today. I think of Dr. Joseph Parker of London's City Temple, recognized as an orator of the first magnitude. A lady once complained to him that his printed sermons were nowhere near as good to read as they were to hear. Parker, who was never noted for his modesty, replied, "Ah! Madame, you cannot print thunder and lightning."

The nickname Thunderer most probably implies that John was possessed of a fiery disposition; he was a short-fused man who never suffered fools gladly, easily giving way to anger, flaring up at the slightest provocation and readily hurting people. There is a warrant for this in the Gospels. Luke records how a Samaritan village refused to receive Jesus when his face was steadfastly set to go to Jerusalem, and James and John were furious, eager to retaliate. "Lord," they cried, "do you want us to bid fire to come down from heaven and consume them?" But Jesus turned and rebuked both disciples. In Mark we read of John coming to Jesus in an indignant mood saying, "Teacher, we saw a man casting out demons in your name, and we forbade him, because he was not following us." Again, Jesus had to rebuke his disciple and give him a lesson in tolerance.

There is, to be sure, a good side to this thunder and lightning. We could do with some passion and fire in our discipleship, some righteous anger in our dealings with the unholy trinity: the world, the flesh, and the devil. Jesus himself could be angry. "The trouble with us," as George Matheson once said, "is that there are times when we do well to be angry, but we have mistaken the times!" That was John's trouble, too, and Jesus called him the Thunderer.

Our second question is this: How did John master the implication of his nickname? How did the son of thunder become the beloved disciple? I think there is only one explanation; he did it by living in the magnetic, transforming friendship of Jesus, by learning at the feet of Jesus, by absorbing the very spirit of Jesus. Yet I am wrong to say he did it. Jesus did it for him, changed him from glory to glory. And in that exhilarating truth is our comfort and hope! His touch has still its ancient power. Take the case of Edward Wilson, the famous doctor who went with Captain Scott's expedition to the Antarctic. In 1891, as an undergraduate at Cambridge University, Edward Wilson was nicknamed "Bill the Cynic." He was argumentative, disagreeable, and he had a bitter tongue. Writing once to a friend he had offended, he confessed, "I know I am hard, proud, conceited, scornful, bitter, and insulting very often, and always selfish; but I don't like you to treat me as though I wasn't trying to do a bit better." Years later, as the physician on that terrible journey to the South Pole and in circumstances of extreme provocation, the same Edward Wilson was nicknamed "Bill the Peacemaker." Captain Scott wrote about him in that last hour as they lay dying in their tent: "If this letter reaches you, Bill and I will have gone out together. We are very near it now; and I should like you to know how splendid he was at the end, everlastingly cheerful and ready to sacrifice himself for others. His eyes have a comfortable blue look of hope, and his mind is peaceful with the satisfaction of his faith in regarding himself as part of the great scheme of the Almighty." The truth is that Edward Wilson fell in love with Christ, write about him in a glowing book of devotion, so lived in his presence that he became a new creation. The old nickname passed away, and a new, Christ-created one took its place. Thank God such mastery is open to every one of us.

II

The second significant nickname is *the Rock*. This too was given by Jesus. John 1:42 tells us how Andrew brought his brother Simon to Jesus, and Jesus, looking at him, said: "So you are Simon the son of John. You shall be called Cephas (which means Peter)—the Rock." We will call Peter *the man who reached the potential of his nickname*. He had a lot of achieving to do! When Jesus first met him, his character was far from rocklike. The nickname must have sounded ironic to those who knew Simon well. The rock-man? He was unstable, unreliable, more like drifting, shifting sand, blown this way and that by the wind. He misunderstands what Jesus means by his Messiahship; he boasts of his unswerving loyalty and then denies Jesus; he fails so dismally as a disciple that even the resurrection of the Lord left him feeling that he had no future. "I am going fishing," he said, "back to the old job. I am a failure as a follower of Jesus."

The wonder of it is that Peter achieved the potential of his nickname. Turn the pages of the New Testament, turn to the Acts of the Apostles, and see Peter standing boldly before all Jerusalem, facing the Jewish Council and daring them to disobey God, rejoicing to be counted worthy to suffer dishonor for the name of Christ, and becoming the strong, courageous, dependable elder of the Jerusalem church. Peter made it by the grace of God and in the power of Christ.

Now, in giving this nickname to Simon Peter, Jesus did two things. He revealed his prophetic confidence in human nature. He was under no illusions about humankind. He knew what was in us. He knew how selfish, frail, fallible, weak, and unreliable we can be. Simon Peter is you and me. Yet Jesus stubbornly kept his confidence in us. He believed we were worth dying for, believed that we could become new creations, ransomed, healed, restored, forgiven, transformed. Jesus Christ looks at us with prophetic confidence, sees us not as we are but as we may become. He has the creative vision of a Savior. "You are Simon the son of John . . . you shall be Peter, the Rock."

At Mount Rushmore, South Dakota, are the carved figures of four United States presidents—Washington, Jefferson, Lincoln, and Theodore Roosevelt. The sculptor was Gutzon Borglum. Asked how he did it, he replied whimsically: "Well, those figures were there for forty million years. All I had to do was dynamite 400,000 tons of granite to bring them into view." Isn't this what Christ is seeking to do: to bring into view the real person he knows us to be? There's another story about Gutzon Borglum. He was working on a head of Abraham Lincoln in his studio. Each day he chipped away at the stone, and each day it was the task of a cleaning woman to sweep up the pieces. Amazed, she watched the head of Lincoln emerge under the sculptor's hands until, at last, when the work was almost finished, she could contain her wonder no longer. "Mr. Borglum," she said, "how did you know Mr. Lincoln was in that stone?" The emergence of strong, stable character from our unshaped lives often seems improbable enough, but Christ knows better than any cynic! He believes in us. All things are possible with him.

Then, in giving this particular nickname, Jesus revealed the true nature of his church. The church is not a community of people who have arrived spiritually; it is a community of people who are achieving spiritually. "The Lord added to the church," says the book of Acts, "those who were being saved."

Go to that dramatic incident at Caesarea Philippi recorded in Matthew 16, when Peter made the great confession: "You are the Christ, the Son of the living God." Jesus responded glowingly, "And I tell you, you are Peter, and on this rock I will build my church, and the powers of death shall not prevail against it." What was Jesus referring to by "the rock"? Was it Peter, the man to whom he had given this very nickname? Or was it Peter's confession of faith in him as the Son of God? The truth surely lies in a combination of both: Peter as a confessing disciple. The church was to be built, is being built, and must be built on the foundation of men and women believing and confessing that Jesus is the Son of God. Yet how frail and fallible Peter still was! Almost with the next breath Jesus had to call him "Satan." But on such common, unreliable, inadequate material Christ consistently chooses to build. We who belong to the church are not what we should be, by a long shot; but, thank God, we are not what we were, or what we will be! By grace we shall justify Christ's strange confidence in us and achieve our potential. This is the true nature of the church, and the powers of death shall not prevail against it.

III

Turn now to the third significant nickname. It is *the Encourager*. It was given by the early church to one of its finest members, Joseph of Cyprus. Acts 4:36 records: "Joseph . . . was surnamed by the apostles Barnabas (which means, Son of Encouragement) . . ." We will call Barnabas *the man who deserved the award of his nickname.* He was a wealthy man and generous. He sold a field and gave the money to the church leaders to strengthen their hands in God. And this was no isolated act. Everything we read about this good man in the New Testament is geared to some act of encouragement. It was Barnabas who encouraged Saul of Tarsus when the church was naturally suspicious of the converted persecutor; it was Barnabas who encouraged a new and unorthodox cause. Always an encourager, Barnabas gave his services freely and fully to the end of his days.

Isn't this a nickname for every Christian to covet? There are always vacancies in the ministry of encouragement. The world is full of discouragers, always ready to pour the cold water of their negativism and criticism over any enthusiasm, love, and vision that they find. Rose McCauley says of a character in one of her novels: "Her worst fault was a cynical unkindness against which she did not strive, because investigating the less admirable traits of human beings amused her." Unfortunately, we encounter people like that in fact as well as in fiction. To encourage, to lift, to offer the tonic of praise, to stand at the side of another person in need of help is a Christ-like service.

There was a logging operation in the northwest of our country, and the superintendent of it had as his deputy a young university student. A time came when this superintendent had to be away for a while, and he confidently left the operation in care of his deputy. Before leaving, he briefed the student on the situation. "You shouldn't have any trouble," he said, "except possibly from one man called Tony. He can be difficult, even rebellious. But on no account are you to fire him. He is the best logger in the northwest." The next day the young deputy went round to see the loggers at work and eventually came to Tony. After chatting pleasantly with him for a time, he said before moving on: "Tony, the boss tells me you are the best logger in the northwest. There isn't anyone who can touch you at the job." That night, when the whistle went, Tony was waiting for his new, temporary boss. He invited him to his home for supper. As they sat around the table enjoying a fragrant meal, Tony told his wife what the student had told him earlier: that the bossman thought he was the best logger in the northwest, and there wasn't a man to touch him. Tony's wife got up from the table, wiped her hands on her apron, went over to their guest and put her arms around him. "Today is like Christmas Day in our house," she said, with tears in her eyes. And Tony, jabbing the air with his fork, said: "Why didn't the boss ever tell me that himself? There were days when I could have killed somebody."

We all need encouragement. All people need a Barnabas to underline their strengths, praise their good qualities, believe in them when they find it hard to believe in themselves, stand by them when they fail, expect great things of them.

To deserve the award of the nickname "Son of Encouragement" is an honor indeed and a sure sign that we are growing in grace and in the knowledge of our Lord Jesus Christ. But how can we deserve it? The secret is in an eloquent tribute paid to Barnabas later in the book of Acts: "For he was a good man, full of the Holy Spirit and of faith." I suspect that none would have been more surprised than Barnabas to read this glowing testimony concerning his life and service. His goodness was not self-conscious goodness. It was the by-product of his faith in Christ and his experience of the indwelling Holy Spirit. The good life becomes ours not by struggle and effort, but by surrender and discipleship. What's in a nickname? Everything true and good—when Christ is enthroned in our hearts by faith, and his Spirit is allowed to have his way with us.

> And every virtue we possess,
> And every victory won,
> And every thought of holiness,
> Are his alone.

12. Saul and the Witch
Richard C. Marius

Scripture: 1 Samuel 28–31

THE STORY of Saul and the witch of En-Dor always frightened me when my mother read it to me in my childhood, and
as an adult I can see why. Saul, Israel's first and doomed king,
sees the gathering of the Philistines to subjugate Israel. The
Philistines have come in from the sea—always a source of mystery and horror for Israel—and they know the secret of iron
and fight with iron swords. There is not a blacksmith in all Israel, and Saul knows that the very existence of his people is at
stake.

The god who has made him king will not speak to him
"whether by dreams or by Urim or by prophets." Since no one
among the living can console him, Saul turns to the dead, to
Samuel the prophet who had anointed Saul and then cursed
him and died. Saul's men locate a witch at En-Dor, and disguis-
ing himself, Saul goes to her at night to ask her to call Samuel
from the grave.

So Samuel's ghost comes up from the earth at this midnight summons, but he pronounced not hope but doom. "You

Richard Curry Marius was born in 1933 in Martel, Tennessee. A
Baptist, he was educated at the University of Tennessee, the Southern
Baptist Theological Seminary, and at Yale University, and currently is
director of expository writing and senior lecturer in English at
Harvard University. One of Dr. Marius' books, the biography *Thomas
More*, was a finalist in the 1984 American Book Award nonfiction
competition. He has written two novels and has a third in progress.

were not bloody enough," the ghost says in effect. Saul had not sacrificed Agag, king of the Amalekites, before Yahweh, and for that offense, says the ghost, "Yahweh will let your people Israel fall into the hands of the Philistines, and, what is more, tomorrow you and your sons will be with me."

So it was. Saul was terrified at Samuel's bloody prophecy, but he was no coward. This was the Saul who had come home one evening from his plowing only to learn that Nahash the Ammonite had besieged Jabesh-Gilead and had offered to lift the siege only if he might gouge out the right eye of every man in the town. Saul, stirred by fury and pity, rallied Israel and fell on the Ammonites and massacred them until, the Bible says, "no two men were left together."

But then came the Philistines, and even Saul's courage could not triumph against iron swords. "Tomorrow, you and your sons will be with me," Samuel's ghost said. The next day, Saul's three sons—Jonathan, Abinadab, and Malchishua—were cut down by the Philistines on Mount Gilboa, and Saul, "wounded in the belly by the archers," as the Bible says, told his armor-bearer, "Draw your sword and run me through, so that these uncircumcised dogs may not come and taunt me and make sport of me." But the armor-bearer refused to strike Yahweh's anointed, and Saul staggered upright in the raging sun and fell on his own sword. The Bible says, "When the armor-bearer saw that Saul was dead, he, too, fell on his sword and died with him. Thus they all died together on that day, Saul, his three sons, and his armor-bearer, as well as his men."

The next day, the Philistines found Saul and cut off his head. The Bible says, "They deposited his armor in the temple of Ashtoreth and nailed his body on the wall of Beth-Shan." The implacable prophecy of Samuel's ghost was fulfilled. But the people of Jabesh-Gilead had not forgotten the savior of their eyes. The Bible says, "When the inhabitants of Jabesh-Gilead heard what the Philistines had done to Saul, the bravest of them journeyed together all night long and recovered the bodies of Saul and his sons from the wall of Beth-Shan; they brought them back to Jabesh and anointed them there with spices. Then they took their bones and buried them under the tamarisk tree in Jabesh and fasted for seven days."

Saul and his brave sons have been dust now for almost three millennia, but desperate mortals still seek prophecy from the ghosts of the dead and hear doom pronounced on tomorrow. Our ghosts speak in the new vision of our history, and in recent years Americans have searched out a diabolical vision of our past that rises from the grave to damn the future. Two extremes have somehow come together in the same midnight to listen to the same prophecy.

On the one hand the Reaganites tell us in effect that America has been historically great because it has been historically greedy; in the last months they have pronounced doom on the national aspirations we once had to clothe the naked, to feed the hungry, to bind up the wounds of the fallen, and to care for the widow and orphan among us. They have discovered that it is not American to care for such things.

But we also have those other folks preaching with bullhorns in Harvard Square on Saturday morning, who believe that our past has been nothing but two centuries of infamy. Now even liberals languish for lack of purpose because we all know that Abraham Lincoln was a racist, Franklin Roosevelt was a politician, and Woodrow Wilson was a Presbyterian. Not long ago a dear friend of mine told me that American attitudes toward the Jews were no better than the Germans' because, given the historical circumstances, we might have had a holocaust, too. The fact that we did not have a holocaust did not make any difference to her.

The obvious conclusion for both these views of the past is doom for the future of justice in this society. The Reaganites and the radicals alike hear the voices of the dead in the night and conclude that anything we do for the people as a whole will finally be judged as contemptuously as we now judge the past. So we may as well eat, drink and be merry—or, in the present jargon, wrap narcissism around ourselves and call it fate. How strange to such people Saul must be, standing bravely in the blazing sun with his back against a mountain, fighting to the end against the overpowering Philistines and killing himself before he would let them dishonor them.

Only a fool would deny that this diabolical past pronouncing doom speaks the truth; but it is not the whole truth. Saul did die as Samuel's ghost promised, but Saul in his life preserved his people, and they endured beyond his death and endure yet— something that might not have happened without him.

We shall certainly die, and we may not win any memorable triumphs in the daunting human struggle to do unselfish good. Our labors for justice will always be corrupted by our nature—as Saul's temper corrupted him. Yet corruption is not depravity, and frail human beings may still honor the good by giving a life and perhaps a death for it. We do remember Saul after all these centuries, and David loved him though Saul had tried to kill him.

There is always a party of hope and a party of despair. Now the party of hope that has always represented the America of our best dreams staggers before the cynicism of the right and the left who have read their history at midnight and hear a murmur of doom for generous aspiration. We could use Saul's courage against our gentle hopes.

When Samuel's ghost uttered his prophecy, Saul might have fled and hidden himself in the pleasures of some remote, private life. Instead he went into battle for his people—and we remember him. We might also imitate him, for there is a softer voice to history than the harsh pronouncements of our hard prophets. It tells us that tomorrow's doom may be but a step along the journey and that hope knows something other than endless defeat.

13. Who Is Supposed to Serve?
Eduard Schweizer

Scripture: 1 Kings 16:19–33; 17:10–16; Mark 1:29–39

My dear brothers and sisters in Christ,

The success of Jesus—there was nothing like it! Talk about him spread over the entire region—and then, so we are told, "the whole city was gathered together about the door." The whole city—think of that! As if for once our entire town, down to the last person, would be gripped by an evangelist, who preaches the word of God! And in that connection, it is clearly a pious, God-fearing city, for they wait until after sundown to bring their sick. Then the Sabbath is over, for they are not permitted to work on the Sabbath, even to carry around a sick person. It is a city that keeps God's law and keeps Sunday holy, we would say, down to the last detail.

And now we read something remarkable: we are told that the demons knew him.

There is a transparent human world that we can penetrate with our understanding, and there is also in each one of us a much darker world. In it there are powers and forces at work

Robert Eduard Schweizer was born in 1913 in Basel, Switzerland. He was educated at the Universities of Basel, Marburg, and Zurich. Dr. Schweizer, a member of the Reformed Church, served as a pastor and as professor of New Testament at the University of Zurich in Switzerland until he retired in 1979. He is the author of more than twenty books and two hundred essays. A number of his sermons appear in *God's Inescapable Nearness.* ("Who Is Supposed to Serve?" has been translated from the German by James W. Cox.)

over which we have no control, very evil, dark, sinister powers and forces. We think of drug addiction or what happened under Hitler in Germany or other such things. There can also be good powers and forces. Many times love and a feeling of happiness will rise up in us without our knowing where it comes from. And sometimes, it is in the world of dark things, which we cannot simply illuminate or explain with our understanding, that we realize something of God's activity. Thus the demons recognize Jesus, long before people reason out what is going on. Just before the events described in our text, such a demon in a possessed man cried out, "I know who you are, the Holy One of God." And quite soon after that, the demons cry out even to him, as the Son of God. So the demons are orthodox; they understand matters better than anyone else; they understand who Jesus is. They are much further along than Peter. After many months he can say one day for the first time, "I actually believe you are the Christ of God." The demons have already long since said that he is not only "the Christ," but even "the Son of God." One could not say it better. Indeed, God himself says it to his son, when Jesus gets baptized by John the Baptist: "You are my beloved Son." Likewise, God will say it also to the trusted disciples in the story of the Transfiguration: "This is my beloved Son, hear him." But not until under the cross will a human being, namely the Roman officer who has just executed him, confess it: "This was truly the Son of God."

Now we are told that Jesus "would not permit the demons to speak, because they knew him." To be acquainted with him, to know precisely who he is, does not necessarily imply faith at all. One can, as we say, be orthodox and not really be in the faith. So it does not follow, therefore, that we may find even better titles for Jesus, like the ones the demons themselves also know—Son of God or something like that. The issue is not whether people now might be even more precisely and better taught. That all has its place. Throughout my life I have attempted only to understand Jesus as well and as clearly as possible and to pass that on to my students. The same happens in confirmation classes and in all kinds of adult education courses. And it has its place. But that is not the central point.

"And in the morning, a great while before day, he rose and went out to a lonely place."

So a tremendous enthusiasm has broken out in this city. And even that is obviously still not the crucial issue. One might experience that on a retreat, perhaps with a church youth group. One might experience that in the family circle. One can experience it as an individual. And all of that has its place and is important too, but it is still not the decisive thing. So our text does not say that the next day even greater miracles did happen, even more beautiful experiences of God did occur. Not at all. Peter cannot grasp that: "And Simon and those who were with him pursued him, and they found him and said to him, 'Every one is searching for you.' " How extraordinary—this is indeed a once-in-a-lifetime opportunity! Now to break through, now to convert the whole city, now to do something one more time more inspiring than ever. They are seeking him: it has started a religious movement. Why does Jesus now withdraw? Even yet not all have heard about him. The ones who perhaps live outside on the fringes learned of it in fact for the first time in the evening and now want to come next morning. Is he then not for them? Here are the warriors for God's kingdom, Peter and his disciples, to whom it is not a matter of indifference that this fabulous opportunity has now slipped by. Now one has to be missionary!

But Jesus withdrew "to a lonely place, and there he prayed."

There is a kind of retreat that is egotistical, a retreat into totally individual solitary piety, where one wants only to be with one's God, and let the world be the world and let the other people go their way on their broad, bright streets, as a well-known pietistic hymn puts it. But that is, of course, not how it is with Jesus. It is daybreak, and the day will certainly follow in which he will once more emerge from this quiet time in isolation from other people. But for him this stillness is essential, perhaps no doubt because one has to learn that one cannot and even must not always do everything, that one may for once turn over to God that which goes beyond personal possibilities and powers. But it is especially important, because we understand for the first time in connection with this withdrawal of Jesus what that means: that God wants to encounter us in him. God is indeed a living God and is not simply present in Jesus like a piece of jewelry that we can place in a strongbox, that will stay put until we want to take it out. It is much more like a child that grows in its mother's body, and that of course must be constantly nourished and breathed for, in order that it may grow. If the mother poisons herself with anything, then she also poisons the child. She may notice nothing at all for some time, though the child is long since dead. That is how it is with God's presence in us: it lives, but it is not simply to be taken for granted; rather, it must be nourished and cared for, be resuscitated. So it is with Jesus. Even in his case, God had to live anew again and again, live anew every day (and it is no different with us today). That continues on to Gethsemane, where he is completely alone in his wrestling and praying and where God becomes so much alive in and through him.

That is one side of the matter. The other is this: he says, "Now I must also go into the other towns and preach there." Jesus wants to sow seeds and must do so, for faith has to be active everywhere, not just in one place. Thus, preaching is for him the decisive factor. He believes that the word has power to create community, to accomplish things, to nourish, and to produce growth; with him it is the kind of word that comes to expression again and again in deeds and thus proves itself. "And he went throughout all Galilee, preaching . . . and casting out demons." Both belong together, but both intend to point our heart entirely to such confidence in the word of God.

There is in our text an account of what happens when God, in his word, breaks in, into the life of a person.

"Now Simon's mother-in-law lay sick with a fever, and immediately they told him of her. And he came and took her by the hand and lifted her up, and the fever left her."

And what about her now? She has had an experience of God, an experience of God that is not simple at all. Experiences of God are never unambiguous. To be sure, her getting well just now can be an accident. It might be the psychological influence of this Master, who comes so unexpectedly. Or he could even be a miracle worker with special powers, as they are known in all times, and certainly in that of Jesus and Peter.

But she *knows* that God has now entered into her life. And what should she do next? She could now go to great pains to believe as correctly as possible; therefore, to listen to advice, perhaps from her son-in-law, and find still more exalted titles for Jesus—not only Rabbi, not only Prophet, but perhaps even Messiah or something like that. To be sure, one can hold to such a conviction for a lifetime, and say precisely the right thing about Jesus, and at the same time the child is long since dead. The demons also can do that, as James writes (2:19). They know it with precision—better than we do, better than the best theologian. She, Peter's mother-in-law, does not know all that. She has no pious words; she could not express formally who Jesus is. And perhaps it is not so bad if, many times, we cannot express precisely who he really is. She knows only one thing: In this Jesus, God has entered into my life.

On the other hand, she could be inspired; she could fall down before him, adore him, and perhaps begin to speak in tongues; and she could expect even more beautiful experiences and inspiration. But one can do all of that, too, and only become proud; one may in this way belong to the elite, letting others go their way is if they were nothing. And it can still be nothing less than plain pride, slightly camouflaged with religion. That is not how it is with her. She remains incredibly calm. Nothing extraordinary happens; there is no evidence of her being inspired. Rather, only a single thing is said about her, and that is the real point: "And she served them." So, it was something very simple.

She is a woman—and women were then looked down on. She was not once permitted to be in the worshiping community; rather, she had to sit way back, behind the barrier. This is a woman who apparently never went outside her little village; whose life by and large is lived out in this little house, and no doubt also ends one day right there; therefore, one who can accomplish nothing at all. And yet she is precisely the one who, out of hundreds who were healed, is now placed center stage in the Gospel.

And in the Old Testament lesson, it is once again a woman, a widow, who does not have a husband through whom she could have some importance, who has learned to render service to Elijah. She had to serve before she saw the miracle, had to dare to bake him a little loaf of bread on credit, so to speak, from the scanty supply of meal that she still had as a last resort. At that point she experienced the help of God.

In the New Testament we are told again and again, by Mark, Matthew, Luke, and John, that women served Jesus. That was, in a way, the form of discipleship for the women of that time. But we must see how progressive it was in Palestine then that a group of men tolerated women among them. And we must see that we cannot remain at a standstill, but rather that this means that women today, according to my view, are permitted to serve together with men on the same level. For on the one hand, even the evangelists use at least at one place (Mark 15:41) the term "following" Jesus, which designates real discipleship, also of women. On the other hand, the male disciples should have served, as Jesus tells them after James and John had asked for the best places in heaven (Mark 10:43–44), but did not actually do so. Thus, according to the Gospel, men are supposed to learn to do what women have already been doing.

In the first chapter of Mark, right at the beginning, it says, "The angels served him." And it is said of Jesus, "The Son of Man did not come to be served, but to serve and to give his life as a ransom for many." On the last day of his earthly life he said to his disciples, "I am among you as one who serves." And in a remarkable parable we are told: then in the age of glory "will he the Lord himself serve us his slaves" (Luke 12:37) as one who serves at table. That is to say, the women have done what the angels do and what Jesus himself does.

Dear friends, the point is not for us to become even more orthodox—that is well and good, but it is still not the crucial matter. The point is not for us to have even more inspiring experiences, which is right and proper, but not of ultimate importance. The point is not that we have higher standing than others, as the chosen ones, higher than the disciples, who were simply obligated to serve.

This is the issue: that we serve Jesus with our total being. To serve Jesus is not always comfortable. But serving is what the angels do; it is what Jesus himself does; it is what ordinary women like Simon's mother-in-law are doing; and it is what all the disciples of Jesus should do.

14. God's Promises Are for Believing

Steven P. Vitrano

Scripture: Genesis 15

IF YOU WERE to draw a picture of Abraham, what would he look like? Tall, dark, handsome, muscular, athletic, the Arnold Schwarzenegger of the Old Testament? Hardly! When the story begins in Genesis 12, where God promises him he will make him the father of a great nation, he is seventy-five years old! And he is much older than that in Genesis 15, where we read of the most important conversation with God he ever had. It goes something like this:

> *God:* Abram [he was later to be called Abraham—Gen. 17], your reward shall be very great!
>
> *Abram:* Lord, how can this be? I continue childless and, according to our custom under such circumstances, the heir of my house is Eliezer of Damascus. How can I be a great nation when you have given me no offspring?

Steven Parfitt Vitrano was born in New London, Wisconsin, in 1922. Dr. Vitrano received degrees from Emmanuel Missionary College (now Andrews University), the Seventh-day Adventist Seminary, and Michigan State University. He is professor of preaching, liturgics, and evangelism at the Seventh-day Adventist Seminary in Berrien Springs, Michigan, and has had published three books and numerous articles.

> *God:* No, Abram, this man shall not be your
> heir. Your own son shall be your heir.
> Abram, look at the heavens. Can you number
> the stars? So shall your descendants be.

Well! What would you have said to that? You are an old man
and your wife is old too. There is no possible way that you can
have children at that age! God means well but this is just plain
silly. It's too late! It was too late when you were seventy-five;
why would anyone in his right mind think it could happen now?

Abraham could have thought that. He could have, but
thank God he did not! You see, he had been talking and walking
with God for some time. He had learned, for the time being at
least, that you don't question God just because he doesn't make
sense. What you do is believe him. And that is just what he did.
It says, in verse 6, "And he believed God." And then it adds,
"And he [God] reckoned it to him as righteousness."

That is righteousness by faith *alone!* There is nothing Abraham could do to make it happen. He couldn't try harder, be
more diligent, more persistent, exercise greater will power. All
he could do was believe, and God reckoned it to him as
righteousness.

So God promised Abraham a son, an heir, so that he could
be a great nation. But there is more. God speaks again:

> *God:* Abram, I brought you from Ur of the
> Chaldeans to give you this land.
> *Abram:* Lord, how am I to know that I will
> possess it?

Incredible! How was Abraham, the nomad, to possess the
promised land? He didn't have the resources, neither the money to buy it nor the armies to conquer it. True, he was not
poor, nor without men who could fight for him, but this was
preposterous! The man of faith was having his doubts.

But God did not rebuke him or chasten him. What he had
him do was prepare for the making of a covenant. As was the
custom in covenant making, he had Abraham cut the ceremonial animals in two and separate the halves so that each party

to the covenant could walk between them. In so doing, they would say, "Let me be so cut asunder if I should not keep the provisions of this covenant." It was a symbol of perpetual fidelity to the provisions of the covenant.

With the going down of the sun, while Abraham was in a deep sleep, God explained to him how it would all work out:

> Abram, your descendants will be slaves for four hundred years in a land that is not theirs. But I will bring judgment on the nation that they serve, and they will be set free and come out with great possessions.
> As for you, you shall go to your rest and be buried at a good old age. But your descendants will come back here in the fourth generation because the iniquity of the Amorites is not yet complete.

When the sun had gone down and it was dark, a smoking fire pot and a flaming torch passed between the pieces of animals. On that day God made a covenant with Abraham. It was a covenant containing two promises; first, the promise of a son, and second, the promise of the land. It was a covenant that revealed God's grace to Abraham and his posterity, and God's long-suffering and patience toward the Amorites. He would not judge them until their iniquity was complete.

And history records that it happened just that way. After some time, Sarah, Abraham's wife, bore him a son, Isaac, but the promise of the land was not fulfilled in Abraham's day. It was many years later that his descendants entered the land of promise, when the iniquity of the Amorites was completed.

A most interesting story! But what does it say to us? Stories are good, I suppose, especially Bible stories. The pious would read and tell them just because they are in the Bible. But there is more to this story than that, at least for the apostle Paul. Many centuries later he wrote in Galatians 3:29:

> And if you are Christ's, then you are Abraham's offspring, heirs according to the promise.

Really? Christians are the offspring of Abraham, and heirs according to the promise God made to him? That's what Paul said! You mean God promised Abraham's offspring a son? Yes. That's what the offspring of Abraham have believed for centuries. Here is Isaiah's version, in Isaiah 9:5–6:

> For to us a child is born, to us a son is given;
> and the government will be upon his shoulders,
> and his name will be called "Wonderful Counselor,
> Mighty God, Everlasting Father, Prince of Peace."

And God promised Abraham's offspring land? Yes. Again, listen to Isaiah:

> For behold, I create new heavens and a new earth;
> and the former things shall not be remembered or
> come into mind. . . . I will rejoice in Jerusalem, and
> be glad in my people; no more shall be heard in it
> the sound of weeping and the cry of distress. . . .
> They shall build houses and inhabit them; they
> shall plant vineyards and eat their fruit. They shall
> not build and another inhabit; they shall not plant
> and another eat. . . . Before they cry I will answer,
> while they are yet speaking I will hear. The wolf
> and the lamb shall feed together, the lion shall eat
> straw like the ox; and dust shall be the serpent's
> food. They shall not hurt or destroy in all my holy
> mountain, says the Lord (Isa. 65:17–25).

Fantastic! But have the promises been fulfilled? Has the promise of the son been fulfilled?

Of course! That's what Christianity is all about. From the day of Jesus' baptism, when God called him his beloved Son, his disciples have proclaimed him to be the fulfillment of that promise,. Like Abraham, every Christian believes that what God has promised he is able to fulfill. Like Isaac, Jesus did not come as the result of human effort. That he was born of a virgin is a miracle, an act of God. All we can do, and all that we are asked to do, is believe, and, like Abraham, it is counted to us as righteousness. It is righteousness by faith. And that is just how Christ becomes your Savior and mine, by faith *alone*.

And has the promise of the land been fulfilled?

No. That promise has been delayed. Why? The apostle Peter, one of the first disciples, in his second epistle, 2 Peter 2:8–10, 13, explains the delay:

> But do not ignore this one fact, beloved, that with the Lord one day is as a thousand years, and a thousand years as one day. The Lord is not slow about his promise as some count slowness, but is forbearing toward you, not wishing that any should perish, but that all should reach repentance. But the day of the Lord will come like a thief, and then the heavens will pass away with a loud noise, and the elements will dissolve with fire, and the earth and the works that are upon it will be burned up. . . . But according to his promise we wait for new heavens and a new earth in which righteousness dwells.

From these words of Peter, we note first of all that the promise of the land was "according to his promise." Peter, of course, understood the word of Jesus recorded in John 14:1–3 to be a confirmation of that promise:

> Let not your hearts be troubled, believe in God, believe also in me. In my Father's house are many rooms; if it were not so, would I have told you that I go to prepare a place for you? And when I go and prepare a place for you, I will come again and will take you to myself, that where I am you may be also.

And again, as recorded in Matthew 25:31–34:

> When the Son of man comes in his glory, and all the angels with him, then he will sit on his glorious throne. Before him will be gathered all

the nations, and he will separate them one from
another as a shepherd separates the sheep from
the goats. . . . Then the King will say to those at
his right hand, "Come, O blessed of my Father,
inherit the kingdom prepared for you from the
foundation of the world."

So the promise of the land is secure, renewed by Christ and
confirmed in the promise of his second coming.

But why the delay?

Because, as Peter put it, God is long-suffering, not willing
that any should perish but that all should reach repentance.
The iniquity of the Amorites is not yet complete. This is what
calls the Christian to mission and evangelism. While the iniquity of the earth is not yet complete (and at times that seems
hard to believe), he has work to do. There are still those who
will accept Christ by faith and become heirs according to the
promise. "And this gospel of the kingdom will be preached
throughout the whole world, as a testimony to all nations; and
then the end will come" (Matt. 24:14).

It is the promise of the land that gives the Christian the impetus to live as a Christian. "Since all these things are thus to
be dissolved, what sort of persons ought you to be in lives of
holiness and godliness, waiting for and hastening the coming
of the day of God?" (2 Pet. 3:11,12). The Christian is not frus-
trated or demoralized by the fact that all of our efforts for personal well-being, social renewal, moral responsibility, and
equality and justice for all, seem to have little effect upon a
godless, materialistic, hedonistic world. The same righteousness we hope to find in the new earth, we seek to demonstrate
in the here and now.

It is the promise of the land that gives the Christian hope in
the face of dehumanizing pain, suffering, and death:

Then I saw a new heaven and a new earth; for
the first heaven and the first earth had passed
away, and the sea was no more. And I saw the
holy city, New Jerusalem, coming down out of

heaven from God, prepared as a bride adorned
for her husband; and I heard a loud voice from
the throne saying, "Behold, the dwelling of
God is with men. He will dwell with them, and
they shall be his people, and God himself will
be with them, he will wipe away every tear
from their eyes, and death shall be no more,
neither shall there be mourning nor crying nor
pain any more, for the former things have
passed away" (Rev. 21:1–4).

Wow! That's heavy! But do you really expect me to believe
all that? After all, this is 1987, not A.D. 100 or 200 or even
1500. With what we know about the world and space and the
universe and the natural sciences and, and, and? For someone
with a medieval mentality, maybe. But today?

Well, it somewhat depends upon whether or not you believe in the promise of the Son. Was Jesus the fulfillment of the
promise? Was he the Son of God, born of a virgin, crucified
and raised the third day? Is he alive, now? After all, this is
1987! It is just as impossible to believe in the promise of the
Son as it is to believe in the promise of the land. It was no easier for Abraham to believe in his day than it is for us to believe
in ours. If God has promised, it really doesn't matter whether
it harmonizes with our "system of knowledge" or not. Jesus
said, "Blessed are the meek, for they shall inherit the earth"
(Matt. 5:5). Now there is no way that that is going to happen in
our world. Given the human situation as we know it today, hell
will freeze over before the meek will inherit the earth! But
God has ways of bringing it off that we know nothing about.
Sarah can give birth to a child in her nineties; Mary, a virgin,
can give birth to the Son of God; Abraham's offspring can oc-
cupy the land of promise; the meek can inherit the earth. One
is just as "impossible" as the other. Yet for the Christian they
are all true.

I was a city boy who saw the milk delivered each day by a
milkman. I took special note of this, no doubt, because of my
thirst for milk. It is something I was born with and from which

I have never really been weaned. There was never enough. The bottle was always too soon empty.

Then one day my parents took me on a visit to my uncle's dairy farm. Imagine my delight when I saw all those cows and was told that that is where the milk comes from. I was in heaven! With all those "milk machines" doing their thing, I could drink until I was drunk!

The next morning I was the first one at the breakfast table. I was prepared to drink five glasses, at least. Imagine my consternation and bitter disappointment when, having finished my first glass, I was gold there would be no seconds; there was only enough for one glass apiece. Why? Have the cows all gone dry? What a revolting development this turned out to be!

Later I was to learn that the cows had not gone dry. They were, in fact, excellent cows, and gave gallons of milk each day. But we were living in a time of depression. Most of the milk had to be sold to buy other necessities such as clothing, fuel, soap, and to pay the electric bill and the payment on the mortgage. "That's not fair!" was my first and quite vehement response. But in time I understood. Such are the vicissitudes of life. We plant and another eats. We build and another inhabits. You can understand, I'm sure, why a broad smile creeps over my face every time I read that figurative description of the promised land—"a land flowing with milk and honey."

Childish? Perhaps. And yet the possibilities and the probabilities of life in the promised land are tremendous. I was leading the singing during a revival one night many years ago and you would know the situation was desperate if you ever heard me sing. So I was overjoyed when I looked down and saw, sitting in the front row, a boy about ten years of age singing from the bottom of his heart. I mean he was doing a number on that song! Actually, he was doing my job for me. He inspired everyone around him.

And then I looked again and almost stopped singing. He had no legs. He had never had any. In the place of legs he had two stumps. He was born that way. He had never known the joy of running and jumping, of playing baseball or football, of racing down the street to beat his friend to the front steps. And then a quiet joy came into my heart. When the promise of the land is fulfilled, all that will change. He will have legs. Not mechanical contraptions (as wonderful and helpful as they are) contrived by the wisdom and genius of man, but real legs. See him jump and run and shout for joy! See him race down the street and get there first. See him hit or catch the ball and run like a deer. Thank God for the promise of the land!

Tell the starving, bloated children of Ethiopia that they will not plant and another eat. Tell the homeless of India who sleep every night in the street that they will not build houses and another inhabit. Tell the frightened people of the village who lock their doors against the maneater each night that the lion will eat straw like the ox. Tell the young woman who has terminal cancer that there will be no more pain. Tell the parents who mourn the untimely loss of their only child that here will be no more death.

Impossible? No way! If you are Christ's, then you are Abraham's offspring and heirs according to the promise. And according to that promise we look for a new heaven according to the promise. And according to that promise we look for a new heaven and a new earth in which righteousness dwells. It is God who has promised. It will be so. Believe it. You cannot make it happen but you can believe. "And Abraham believed God, and he reckoned it to him as righteousness."

15. Old Hundredth
James R. Shott

Scripture: Psalm 100

IN YOUR IMAGINATION, come back with me in time, back about twenty-five hundred years. The date is approximately 500 B.C. The place is Jerusalem. The exile is over, the people have come home to Jerusalem after about a century of captivity in a foreign country. The city is new. The Temple is new. There is that new feeling, that starting-over feeling, when the nation feels young and fresh. Here we are in Jerusalem on a festival day, and it's time to worship God.

Look there! What a magnificent sight!

Winding through the streets of Jerusalem is a body of Hebrew men, led by a group of Levite singers. They approach the Temple. As they march, they sing, and their voices are loud and triumphant. Do you feel it? There is a vibrant joy, a thrill of excitement, in their song!

In keeping with the spirit of Hebrew music, we hear a kind of chant, but it is certainly joyful! The Levites and others are walking slowly, but with a spring in their step and a smile on their faces. The music is bold and cheerful. Let's listen carefully to it, and we can hear the ancient Hebrew words translated for us by the Living Bible into English:

James R. Shott is a retired Presbyterian minister. He served as pastor of Flemington Presbyterian Church in Hinesville, Georgia, as well as other pastorates in Texas, West Virginia, Florida, and Pennsylvania. A graduate of Westminster College and Pittsburgh Theological Seminary, Shott is the author of the juvenile novel *The House Across the Street.*

Shout with joy before the Lord, O earth!
Obey him gladly; come before him, singing with joy!
Try to realize what this means: the Lord is God!
He made us; we are his people, the sheep of his pasture!

And there is the Temple before them, in all its splendor.
And there, at the Temple gates, in the inner court, another
group of Hebrews waits for them. Another Levite choir! And
they are all primed and rehearsed with a response to the approaching choir:

> Go through his open gates with great
> thanksgiving!
> Enter his courts with praise!
> Give thanks to him and bless his name!
> For the Lord is always good,
> He is always loving and kind,
> And his faithfulness goes on and on to each
> succeeding generation!

The choirs meet, the singing merges, and the worship at
the Temple has begun.

What strikes me more than anything else about this experience that we saw in our imagination is the joy of the occasion.
The tenor of the hundredth psalm is obviously happy. This is
particularly true of the first verse. Any time this psalm is sung
by any worshiping congregation, it *must* be sung with great joy!

My earliest recollections of church include the singing of
"Old Hundredth." In the dignified and reserved congregation in which I grew up, this was the opening hymn Sunday
after Sunday, going back to the time Adam and Eve founded
that church. It was a very old-fashioned, straightlaced congregation, and every Sunday the magnificent pipe organ brought
everyone to their feet and they sang the sixteenth-century
paraphrase of Psalm 100:

> All people that on earth do dwell,
> Sing to the Lord with cheerful voice.

> Him serve with mirth, his praise forth tell,
> Come ye before him and rejoice.

. . . and if anyone so much as smiled, I'm sure they would have thrown him out!

The tune of Old Hundredth is a little too solemn to express the jubilant excitement of this psalm. Even the words of that old Geneva paraphrase don't catch it. But if you think the Presbyterians botched it up, you should see what the Methodists did to it! This hymn, paraphrased by Isaac Watts, with the first stanza altered by John Wesley, reads like this:

> Before Jehovah's awesome throne,
> Ye nations, bow with sacred joy;
> Know that the Lord is God alone,
> He can create, and he destroy;
> He can create, and he destroy!

That is a good hymn, expressing the greatness of God over all things, but that isn't the hundredth psalm! Any paraphrase that omits the note of joyous exaltation from this psalm is missing the point.

The best paraphrase I have found is this one:

> O shout for joy unto the Lord,
> Earth's people far and near!
> With gladness serve the Lord; O come
> To him with songs of cheer!

Now, *that's* the way the hundredth psalm should be sung!

I found that paraphrase in the song book of the Reformed Presbyterian Church, and in that small conservative denomination they sing nothing but psalms. The only clue to its origin was the title, which was "Glasgow," so I assume it has a Scottish origin. No wonder Queen Elizabeth I scornfully referred to the Scottish Psalter as "those Geneva jigs!"

How appropriate that we approach the Lord in worship with joy! The second verse of the psalm tells us why, as translated by the New English Bible:

Know that the Lord is God!
He has made us, and we are his own,
his people, the flock which he
shepherds.

This is a very good reason to be so joyous, because God is God, and we are his!

The Hebrews particularly were very much aware of this strong tie to their covenant-making and covenant-keeping God. This was the God who made and kept his ancient agreements with his chosen people. These covenants were sealed in the blood of the paschal lamb that night when they left Egypt, and they were aware of the covenant-keeping God through the wilderness, in the Promised Land, through the exile and the return. No wonder, when they came to the Temple to worship, they came with joy! They had a lot to be joyful about. They felt very secure with the God who made them, redeemed them, and nurtured them. They belonged to him; they were his people, his flock.

We can say the same thing about our covenant-making and covenant-keeping God. Our new covenant was sealed in the blood of the Lamb also, with the New Testament meaning of that phrase. The early church found much to celebrate each Sunday. In fact, they changed the worship time from the Hebrew Sabbath (that's Saturday) to the Lord's Day (Sunday) to celebrate every week the day Jesus rose from the dead. Each Sunday, then, as an Easter celebration. No wonder they celebrated with triumphant joy, because he lives! And we too shall live!

Even their funerals reflected this note of joy. Why not? They firmly believed (and we still do) that for the Christian, death is not an end but a beginning. It is a time to celebrate the resurrection, to rejoice that death has been conquered and eternal life awaits us beyond the grave. Even in the valley of the shadow of death, rejoice!

All worship should be characterized by this note of joy. Our covenant God is present, to welcome us to his Temple and to call our attention to him. He made us, and we are his! He bought us with an exorbitant price, and so we are doubly his! We are his people; he is our God. We are his flock; he is our Shepherd. We are his children; he is our Father. Therefore make a joyful noise, serve him with gladness, come into his presence with singing . . . rejoice! For we are his people, and he shepherds us.

The third verse calls on us to worship God with thanksgiving, as translated by the Jerusalem Bible:

> Walk through his gates giving thanks, enter his
> courts praising him, give thanks to him, bless
> his name!

The title above the hundredth psalm is, "A Psalm for the Thank Offering." Evidently it was one of many psalms they used when they brought a thank offering to the Temple. We in our time have an annual Thanksgiving service, but there ought to be thanksgiving offered at every service of worship.

And we do. In our bulletin there is a prayer of thanksgiving. Do you see where it is? In connection with the offering! Because thanksgiving and thank offering go together. How appropriate it is to say thanks to God with our lips and with our money!

Psalm 96 says: "Ascribe to the Lord the glory due his name! Bring an offering, and come into his courts!" (RSV) This is one of the best ways to praise God, by giving him a gift as a part of the worship service!

I hope none of you thinks an offering is just a collection. A collection implies gathering up some money so we can pay our bills. An offering is more: it is an act of worship in which we give something to God. And the prayer with which we dedicate it is a prayer of thanksgiving. With these gifts we say thanks to God.

But there is something more involved in this act of thank offering. Notice that in our worship service it comes last. A climax. Our final act of dedication before we leave the worship service. The giving of our money is a symbol; it symbolizes the giving of ourselves. The best way to worship God is to give ourselves to him, as symbolized in the giving of money. "Enter his gates with thanksgiving . . . bring an offering, and come into his courts!"

Why? That's in the last verse of the hundredth psalm. Because . . .

> The Lord is always good!
> He is always loving and kind,
> and his faithfulness goes on and on
> to each succeeding generation.

I'm sure that as those Hebrews approached the Temple that day singing their psalm of joy, each one had his own burdens. Look at them again, in your imagination. One of them has health problems; you can tell by his stumbling step, the way he's hunched over, and his shortness of breath. Another has a wife at home who is sick, and he is worried about her. Still another has recently lost a loved one, and the sorrow weighs heavily upon him. And another has financial problems which worry him. And another . . . and another . . . and another . . . each one of them walking in that procession to the Temple has his own needs and burdens and worries.

But look closely at this group of worshipers.

Something is happening in the singing of that joyous song. They are giving thanks! Their attention is focused not on their problems, but on God! And God is good! His steadfast love is not something that comes and goes, but it endures forever. And his constancy endures from one generation to another.

As they sing their song of joy and thanksgiving, their steps become lighter, and their burden—while it doesn't go away—is not quite so heavy. Some unseen presence walks beside them, sharing that burden. Look at them! Their step is a little stronger, their shoulders straighten, and they are smiling! And listen! There's that vibrant note of joy and thanksgiving in their song!

We too sing that song of joy. We sing it with gladness, as a celebration, a thanksgiving. We sing it with smiles, with head lifted high, with hearts rejoicing! The burden which each one of us carries is not quite so heavy now, because we have lifted our voices and our hearts in praise to God! Therefore, "Give thanks to God, bless his name, for he is always good, he is always loving and kind, and his faithfulness goes on and on to each succeeding generation!"

What a magnificent psalm is Old Hundredth!

"Come into God's presence with joy," it sings, "for God is God, and we are his. Give thanks, because God is good, constantly loving us, and this is forever!"

Let's answer the psalmist's invitation to worship God with joy!

16. The Marks of Jesus
Joseph A. Hill

> Henceforth let no man trouble me; for I bear on my body the marks of Jesus.—Galatians 6:17

THE RENOWNED Roman statesman and orator, Cicero, would sometimes defend an accused person by pointing to the scars on the defendant's body as evidence of his worth, especially his manly traits. The apostle Paul, too, bore scars that had been inflicted upon him in the course of his apostolic mission. He had suffered persecution and injury because he had preached the good news of salvation by grace, through faith in Jesus Christ.

Paul's opponents accused him of preaching a false gospel, one that made circumcision the mark of true religion. But Paul declared, "I bear on my body the marks of Jesus." The scars that disfigured him were proof of his uncompromising devotion to his Master. He wished that his detractors might consider those marks of loyalty to Jesus and give him no more trouble.

Joseph A. Hill is associate professor of biblical studies and Greek at Geneva College, Beaver Falls, Pennsylvania. He has also pastored churches in Colorado, New York, and Pennsylvania. Hill pursued his education at Geneva College, Reformed Presbyterian Theological Seminary, and Pittsburgh Theological Seminary, where he was awarded a master of theology degree in 1971. He was an advisor for the translation of the New International Version of the Bible, and he has written for *Christianity Today*.

I

I am convinced that every Christian is privileged to bear the marks of Jesus. There should be in your life and mine distinguishing signs that we are followers of Jesus. Foremost among them will be Christ-like traits of character.

In Bunyan's timeless allegory of the pilgrim's progress toward the celestial city, Christian at the cross received four gifts from the angels—peace, new garments, a mark, and a sealed scroll. The mark had to do with Christian's appearance; it distinguished him from worldly men and identified him as a follower of Christ. We too may have distinguishing signs of God's grace. Kindness and compassion, gentleness and goodness, honesty and fidelity—these are some of the marks of Jesus that distinguish Christians and plainly exhibit the grace of God within them.

Tolstoy in one of his books portrays an ideal czar who keeps an open house and spreads a table for all comers. But his guests must comply with one condition: each man has to show his hands before sitting down to the feast. Those whose hands are rough and hard with honest toil are welcomed to the best of the board, but those whose hands are soft and pale receive only the crusts and crumbs. The hands were the index of character. The hard rough hands told of a life of toil and sacrifice and suffering, and for these the best of the feast was spread.

Can we not see in the *face* of the devout Christian man or woman the distinguishing marks of Jesus? Perhaps more than we realize, a person's countenance reveals his character. It may be a plain face, a homely face, a face furrowed by care or marred by disease or wrinkled by age, but it can nonetheless reflect the character of Christ.

> As in Christ, though men behold no beauty—
> Only the marks of suffering and care,
> God, from the first, beheld his own bright image,
> Rejoicing in the revelation fair.[1]

II

Paul, when referring to the marks of Jesus on his own body, used an interesting Greek word: *stigma.* A stigma as we know it is a mark of disgrace or reproach—like the scarlet letter A that marked Hester Prynne as an adulteress in Hawthorne's classic story of the stern and rigid morality of the Puritans in New England. In the Roman world of Paul's day, a slave who attempted to escape or steal from his master was marked with a red-hot branding iron. The resulting scar was called a *stigma,* and of course it was a mark of disgrace. But not all bodily marks were signs of reproach. It is said that people at that time proudly wore religious tattoos on their bodies, and these marks also were called *stigmas.* It is possible that the early Christians had themselves tattooed with symbols of their faith—a cross, perhaps, or the greek letter *chi* (which looks like an X) representing Christ.

I seriously doubt that Paul had any religious tattoos on his arm or hand or forehead. More than likely, the marks of Jesus on the apostle's body were the visible signs of his suffering with Christ during his missionary expeditions. "I bear on my body the 'stigmas' of Jesus," declared Paul.

Like the apostle, we are called to a life of sacrifice and suffering for the sake of Jesus, beginning with the crucifixion of the flesh—the death of the old nature. But being Christ-marked entails much more; it requires that we identify with Christ in his suffering by taking up our cross and following him. Paul, in fact, went so far as to say: "I am crucified with Christ." His union with Christ and devotion to him were such that he could glory in "the scars of Jesus" that marked his body.

It is reported that St. Francis of Assisi in the year A.D. 1224 received in a trance the wound-prints of the crucified Savior on his body. From that time until his death he had the physical appearance of one who had suffered crucifixion. I cannot vouch for the veracity of that report, but one thing I know is true, for we have the inspired word of the apostle who bore on his own body the brand marks of Jesus: If we suffer with him, we shall also be glorified with him.

Dietrich Bonhoeffer, who gave up his life in the conflict between the German church and the demonic forces of the Third Reich, knew what it meant to suffer for and with Christ. While in a concentration camp waiting to die for his outspoken attack on Nazi policies, Bonhoeffer issued an unambiguous statement regarding the cost of following Christ. He wrote: "The call of Christ . . . sets the Christian in the middle of the daily arena against sin and the devil. . . . Every day . . . he must suffer anew for Jesus Christ's sake. The wounds and scars he receives in the fray are living tokens of this participation in the cross of his Lord."[2]

But there is another kind of suffering with Christ which the Christian is not spared. It is the suffering we share with others when we bear their burdens and enter into their sorrows and troubles. Caring concern for others will be rewarded generously, for our Lord from his throne in heaven will one day beckon his followers to share in his glory, saying to them, "I was hungry and you gave me food, I was thirsty and you gave me drink, I was a stranger and you welcomed me, I was naked and you clothed me, I was sick and you visited me, I was in prison and you came to me." All of these deeds of benevolence were done to relieve the suffering of God's children, but our Lord declares, "As you did it to one of the least of these my brethren, you did it to me."

As Christ suffers with us, so we ought to share in the sufferings of others. By taking on ourselves the burdens of our fellow men, and by bearing their pain and feeling their sorrow and relieving their needs, we bear the marks of Jesus.

Making a profession of faith in Christ or reaffirming faith in Christ does not, in itself, marks us as Christians; and it does not fulfill the law of Christ. The law of Christ is the obligation to live not for ourselves but for others and, above all, for Christ.

III

When Jesus Christ marks us, he places upon our lives the imprint of his own character and makes us heartily willing to suffer with him and with others. But we bear his mark in yet another sense: we *belong* to him. Ownership by Christ is one of the great realities of the Christian life. Like slaves in the ancient marketplace, we are bought with a price; we are not our own. We belong body and soul to our faithful Savior, Jesus Christ, who has redeemed us and placed on us his own brand mark.

One of our contemporary translations of the Bible, Today's English Version, brings out, in its rendering of our text, ownership by Christ: "The scars I have on my body show that I am a slave of Jesus."

In our day when liberation movements would break every shackle that binds people to servitude or diminishes their worth as human beings, the mere mention of slavery seems repugnant. But the surrender of our lives to Christ is not demeaning in the least: it is the highest act of love and the noblest form of freedom. If it entails sacrifice and hardship and suffering, it also leads to honor and glory.

In the battle of Busaco in Portugal in the early nineteenth century, a man was shot in the face. His two brothers also had been wounded a short time before, and when he wrote to his mother he said: "You have the pride of saying your three sons have been wounded and are all alive. . . . There is no shame in such wounds," he continued. "The scars on my face will be as good as medals; better, for they were not gained by hiding behind a wall."

If you are courageous and uncompromising in the service of Jesus Christ, you will inevitably wear the telltale scars of spiritual conflict. But there is no shame in such scars. Shame, rather, is on those who have promised to follow Christ but do not bear the distinguishing marks of a Christian—the marks of Jesus.

How would you reply—what would I answer—if Christ were to say, "Show me *your* marks of valor"?

> If Thou shouldst speak, my Christ,
> My Leader and my King,
> And bid me lay my wounds in sight,
> The scars borne just for Thee in fight,
> What love-scars could I bring?

If Christ is your Master, the marks of his ownership will be clear and unmistakable: his likeness branded into your character, his love manifested in your deeds, and his lordship impressed upon your life.

NOTES

1. Edith Divall, "A Believer's Rest," in *The Great Text of the Bible*, ed. James Hastings (New York and Edinburgh: T & T Clark, 1910–1915).
2. Dietrich Bonhoeffer, *The Cost of Discipleship* (New York: The Macmillan Company, 1959), p. 79.

17. The Suffering Man and the Silent God

Charles E. Crain

Scripture: Psalm 88

IT IS PROBABLY safe to say that no book of the Bible is more loved than the Book of Psalms. Over the centuries, myriad readers have found it to be "a very present help in time of trouble." How often have the voices of the psalmists brought to us comfort and consolation. "The Lord is my Shepherd, I shall not want." "The Lord is my light and my salvation; whom shall I fear. The Lord is the stronghold of my life; of whom shall I be afraid?" (Ps. 27:1). But the Book of Psalms is far different from so many modern devotional books that are full of soft, sentimental soporifics. It is not pietistic but realistic. In it we come across not only cries of penitence but violent outbursts demanding vindication or vengeance. And in it we come across protests of perplexity and bafflement that God seemingly remains silent to man's cry for help in the midst of frightful suffering. Such a psalm is Psalm 88:

> But I, O Lord, cry to thee;
> in the morning my prayer comes before thee.

Charles E. Crain is professor of religion emeritus at Western Maryland College. A United Methodist, Crain pursued his education at Asbury College, Drew University School of Theology, and was awarded a Ph.D. from Drew University in 1951. Since his retirement, Dr. Crain has continued to preach, teach, and lecture.

> O Lord, why dost thou cast me off?
> Why dost thou hide thy face from me?
> Afflicted and close to death from my youth up,
> I suffer thy terrors: I am helpless.

And Psalm 88 is no exception. It may be surprising to learn that the largest classification of psalms is called laments, either national or individual lamentations. It is true that often in such psalms of lament there are also shafts of light, assertions of trust and hope. So, for example, Psalm 22, which begins "My God, my God, why hast thou forsaken me?" But here complaint is soon followed by confidence:

> Yet thou art holy,
> enthroned on the praises of Israel.
> In thee our fathers trusted;
> they trusted, and thou didst deliver them.
> In thee they cried, and were saved;
> In thee they trusted, and were not disappointed.
> (Ps. 22:3–5)

But in Psalm 88 there are no flashes of light; here there is only gloom and unrelieved darkness. So there follow upon the lines just quoted from this Psalm these concluding words:

> Thy wrath has swept over me;
> thy dread assaults destroy me,
> They surround me like a flood all day long;
> they close in upon me together.
> Thou hast caused lover and friend to shun me;
> my companions are in darkness.

Or as another translation puts it, "Darkness is my only companion left." No compensating beams of light are to be found here. To the persistent prayers of the psalmist, there is not the slightest glimmer of divine response.

If laments are the most numerous of the psalms, Psalm 88 might well be characterized as the most pessimistic of the laments. How could a psalm like that survive? How could it be included in this ancient book of hymns? Might it not be well for us, even at this late date, to excise it from the Bible? What does it have to offer to the modern reader except perhaps to deepen an already black state of depression?

It seems almost sacrilegious to intrude an analysis into the anguished outpourings of this suffering poet. Yet there must have been some purpose that he had in the composition of this psalm, and some meaning for those who have read it across the centuries. May I suggest that three facets stand out in this record of suffering: first, the intensity of pain; second, the isolation from friends; and third, the interrogation of God.

1. The Intensity of Pain.

C. S. Lewis has argued that pain has certain benefits. It may alert us to a dangerous situation, whether physical or moral. It may serve as a warning that persistence in the wrong lifestyle may bring us to self-destruction. Of course, it does not follow from this beneficial aspect of pain that we are inclined to pray, "God, bring on more pain so that we may be more vividly aware of our condition." In fact, what troubles us is the "surplus" of pain. Why does the alarm bell of pain have to shriek so loudly? Can't we have more gentle kinds of pain?

It is this very intensity of pain that turns us inward upon ourselves, which cuts us off from our friends, which leads us to question the goodness of God. "Why did this have to happen to *me?*" So the psalmist describes his experience as one of imprisonment: "I am shut in so that I cannot escape" (v. 8c). Intensity of pain induces a sense of solitary confinement.

It has been surmised that the particular affliction from which this psalmist suffers may have been leprosy. Certainly it has been a long-standing kind of suffering:

> Afflicted and close to death from my youth up,
> I suffer thy terrors; I am helpless. (v. 15)

And in a very literal sense, leprosy would have isolated him from his friends. The cry of the leper—"Unclean, unclean"—warned off those who might approach too closely and expose themselves to contagion. "Thou hast caused my companions to shun me," says the psalmist, "thou hast made me a thing of horror to them" (v. 8ab, cf. v. 18). Leprosy in the ancient world aroused the same fear of infection that AIDS does in our time.

Actually, my attention was called to this psalm by an article in which the writer was making the point that the church must undertake a mission to those afflicted with Alzheimer's dementia. In the ancient poet's description of disintegration and "his relentless progression toward death," the author saw a reflection of the stages of the steady process of decline characteristic of Alzheimer's disease.

> Thy wrath has swept over me;
> thy dread assaults destroy me.
> They surround me like a flood, all day long
> they close in before me altogether. (vv. 16,17)

But whatever the affliction from which the psalmist suffers, its intensity has isolated him from his friends and it has led him to question God.

2. The Isolation from Friends

That he finds himself bereft of his friends is a second facet of the pain of this ancient sufferer. His protest is translated in this way in the Jerusalem Bible:

> You have turned my friends against me
> and made me repulsive to them. (v. 8)

Or again, those closing words:

> You have turned my friends and neighbors against me,
> now darkness is my one companion left. (v. 18)

What kind of companionship is provided by "darkness?"

Writing about the communal nature of religion, Gerhardus van der Leeuw asserts:

> . . . man cannot be solitary. Whoever is
> thoroughly isolated weeps like an abandoned
> child; or like Christ in Gethsemane. From the
> child to the God-Man, solitude excites dread in
> us all; for we possess power and life only in
> community . . . Loneliness is the culmination of
> the insecurity and *care* wherein we live.[1]

Darkness is no companion. Darkness is the absence of all companionship. So part of the anguish of the psalmist stems from a longing for friendship which might help to alleviate somewhat the intensity of his suffering.

We think almost immediately of another ancient sufferer who *had* friends and who might have been better off without them. Job sought sympathy from his friends in the midst of terrible suffering. But their acceptance of neat orthodoxy, which concluded that all suffering was to be explained as a punishment sent by God because of sins committed, turned his friends into accusers rather than sympathizers. Of them it has been said:

> They let their attitude be determined by an
> intellectual theory rather than by brotherly
> affection. As the guardians of traditions in
> religion which form a trust they cannot betray,
> they dare not extend their sympathy to one
> from whom God is evidently hiding his face.[2]

So Job is led to compare his friends to those Palestinian wadis which bubble with water during the winter storms but, when the heat of summer comes, turn into dry and dusty ravines.

> He who withholds kindness from a friend,
> forsakes the fear of the Almighty.
> My brethren are treacherous as a torrent-bed,
> as freshets that pass away,
> which are dark with ice,
> and where the snow hides itself.

In time of heat they disappear;
when it is hot, they vanish from their place.

(Job 6:14–17)

"Thirsting for the living waters of sympathy," says James Strahan, "he is offered the arid sands of dogma."[3]

Yet the protests of both Job and the psalmist underline the same truth—the need for sympathetic friends in time of great suffering. If Job complains of their accusations, the psalmist protests their absence.

But note that the psalmist does not charge his friends with desertion. It is God's doing that has cut them off from him.

You have turned my friends against me
and made me repulsive to them;
You have turned my friends and neighbors against me,
now darkness is my one companion left.

Is this the tormented exaggeration of an anguished sufferer? Or is it an oblique recognition that great as the blessing of human friendship may be, the ultimate answer to his suffering lies with the silent God?

3. The Interrogation of God

So we come to a third, and most profound facet of the pains of this psalmist—his interrogation of God:

But I, O Lord, cry to thee;
in the morning my prayer comes before thee.
O Lord, why dost thou cast me off:
why dost thou hide thy face from me?
Afflicted and close to death from my youth up,
I suffer thy terrors; I am helpless. (v. 13–15)

God's heedlessness of man's helplessness—what can be worse than that? "Slow physical deterioration and loosened social relationships have a profound spiritual significance," writes Glenn Weaver, "for they can separate a person from God. It is remarkable that the laments which so vividly portray this human despair should dominate the Psalter—Israel's book of praise."[4]

Why? Why? Why? Isn't that the word that trembles on our lips when experiences of accident, or tragedy, or suffering, or death, come to us? Why? We long for some explanation that will help us to make sense of such experiences. We might even be tempted to settle for that bankrupt theory of Job's friends: all suffering is a punishment sent by God because of committed sin. Well, that theory may explain some suffering, but a huge surplus remains that defies an intelligible answer.

But if there is no explanation for so much suffering, why not give up trying to explain it? Why interrogate God? Let's repudiate him; that would at least save us from some mental anguish. Why not be content with the sentiments of one of Job's friends:

> Man is born to trouble
> as the sparks fly upward. (Job. 5:7)

Or why not concur with the familiar words of Matthew Arnold (from "Dover Beach"):

> . . . the world, which seems
> To lie before us like a land of dreams,
> So various, so beautiful, so new,
> Hath really neither joy, nor love, nor light,
> No certitude, nor peace, nor help for pain;
> And we are here as on a darkling plain
> Swept with confused alarms of struggle and flight,
> Where ignorant armies clash by night.

To give up on God might save us from some mental anguish, but only at the price of giving up the search for some meaning in life. Some of our own pain, and much of the world's pain, remains unintelligible; but does it help to write off the whole human experiment as an incomprehensible mistake?

In this psalm of personal lamentation we search earnestly for some note of comfort. But certainly there is no sunburst at the end giving assurance at last of God's attentive presence.

Rather, it ends in darkness. "Darkness is my only companion left." Yet the psalmist has not given up on God. This is clear from the words with which his protest begins:

> O Lord, my God, by day I call for
> help,
> by night I cry aloud *in thy presence.*
> Let my prayer come *before thee,*
> hear my loud lament . . .

"I cry aloud in thy presence. . . ." God's silence has not deprived the psalmist of faith in God's presence. Long ago John Calvin wrote:

> In the psalms we may frequently observe how
> . . . faithful men, when almost wearied with
> praying, . . . seemed to beat the air, and God
> seemed deaf to their petitions, yet [they] did
> not desist from praying; because the authority
> of the divine word is not maintained, unless it
> be fully credited, notwithstanding the
> appearance of any circumstances to the
> contrary.[5]

Is it too much to suggest that it is only as the psalmist continues his prayer of protest that there is hope of recovery? I do not mean recovery from his illness, or from his isolation, or even from interrogation of God, but a recovery of the sense of God's presence in the midst of them all.

The silence of God does not mean the absence of God. God is present even in and through his silence. God stands "within the shadow, keeping watch above his own." There is no proof of this. There is only the cry of faith, "Lord, I believe, help thou my unbelief."

> O Lord, my God, by day I call for
> help,
> by night I cry aloud *in thy presence.*
> Let my prayer come *before thee,*
> hear my loud lament . . .

NOTES

1. Gerardus van der Leeuw, *Religion in Essence and Manifestation* I. 242 (London: G. Allen & Unwin, 1938).

2. J. Strahan, *The Book of Job* (Edinburgh: T & T Clark, 2nd ed., 1914), p. 75.

3. Ibid., p. 76.

4. Glenn Weaver, "Senile Dementia and a Resurrection Theology," *Theology Today* 42/4, January 1986, p. 448.

5. Quoted in S. Terrien, *The Psalms and Their Meaning for Today* (Indianapolis: Bobbs-Merrill, 1952), pp. 160f.

18. Forsaken with Jesus
Martin B. Copenhaver

Text: Mark 15:29–34

"MY GOD, My God, why hast thou forsaken me?" These words are difficult for a Christian to hear. They are raw and threatening, like an open wound. They sound like words of despair, of hopelessness, of doubt even, which, of course, is just what they are. We are never very good at letting those we admire be fully human, shed human tears, or express human agony. And when the one we hear expressing despair is Jesus of Nazareth, it is not just our view of Jesus that is shaken, but our view of God and our view of ourselves as well. If Jesus doubts, even for a moment, it is enough to scatter our light and fragile faith.

So these words are seldom left to stand on their own in their stark and raw simplicity. Biblical commentators and preachers alike often interpret these words in such a way that they become easier to hear, softening the hard edges, muffling the piercing cry so that it will not echo so painfully through out hearts and minds. We are reminded by some that these words are the first words of the twenty-second psalm, which begins as a desperate cry, "My God, My God, why hast thou forsaken me?" but which ends with the great affirmation:

Martin B. Copenhaver is senior minister of the First Congregational Church in Burlington, Vermont. Copenhaver attended Dickinson College and was awarded a master of divinity degree from Yale Divinity School in 1980. He received the Mersick Prize for Preaching from Yale in 1980 and is the author of many articles. He has also written a full-length play entitled *The Evening Edition of the Morning Star.*

> You who fear the Lord, praise the Lord! all you
> children of Israel, glorify God, and stand in
> awe of God, all of you; For God has not
> despised or abhorred the affliction of the
> afflicted; and God has not hid God's face from
> us, but has heard when we cried to the Lord.

Jesus knew how the Psalm ends, as would his hearers. Even if only the agony of the psalm is voiced, the concluding affirmation would be supplied by the mind's ear of the person hearing Jesus.

Others come to terms with the difficulty of these words on the lips of Jesus by pointing out that as despairing as these words sound, they are still the words of a believer, even in pain, still directed to God. It is, after all, *"My* God, *My* God" to whom he cries.

Elie Wiesel tells of one scene he observed during his imprisonment in Aushwitz:

> Inside the kingdom of night I witnessed a
> strange trial. Three rabbis, all erudite and
> pious men, decided one winter evening to
> indict God for having allowed his children to
> be massacred. An awesome conclave,
> particularly in view of the fact that it was held
> in a concentration camp. But what happened
> next is to me even more awesome still. After
> the trial at which God had been found guilty as
> charged, one of the rabbis looked at the watch
> which he had somehow managed to preserve in
> the kingdom of night and said, "Ah, it is time
> for prayers." And with that the three rabbis, all
> erudite and pious men, all bowed their heads
> and prayed.

It seems to me that the words of the persecuted Jesus may be viewed in the same way. The God who has been found guilty of absence remains a God to be approached through prayer. The God who is absent is still *"My* God, *My* God." In moments of agony that is sometimes the closest we can come to a statement of faith.

These interpretations of Jesus' words of agony are fitting and valuable. They are helpful insofar as they set a context in which we can better understand Jesus' words. They are not helpful, however, if we let such interpretations take the stinging edge off Jesus' words, which somehow manage to stand as powerful as ever anyway, beyond our ability to mute or diminish. Besides, I am convinced that, as difficult as it may be to let these words stand as stark and threatening as they sound, it is only when we do so that we can receive their true blessing.

So, let us assume that Jesus actually felt forsaken, that what we read and hear from Jesus is true, true despair, a true sense of being forsaken. The hour was dark, we are told, and in more ways than one. It was dark, with the kind of eerie darkness that can fall like a pall over the world in midday. And it was a dark time for Jesus, what has been called the dark night of the soul, which can lengthen ominous shadows any day at any time. Although death is the greatest isolator of all, it is clear that Jesus is not here expressing the fear of death. Rather, as he faces death, what prompts his cry is the sense of being forsaken by all who loved him, even forsaken by God.

"Misery loves company," or so the old adage has it. But abject misery is isolating as nothing else this side of death has the power to be. Abject misery does not seek company; it knows no company. A cry of misery can have no accompaniment. Into the most important areas of life we go single file. We are born single file. We die single file. We enter life's darkest days single file, face our greatest disappointments single file, without companions, and necessarily so. Where we go in those moments, no one else can follow. And those are lonely moments, with a kind of loneliness that cannot be quenched, because there is no companion anywhere to be found that can share them.

But, certainly, God is the exception. We are never forsaken by God. God can accompany us into the dark times, the despairing, doubting, dark times. And yet, even if God is not absent, God may be perceived as absent, which is just as ago-nizing. "My God, My God, why hast thou forsaken me?" It is the cry of those who wonder how it is that circumstances seem to conspire against them, and who begin to conclude that God is in on the conspiracy. It is the cry of the patient clutching the sheets of the hospital bed, the cry of the prisoner in Auschwitz who watches a grim parade of family and friends being led to their deaths, the cry of any who, out of their misery, cry with Coleridge, "Alone, alone, all, all alone, alone on a wide, wide sea."

No one feels so alone as the one who feels deserted by God. And note the cruel irony that the absence of God is only a problem for the believer. It is only the believer who even ex-periences the absence of God. Furthermore, the greater one's faith, the greater the potential for disillusionment when that faith is directed toward a God who seems to have left without a trace. It is the one who rejoices most in God's presence who is the one most bereft when God is gone. By this measure, could anyone have felt so deserted, so alone, all, all alone, as Jesus on the cross?

"My God, My God, why hast thou forsaken me?" It is diffi-cult to let those words stand, raw and not explained away, yet there are gracious benefits in doing just that. A Jesus who would experience the full range of human circumstances and human emotions must surely experience the sense of being forsaken. He came to live among us, not as God in a human costume that can be shed whenever things begin to get hard and rough. But, rather, in Jesus God came as human to the bone, which means human enough to experience human doubts, bone-deep despair, and even the perceived absence of God. If Jesus never experienced these, that would mean that he never experienced the kind of human life that we live, which is filled with such things.

The Apostle's Creed contains this affirmation about Jesus: "Jesus Christ was crucified, dead, and buried. He descended to hell." The last part of that statement used to always trouble me, until one day someone told me that, for her, it was the most treasured part of the creed. When I asked why, she answered with the simplicity of truth: "Because hell is where I spend much of my life." Hell—the dark night of the soul, a sense of being forsaken, the absence even of God, a place of despair. We have been there. And Jesus has been there. He has been with us. And having been there, Jesus transformed it, transformed hell by his presence, transforming the experience of any and all who have been in hell, transforming it by his very presence, a presence which cannot help but transform even the darkest regions.

One who would rescue those trapped in a mine shaft must enter into the danger and darkness of that place himself. How else can those who are trapped be saved, if the one who knows the way out is not willing to be trapped with them? Before a savior can share his light with us, he must first enter into our darkness, including the darkness of agony and despair. The story of Jesus despairing on the cross is the story of a God willing to experience our hopelessness, that we might have hope, and the story of a God willing to share human defeat, that we might, in turn, share God's victory.

III. DOCTRINAL/
THEOLOGICAL

19. What is Truth? Or Shirley MacLaine, Meet the Master
John Killinger

Scripture: John 18:28–38

"WHAT IS TRUTH?" We have to sympathize with Pilate, don't we? He wasn't in an easy situation. He was a Roman politician far from home, set down in a strange culture. Perhaps he had been the secretary of a senator or the son of a local potentate and had been given preferment in foreign service as a gift. One didn't look gift horses in the mouth. But it had not been an easy adjustment. The distance from Rome was itself a problem; transportation and communication were not easy. His wife was probably unhappy, stuck off in that bizarre little land a month's sea-travel from her family and friends and the gossip of the Imperial City. The food and language weren't what they were accustomed to, nor were the people, with their extraordinary, fanatic religious customs.

Anyone who gets caught up in the whirlpool of life in a foreign country begins to wonder about the nature of truth, and Pilate was no exception. The Jews said there is one God; Pilate

John Killinger was born in 1933 in Germantown, Kentucky. He received his education at Baylor University, the University of Kentucky, Harvard Divinity School, and Princeton Theological Seminary. Dr. Killinger currently is senior minister of the First Congregational Church in Los Angeles, California. He is the author of many books, including *Bread for the Wilderness, Wine for the Journey* and the text *The Fundamentals of Preaching.*

was accustomed to acknowledging many. The Jews had strict laws and customs from their God; Pilate's laws all came from the state; his gods tended to disport themselves like spoiled children. The Jews kept to themselves to protect the purity of their race; Pilate had become a cosmopolitan, adapting to the scene where he lived. It is no wonder that, when he became unintentionally involved in the trial of Jesus, which he regarded as a Jewish matter, he was puzzled and asked, "What is truth?" Under the circumstances, we would have wondered the same.

In fact, we often wonder today, don't we? We live, like Pilate, in a strange, sometimes bewildering world. Our parents, we fancy, didn't. Their world was smaller, tighter, more surely structured. They knew what they believed about everything. They had been taught by their parents and grandparents. Society reinforced their understanding of life and the world around them. If they wanted to know what they thought about something, they had but to consult the opinions bequeathed by an earlier generation.

A friend who owns a tenant farm in Kentucky told me this little story that illustrates the way it used to be for most of us. On a visit to the farm, he was walking about with the tenant, an old man from a rigid, Pentecostalist background. The tenant's blond-headed little granddaughter, three or four years old, was running about with them. Whenever something contrary to the old man's way of thinking came up in the conversation, he made a point of saying, so the little girl could hear, "We don't believe in that, do we?" It was always the same, whether it was the subject of dancing, smoking, working on Sunday, or giving equal rights to women: "We don't believe in that, do we?"

As the three of them approached the farm pond, they discovered that one of the ducks had hatched her eggs and was now surrounded by a dozen scurrying, cheeping balls of yellow fluff. The little girl ran to them and squatted in their midst. For a few moments, she was entranced. Then, suddenly remembering herself, she looked up at her grandfather and said, "Granddaddy, do we beweeve in ducks?"

Her conditioning was almost complete.

So was ours, until a few years ago. Our white, Anglo-Saxon, Protestant culture, protected by our country's insularity, had easily maintained control of popular thinking. Combined with the cocksure rationalism of the eighteenth century, it was a balanced, sober way of looking at life and its meaning. God was in heaven, man was put on the earth to work hard and maintain order, prayer was a neat recitation of our common needs, and one simply didn't inquire into matters of mystery and metaphysics. The afterlife was divided into heaven and hell, and any thirst for knowledge beyond that was deemed akin to witchcraft and devil-worship.

But the first truly global war in the history of the world, with the enormous transcultural migrations it produced, plus the growth of modern travel and the development of television and an era of instant communication, changed all that, didn't it? A generation of American young people began going to India and Tibet to study Buddhist meditation. Well-to-do natives in Pango Pango began importing Japanese TV sets and American air conditioners. Beatlemania encircled the globe. Llama rugs from Bolivia and Peru were sold at roadside stands in Georgia and Alabama. Teenagers in Greenland, Italy, and Korea went crazy over blue jeans. Primitive dances in Borneo and Zimbabwe were shown on television screens all over the Western Hemisphere. Centuries-old world views and belief structures began to crumble. We all found ourselves asking Pilate's question, "What is truth?"

We're still asking, more often than ever.

After hundreds of years of a great philosophical tradition, from Thomas Hobbes and Emmanuel Kant to Whitehead and Husserl and Heidegger, Shirley MacLaine is the most talked-about thinker of our time. Her book *Out on a Limb*, with its description of seances, out-of-body experiences, and channeling, has become a runaway best-seller among people who sense that the wholeness of truth lies beyond the conventional little systems most of us grew up with and that, even if she's a kind of lovable kook, she is toying with a dimension of human existence as real and significant as mainline Protestantism, the Mona Lisa, and the Dow Jones Average.

Recent surveys show that the percentage of people in America who admit to having had ESP, extraterrestrial, life-after-life, out-of-body, or reincarnation experiences has shot up from 40 percent ten years ago to about 75 percent today. Think of that: three out of four Americans professing to have had superphenomenal experiences, experiences that cannot be subsumed under the old classifications of religion and reality.

Does that mean that the nature of reality has drastically changed in our lifetime? Does it mean that the end of the world is approaching? No. It means that the old ways of thinking and perceiving are breaking down. We are shedding some of our straitjackets. We are more open to a variety of visions and perceptions than our parents and grandparents. We understand something about the extraordinary versatility of truth. We are entering a period predicted by André Breton, the remarkable surrealist, when our dreams and unconscious life are valued as highly as the tough-minded realism of everyday existence.

A woman who lived alone had gone to bed in the upstairs of her large house. In the middle of the night, she was awakened by a dream of her long-dead mother, who told her to get up; there was danger in the basement. Slipping on her robe, the woman descended to the basement and found a fire just starting in some old papers near the water heater.

A splendid young Air Force chaplain I met in Japan had begun his military career as a nineteen-year-old marine in Vietnam. One day, as he was entering the rest room of his barracks, a great pain struck him in his side, knocking him to the floor. Gasping for breath, he dragged himself across the floor and pulled up to the sink. Later, he learned that his father in Georgia had been thrown from a car wreck and was killed at precisely the same moment the pain had struck him. This incredible moment of sympathetic pain became a key element in the young man's decision to study for the ministry.

A businessman in Washington, D.C., was "killed" on a bridge when his car skidded on wet pavement, and later wrote the story of it himself. When it happened, he said, it was as if everything were occurring in slow motion. He felt himself being thrown from his body, and for several minutes he hovered a few feet above the scene of the accident. He watched the police and medics arrive and saw them working over his body. He felt completely serene and joyous; in fact, he had never felt so good in his whole life. Then he heard a voice calling him back to his body. He resisted; he didn't want to return. "You still have much to do," said the voice. Reluctantly, he went back. The medics were startled, for they had found no pulse or heartbeat and were sure he was dead. His whole life was reoriented by the experience. Now, he says, he is loving and generous; he never becomes anxious about the things that once troubled him; and his entire existence has become "beautifully religious."

What is truth? We dare not draw the circle too small, do we?

So we swarm to church on Easter to pay homage to one who rose from the dead—or supposedly rose from the dead. That's what our faith teaches, isn't it? Perhaps it's the one place where our narrow old faith and the wild new world of speculation converge. They agree on the possibility, and provide a double reason for our being here.

Maybe we don't all come very often, for we're not convinced. But on Easter something draws us—something primordial, immemorial; something instinctive; something that says, "This mystery lies at the heart of all life, even all truth."

What if we reoriented our lives around it? I mean, suppose it is true that Christ rose from the dead, that the tomb was empty and he appeared to his disciples in spectral form, that Christianity has been proclaiming the truth all these years, that God was in Christ showing us the nature of reality and inviting us to a new way of seeing everything. What would happen if we restructured our entire existence around this truth, made it the linchpin of everything we believed and did in the future?

What if Shirley MacLaine were to come face-to-face with the Master? It would be the best proof she ever had, wouldn't it, that the spirit world is as real as the physical world? She would see love as the primary modality for all true and lasting action. She would experience herself as belonging to God, the way Mary Magdalene did that first Easter in the garden when she fell at Christ's feet crying, "Rabboni! Rabboni! Master!" She would see the whole future in terms of the kingdom of God, and begin to serve that kingdom with a fervor that would surprise even her. And she would never, never again be afraid of death.

That's the way it would be for us. Our lives would be completely transformed. Nothing would ever be the same again.

I remember a professor of philosophy I knew when I was in graduate school. He had studied in Holland and Sweden and Great Britain as well as in America, pursuing truth with the finest minds in the world. There was nothing he liked better than to pore over old books and argue with their authors. He was a brilliant man, and his head was filled with postulates and systems and ideas. He had been an agnostic, suspending commitment to any final system of thought, lest it hamper him in his exploration of other systems. But he told of an experience he had when his second child was only a few months old. She had fallen ill with a high fever and the doctor put her in the hospital. The mother was exhausted and the father told her to go home and get some sleep while he stayed in the room with the child.

"I was sitting there feeling so helpless," he said. "My mind raced from one thing to another, from this idea to the other. Finally, when I thought I would go crazy with worry and grief, I began thinking the words of an old hymn I must have learned when I was a boy: 'O Jesus, I have promised to serve thee to the end.'

"Over and over I sang them in my head, until finally I found myself singing them aloud. I got down on my knees by my daughter's bed and I prayed, 'O Lord, I *did* promise, I remember; but I have gone away from you. I have let all my learning turn my head. In searching for the truth with a little *t*, I have lost the Truth with a capital *T.*' "

Before he got up, he committed himself to Christ again, and then committed his little daughter to God's care. During the night her fever broke, and two days later she was able to leave the hospital. "But even if she had died," he said, "I believe I would have remained committed to Christ. I learned that night that there isn't any truth apart from him."

That's the way it was with Pilate, wasn't it? He began by asking, "What is truth?" And then, after he had been with Jesus for a little while, had spoken with him and observed his behavior under enormous pressure, he saw that truth somehow had its dwelling place in this strangely dignified and otherworldly man. Jesus' enemies had accused him of posing as the king of the Jews and trying to start a rebellion against Rome. They brought pressure on Pilate to commit him to death by crucifixion. But Pilate had the last word. When they took Jesus off to Golgotha, the site of execution, he sent them with a sign to put over his head. It said, "Jesus of Nazareth, King of the Jews."

"Don't write 'The King of the Jews,'" said the chief priests; "write, 'This man said, I am King of the Jews.'"

"What I have written," said Pilate, "I have written."

Pilate knew he had come face-to-face with the Truth. Jesus was truly a king.

Unfortunately, Pilate didn't restructure his life around his discovery.

Perhaps we shall do better.

20. The Reformation Continues
Charles P. Price

"... for all who exalt themselves will be humbled, but they who
humble themselves will be exalted."—Luke 18:14
Readings: Psalm 84; Jeremiah 14:7–10, 19–22; Luke 18:9–14

THE LAST SUNDAY in October is designated as Reformation Sunday. It commemorates the day of October 31, 1517,
when Martin Luther nailed his ninety-five theses to the church
door in Wittenberg. Those hammer blows began the Protestant Reformation. They broke the visible unity of the church.

In this era of ecumenical good feelings, does that action
have any continuing validity? Was it a cosmic mistake, an act of
human pride rather than obedience to God? Most of the issues
that tore the church apart in the sixteenth century no longer
seem so divisive. Indulgences, the sole authority of scripture,
justification, transubstantiation, predestination—no longer
are these fighting words; they are scarcely household words.
Roman Catholic and Lutheran theologians have come to at
least preliminary agreement about justification. Roman
Catholic and Anglican theologians have come to at least preliminary agreement about transubstantiation. Is the Reformation over then? Was it for nothing?

Charles P. Price was born in 1920 in Pittsburgh, Pennsylvania. He
received degrees from Harvard University, Virginia Theological
Seminary, and Union Theological Seminary in New York. Dr. Price,
an Episcopalian, has served as preacher to the University and Plummer Professor of Christian Morals at Harvard University and currently is professor of systematic theology at Virginia Theological Seminary
in Alexandria, Virginia.

The one point I want to make in this sermon is that the Reformation continues. And it continues around at least three issues that should move the church to protest; in fact, which do move the church to protest against "the stale cake of custom" in every age. I present them in the spirit of the day as three theses, which are designed to make Protestants of us all, whether we are Roman Catholic, Lutheran, Greek Orthodox, Presbyterian, Methodist, Baptist, or even Episcopalian. These theses concern the continuing reformation of the church.

I.

Thesis one: God is a living God. God, the ultimate reality we have to deal with in this life of ours, is not under our control. God is not our invention. We are God's creation. God controls us.

A few years ago I walked through the Pitti Palace in Florence, overwhelmed by that collection of Renaissance paintings. What struck me, among many other things, was the omnipresence of angels. Scene after scene was filled with them. Now angels are not an omnipresent reality for me. What do they mean? What do they signify? It finally dawned on me that that overpopulation of angels was a way of communicating the reality that I am talking about now, that the world is full of life beyond anything we can experience, and almost beyond anything we can describe in words or signs. Those angels tell us that the universe is not dark, empty, or silent. It is full of glory inexpressible, unutterable. For God, the ultimate reality, in, with, and under everything that is, is a living God.

It is easy to lose faith in the living God as long as we grant reality only to what our five senses perceive. In the years before Martin Luther's protest, the church lost faith in the God who works through human agents. The church, which ought to be transparent to the glory of God, which ought to be obedient to the reality of God, which ought to be humble before the power of God, began to put itself in the place of God. It acted, not for God, but instead of God. Maybe not the whole church, but enough of the church to give that impression to an angry host of people. It seemed to deny that God lived. To be a Protestant is to protest that denial.

We have a different way of denying the living God, an even more drastic way, I think. God is dead, we say, or asleep, or in eclipse. Or God is just another name for the natural forces which we can calculate and control. Religion becomes a facade for applying psychological therapy or social reform. Let me be clear. There is nothing wrong with psychological insight or with the demand for social justice. But when the church is truly the church, it is open to the Spirit of the living God. The living God works through our commitment to psychological insight and social action. The living God shapes those ministries. The church acts for God and not instead of God. So the question abides. Do we acknowledge the power of the living God, whom we cannot control and whom we did not invent? Are we open to God, or do we deny that God lives? To be a Protestant is to protest that denial. Protestants affirm the living God, whether they are Catholic, Orthodox, Lutheran, Baptist, or even Episcopalian.

II.

Second thesis: human alienation from God is massive and radical. A great abyss yawns between the divine and the human. Its traditional name is sin.

The more you are grasped by the power and glory of the living God, the more your own weakness, inadequacy—indeed perversity and disobedience—come home to roost. At least that has been true for me, and I read that result in the writings of those who wrestle deeply with God: the lesson from Jeremiah is a case in point. "Though our iniquities testify against us, act, O Lord, for thy name's sake. Thou art in the midst of us and we are called by thy name. Leave us not."

The connection between the living God and human alienation is disconcerting. It always has been and continues to be a terrible temptation to Christians and to the Christian church to hide from it. In the years before Martin Luther's protest, the church developed a system for doing just that. Of course it did not mean to do that. But that was the result. If you went through the motions of making an act of contrition, confessing sin, doing penance, receiving absolution, you would in fact be reconciled to neighbor, self, and God. But, you see, it is possible to go through those motions without encountering the living God at all.

Our situation is not the same. We don't have an elaborate penitential system in place. We have virtually none. But we still have a way of avoiding the truth. We face a world—and (let's admit it) a church—which says, "I'm OK and you're OK." Not everywhere of course. But more than it's comfortable to think about. We can shield ourselves from the living God and from the depth of sin.

The cost of that protection is the incomplete development of ourselves. I used the angels in Renaissance art as a way to get at the presence of the living God. Let me suggest the faces of Rembrandt paintings as a way to get at the reality of the self revealed when one admits one's sin. Out of shadowy and gloomy backgrounds loom faces of extraordinary vitality; we see recognizable persons, warts, quirks, and all. That development is made possible by this second Reformation thesis.

It is a perennial temptation of the church to deny the reality and depth of sin. To be a Protestant is to protest that denial—whether one is Catholic, Orthodox, Presbyterian, Methodist, or even Episcopalian.

III.

Thesis three: grace is amazing. Where sin abounds, grace much more abounds. Forgiveness abounds. Love abides.

The greatest of the sixteenth-century Protestant affirmations was not that God is a living God nor that human alienation is profound and radical. The greatest affirmation of all was that God overcomes that estrangement. We are justified by grace.

God is living. That discovery may be bad news. When the presence of God convinces us of sin, it may undo us. Men and women to this day are unhinged by confronting their own depths.

But the heart of the Christian message is quite different. The heart of the Christian message is that God does not intend our alienation from him to be the last word of the process. God loves us too much. In Jesus he shared our estrangement. In Jesus he died the death we die, and in spite of that he lives. In the risen life of Jesus we have the forgiveness of our sins. The yawning gap has been closed. We have been reconciled to the ultimate reality of this universe, able now to live in communion with the living God, at peace with the depths of our own selves, in love and charity with our neighbors. Grace is amazing. "If God is for us, who can be against us . . . ?"

To be a Protestant is to testify for that grace, whether one is Catholic, Lutheran, Calvinist, or even Episcopalian.

IV.

God lives. Sin is massive. Grace abounds. Those are three theses about the continuing Reformation. You may ask at the end of the sermon what they have to do with the text. Well, just about everything. Because God is the living God, the publican does not talk to himself. His prayers are answered. He acknowledges the depth of his sin. And just because he acknowledges it, just as he is, without one plea, he is justified, reconciled with God by God's amazing grace. The publican is the enduring symbol of the continuing Reformation.

> "For all who exalt themselves will be humbled,
> but they who humble themselves will be exalted."

21. Don't Doubt God's Goodness: A Case Study in Temptation

Haddon W. Robinson

Scripture: Genesis 3:1–6

A FEW MONTHS ago I received a letter from a young man in a penitentiary in Texas. He is serving from ten to twenty years for attempted rape. He is a Christian, and he asked if I would send him a book that was not available to him in the prison. I gladly responded to his request. But his letter deeply disturbed me, because the young man had been a student of mine when I taught at another theological seminary.

When he left the seminary, he left with great gifts and great vision. He pastored two different churches, and both of them, humanly speaking, were successful congregations. In the second church, which I knew better, he demonstrated the gift of evangelism—many of the people in that church were led to Christ as a result of his witness. He was a careful student of the Scriptures. There were those in the congregation who testified that again and again as he stood to speak they could sense the power and the presence of God. He had a discipling

Haddon William Robinson, a native of New York City, was born in 1931. His graduate studies include degrees from Dallas Theological Seminary, Southern Methodist University, and the University of Illinois. Dr. Robinson currently is president of the Denver Conservative Baptist Seminary. His books include the widely read *Biblical Preaching*.

ministry; he left his thumbprint upon the people in that congregation. In fact, when his crime was discovered and he had admitted his guilt, people in his church raised over twenty thousand dollars for his legal defense. And now he is a prisoner in a penitentiary in Texas. In one dark hour of temptation he fell into the abyss. He ruined his reputation, destroyed his ministry, and left an ugly stain on the testimony of Christ in that community.

When I read that letter and knew what had happened, I found myself wrestling with all kinds of questions and emotions. What happens in a person's life who does that? What went through his mind? What was it that caused him to turn his back on all that he had given his life to?

I realized as I was asking those questions that I was not simply asking about him, but about myself. I was asking about men and women who have graduated from seminary who, in some act of disobedience, have destroyed the ministry to which they have given themselves. What is it that causes someone to mortgage his ministry to pay the high price of sin? What is it that lures us to destruction?

It's a question you face. You're a Christian; temptation dogs your path and trips you at every turn. The question you must face someplace in your life is, "How does the Tempter do his work? How does he come to us? How does he destroy us?" Here, early in the ancient record, we have one of the themes woven again and again throughout the Scripture, the theme of sin and its destructive power.

What we have here in Genesis 3 is a case study in temptation. In a case study, you get rid of the independent variables to study the thing itself. And certainly as Eve is approached by the Tempter, many things were true of her that are not true of us. For example, she has no poisoned blood in her veins. She does not have a heritage on which she can blame her sin. Eve comes, as Adam does, as the direct creation of God, and when God created Adam and Eve, God declared that the creation was very good. Unlike people today, she was not half-damned in her birth. What is more, Eve and Adam live in a perfect environment. Nothing in the pollution of that atmosphere would lead them away from God. She stands there in the morning of creation, a creature of great wonder. No sinful heritage, no sinful environment. We have a case study in temptation.

As we watch the way the Tempter comes to Eve, we recognize that while this story comes to us out of the ancient past, it's as up-to-date as the temptation you faced last night—the temptation you may be feeling this morning, the temptation you face in your study, in your home, in your ministry, in your life. The scene has changed, but the methodology has not.

As you read this story, one thing you discover is that when the Tempter comes, he comes to us in disguise. The writer of Genesis notes that the serpent was more crafty than all the wild animals the Lord God had made. When the serpent came, he did not come as a creature of ugliness. This scene happens before the curse, before the serpent crawls on its belly over the ground. No rattlers here warn of an approaching danger. There's nothing here that would make Eve feel alarmed.

When Satan comes to you, he does not come in the form of a coiled snake. He does not approach with the roar of a lion. He does not come with the wail of a siren. He does not come waving a red flag. Satan simply slides into your life. When he appears he seems almost like a comfortable companion. There's nothing about him that you would dread. The New Testament warns that he dresses as an angel of light, a minister of God, as a minister of righteousness. One point seems quite clear; when the Enemy attacks you, he wears a disguise. As Mephistopheles says in *Faust,* "The people do not know the devil is there even when he has them by the throat."

Not only is he disguised in his person, he disguises his purposes. He does not whisper to Eve, "I am here to tempt you." He wants to conduct a religious discussion. He would like to discuss theology; certainly he doesn't intend to talk about sin. He begins the temptation by asking, "Did God really say you must not eat from any tree in the garden?" You can't argue with that. Satan merely says, "Look, I only want to be sure of your exegesis, I want to establish the idea God was trying to get across. Did he really say you can't eat of any of the trees of the garden?" You see, he is a religious devil. He doesn't come and knock on the door of your soul and say, "Pardon me, buddy, allow me a half hour of your life. I'd like to damn and destroy you." No, all he wants to do is talk about a point of theology. He only desires to understand the Word of God. It is possible, isn't it, to discuss theology to our peril? We can talk about God in an abstract way, as though he were a mathematical formula. You can construct a theology that leads you to disobey God.

You're big on grace, very strong on Christian liberty. You know the freedom of the sons and daughters of God and you will debate grace with anyone. You can do anything you want, at any time you want, with anyone you want. No restrictions, no hangups; you're free, you know God's grace. Every person who has ever turned liberty into license has done so on theological grounds. "Even when I sin, God's grace abounds. Isn't it wonderful that I always have God's grace because even when I sin I demonstrate his forgiveness?"

You can be strong on God's sovereignty. No one will outpace you when it comes to that doctrine. God is sovereign over the affairs of men and nations. God's eye is not only over history, his hand is on history. His hand rests upon your life, but before long God is so sovereign that you have no responsibility. In a sense "all the world's a stage, all the men and women merely players." God maps out the action, plans the dialogue. We go through our paces, but it's all of God. Even our sin. And out of that discussion you find good sound reasons—or reasons that sound good—for disobeying God. All because you discuss theology with the wrong motive. One advantage of graduating from seminary is that you can manufacture a lot of excuses for doing wrong, and be theological in your disobedience.

Another thing that Satan does in this conversation, this discussion about God, is to focus Eve's attention on that single tree in the center of the garden. He says, "It seems to me a thing inconceivable that God wouldn't let you have any of these trees." Now Eve jumps to God's defense. She's a witness for God. "No, we can eat of all of the trees in the garden but that one tree—that tree there in the center—we can't eat from that, we can't touch that tree." God didn't say that. He didn't say anything about touching it. Some people defend God by becoming stricter than God. They not only know God's commands, but they believe they are holier if they go beyond those commands. There is destruction in that. Eve says, "You know we can't taste it; we can't even touch it." What Satan has done, of course, is to focus her mind on that single tree, the one thing prohibited.

Sometimes people turn their backs on all the good things, all the blessings that have been poured into their lives—throw all that away for a single sin in their lives. They no longer can see God's blessings. Satan shifts your focus, and there emerges that one thing you want so desperately you'll do anything to get it. It becomes the obsession of your life, and everything else God does for you, you forget. So Satan comes in disguise. He conceals who he is. He conceals what he wants to do.

The second part of his strategy is to attack God's Word. When Eve responds, "We may eat from all the trees in the garden, but we must not eat the fruit from the tree that's in the middle of the garden. We must not touch it or we will die," then Satan throws his head back and with irrepressible laughter says, "Surely you don't believe that, do you? That you will surely die? Oh, come now. A bit of fruit? Surely die? That's just a bit of exaggeration God's using to get your attention. He doesn't mean that. Surely die? Come now, you're too sophisticated to believe that God who gave you this marvelous garden and all these trees, and that bountiful fruit is going to be that upset about your taking that one piece of fruit from the. . . . Surely die? You don't believe that, do you? God doesn't mean that. God certainly doesn't mean that."

We can believe in inerrancy of the Bible as a whole, except on this one particular issue between me and God; we're sure God doesn't mean it when he says, "You will surely die."

For thousands of years Satan has repeated that strategy. It

is the theme of modern novels. The author manipulates the plot so that his characters live in deep disobedience of God, yet at the end everything has turned out well. It's the subject of modern movies in which the characters rebel against the moral laws of God but live happily ever after. It's the word from the sponsor on television. It appears in four-color ads. Here's a perfume—it has been on the market for a long time—called "My Sin." A huckster on Madison Avenue named that fragrance. "Here is a fragrance that is so alluring, so charming, so exciting," he whispers, "you can call it 'My Sin.'" You would never guess the fragrance of sin arises as a stench in the nostrils of God.

How do you respond to the warnings against disobedience that fill the pages of Scripture? Does God mean it when he says, "They who live after the flesh shall die?" Does God mean it when he says, "If you sow to your flesh, you will reap corruption?" Does God mean it when he says, "Be not deceived; God is not mocked. Whatever a man sows, that shall he also reap." Does God mean it when he says, "The eye of the Lord is against the wicked?" Does God mean it when he says, "He shall judge his people?" Does God mean it when he says, "Fornicators and adulterers God will judge?" Does God mean it when he warns us that sin brings punishment?

God is serious about sin because God is serious about you. God is serious about sin because God loves you and God knows the devastation that sin can have in your life, in your relationships, in your character, in your ministry. God is serious about sin as a loving parent is serious about fire and warns a child about it, knowing that it can maim that child for life, destroy the home he lives in, and do untold damage. But how do you feel about it? Does God mean it when he utters those warnings?

Not only does Satan attack God's Word, but he drives deeper and attacks God's character, which lies behind his Word. The serpent explains to the woman, "For God knows that when you eat of that tree your eyes will be opened and you will be like God, knowing good and evil." Satan slanders

God's goodness. He implies, "Do you know why God gave you that command? He wants to spoil your fun. He wants to hold you on a tight leash. He doesn't want you to be free and experience the good life. He is out to deny your pleasures. He desires to hold you down. He wants to keep you from the excitement that life offers. He knows very well that when you eat that fruit you'll be able like him to know good and evil. Then you'll enjoy experiences beyond your wildest dreams. God has an ulterior motive, a hidden agenda, and it's an evil one."

Once the well is poisoned, all the water is polluted. One of the most beautiful confessions of love and faith in the Bible is the confession Ruth makes to Naomi. June embraces November. Ruth pleads, "Entreat me not to turn away from you. Where you go, I will go. Where you abide, I will abide. Your people will be my people, your God will be my God. Where you die I will be buried." An expression of loyal devotion as beautiful as any in all of literature.

But suppose someone whispered to Naomi, "Naomi, listen. Ruth's a gold digger. She's a manipulator. What Ruth, this Moabitess, really wants to do is get into Israel to marry a wealthy Jew. She knows you are her passport. She'll tell you anything to get a free pass into Israel." If Naomi believes that, the well is poisoned. Every good word Ruth speaks, Naomi now suspects. Every kind act Ruth does, Naomi will reject. When you poison the well, all the water is contaminated. If you question God's Word because you doubt God's goodness, then Satan has done his work. How easily we succumb. All of us have served the Prince of Darkness and lived in his realm too long. When we enter the kingdom of God's Son, we bring our doubts and suspicions with us. Something painful happens in your life and you ask *Why?*—and that question mark is like a dagger pointed at the heart of God. How easily we suspect that when some reversal happens in our lives God is against us. We suffer such a twisted will that, even when good things happen to us, we doubt God's goodness. If something marvelous comes into your life, something completely unexpected, at first you're delighted. Then all at once a shadow crosses your mind that before long it will be snatched away. God doesn't really want me to enjoy this expression of his goodness; just as I start to enjoy it, he'll pull it back like a sadistic parent. So we "knock on wood" and hammer at the heart of God. When you doubt God's goodness, you'll doubt his Word. If you believe God restricts you and wants to hold you back from enjoying life, then the work of the Tempter is complete.

At that moment, "When the woman saw that the fruit of the tree was god for food and pleasing to the eye and also desirable for gaining wisdom, she took some and ate it." Now the forbidden fruit pleases her eye. She has listened to the lie of the Tempter and her senses take control. When you get God out of your life, when you come to question God's Word and God's goodness, then your senses comes alive to what is evil; what was once out of bounds to you becomes what you desire more than anything else on earth, even if it is something that can destroy you.

"Piece of fruit?" someone might say. "Surely not a piece of fruit. You're not going to tell me that Eve sinned by eating a piece of fruit in the orchard. You're not going to tell me that's why Adam sinned and why murder came into their family. You're not going to tell me that a piece of fruit damned the race."

No, not a piece of fruit, but disobedience to God's Word, a suspicion of God's character. The fruit is out at the periphery; the sin stands at the center. Whenever you come to doubt or deny the goodness of God, then at that point you'll come to reject his Word—the fruit is only the point of disobedience.

If Satan had come to Eve in that early morning and said, "Look, sign this paper. Say that you are done with God," she would never have signed it. When Satan approaches us he never comes dragging the chains that will enslave us. He comes bringing a crown that will ennoble us. He comes offering us pleasure, expansiveness, money, popularity, freedom, enjoyment. In fact, he never hints about the consequences, he only promises we will fill all the desires of our hearts. That is how we are destroyed. That's the lesson: the temptations that destroy us strike at the heart of God, at God's integrity and God's goodness. When we deny God's goodness, we reject his Word. When we reject his Word, we do so at our peril.

Hear me well. I do not advocate some kind of tight religion. Christianity is not morality, toeing the line and keeping the rules. Christianity is a relationship with God who loves you so much that he gave you his Son, and values you so much he has made you his child. God's every gift is good and perfect. He can never cast a shadow on your life by turning from his goodness. The essence of sin lies in doubting God's goodness and then rejecting his Word. The garden belongs to you as a gift from his hand. Enjoy it. Trust him.

22. The View from the Screened-in Porch

W. Sibley Towner

Scripture: Romans 8:19–24a; Psalm 8; Genesis 1:26–28

I'M RATHER glad that this church does not have the custom of putting sermon titles out on the notice board, because I'm not sure I would want this one ballyhooed around. But it seemed good to me to try to capture in words some of the deep stirrings that happen in those who have newly arrived in the country from the urban scene and are, perhaps for the first time, engaged in an intense encounter with this beautiful world in which we live. I'll do so in relation to three texts of scripture which I will read along the way.

Here, then, is the view from our screened-in porch. The lovely blue sky bends down over the distant shoreline across the bay. A neighboring waterman works his crab-pots under the watchful eye of an osprey whom we call Oscar. The air is clear and refreshing, ringing with bird songs in the daytime and so loud with insect noises at night that an Englishman who came to visit said, "This sounds like a jungle, not the edge of megalopolis!"

Wayne Sibley Towner is professor of biblical interpretation at Union Theological Seminary in Richmond, Virginia. Towner attended Yale University and was awarded his Ph.D. in 1965. He has taught at Princeton Theological Seminary, Yale Divinity School, and the University of Dubuque Theoctrical Seminary. He is the author of many articles and several books, including *How God Deals with Evil* and *Daniel* in the Interpretation Bible Commentary series.

From the peace and the joy, the color and the song, one can derive a simple lesson: this is our Father's world. Sometimes I've even thought that I've heard the great big "Good!," which God uttered over the Creation in the beginning, still echoing around the edges.

And yet, the more I sit and watch and listen, the more I also sense that the dynamic issue of life and death is constantly being fought out right there in our own front yard. Some mornings I see Slinky the water snake making its way down the little channel beside our house looking for prey. It finds some, too, and so do the crabs that reach into the minnow trap and snip the minnows in two. The hummingbirds get into nasty fencing matches with their bills. One of the ducks that walked on our shore is missing one morning because a fox has torn it to bits during the night. Innocent Oscar drops out of the sky and comes up with a bleeding fish in its talons. The doe that used to visit the front yard in the summer is missing in the fall. Rachel Carson warned us not to romanticize this beautiful world. The Englishman was right, in a way. Frankly, folks, it's a jungle out there, where creatures lie in wait for each other day and night. You and I, too—perhaps supremely—participate in this life-and-death struggle in our constant battle to keep the mosquitos and the gnats, God bless 'em, away from our turf and onto their turf, to drive the snake and mouse away from our house, and to lay some tasty crabs and fish and venison on the table. Couldn't God have done it some other way?, one wonders. Couldn't God have nitched the great chain of being together in some way that did not involve constant suffering and killing? In one sense this very same beautiful creation which we view from our windows and our porches is groaning in travail because it is gripped in the iron hand of mortality. Paul discussed the matter with the church in Rome, and spoke of an ultimate release from that grip. Listen for the Word of God in his words in Romans 8:19–24:

> For the creation waits with eager longing for
> the revealing of the sons of God; for the
> creation was subjected to futility, not of its own

will but by the will of him who subjected it in
hope; because the creation itself will be set free
from its bondage to decay and obtain the
glorious liberty of the children of God. We
know that the whole creation has been groaning in travail together until now; and not only
the creation, but we ourselves, who have the
first fruits of the Spirit, groan inwardly as we
wait for the adoption as sons, the redemption
of our bodies. For in this hope we were saved.

It is not pleasant to be "subjected to futility," to be bound
to decay. And yet, in the beautiful world in which we live, the
rampant plurality of life is founded upon competition and
death. Yes, vitality depends upon death. We creatures give up
our lives for each other. It is an old idea, not a new one. People
accustomed to living in close proximity to the natural order
have always known that we human beings survive and flourish
only because humble creatures lower down the great chain of
being yield up their lives on our behalf. The fish and the crabs
owe it to us, just as the pears and apples do. And what do we
owe them? Tender husbandry, plenty of good will, and feelings of pleasure when we eat them.

All these things you know. But now here is a new idea for
your reflection. I'll put it in the form of a theological (not a
scientific) proposition. God set this teeming and dynamic pool
of life to churning for one reason above all—in order to make
human life possible. This is not to imply that God designed a
gigantic computer model, factored in each of the numberless
species, and then ordered up graphics on each of them, from
the high-bush cranberry and the mosquito to the noble creatures of the jungle and the deep. Frankly, I rather doubt that
it worked that way, not only because it's hard to see why God
would make a mosquito, but more important because the process of evolution itself—quite apart from God's hand—
thrusts out many branches from the great stem of life in accordance with the inexorable laws of natural selection. But this I
do believe, and it is the testimony of scripture as well: little by

little, God teases out of the teeming mass of life an exquisite creature, one like God's own self, and keeps drawing this creature closer and closer. God loves all of the creation and enjoys fellowship with all the creatures, but uniquely with this earth-creature, Adam, male and female, the culminating achievement of creation. You know who I'm talking about. Don't blush! It is you whom God loves in this special way—you and your spouse and your mother and your tender little children and your great-aunt Agatha and Thomas Jefferson and Napoleon and the criminal behind bars. The universe revolves around us, dear friends. All the other creatures live for our sakes. We are at the very center, alone enjoying a direct relationship with God. Does that sound presumptuous and arrogant? Take it up with the psalmist, then. Listen to his witness to the Word of God, in Psalm 8:

> O Lord, our Lord, how majestic is thy name in all the
> earth! Thou whose glory above the heaven is chanted
> by the mouths of babes and infants, thou hast
> founded a bulwark because of thy foes, to still the
> enemy and the avenger.
> When I look at thy heavens, the work of thy
> fingers, the moon and stars which thou hast
> established; what is man that thou art mindful of him,
> and the son of man that thou dost care for him? Yet
> thou hast made him little less than God, and dost
> crown him with glory and honor. Thou has given him
> dominion over the works of thy hands; thou hast put
> all things under his feet, all sheep and oxen, and also
> the beasts of the field, the birds of the air, and the fish
> of the sea, whatever passes along the paths of the sea.
> O Lord, our Lord, how majestic is thy name in all
> the earth!

Whatever the phrase "little less than God" (or as many of us learned it in Sunday school, "a little lower than the angels") means exactly, it seems to fit very well with the testimony which I have just offered. Tiny little specks we are indeed when compared with the great reaches of space, and yet the Bible says we have no peer in the whole realm of creation and that we are the only creatures who are personally invited into fellowship with God.

But for this very reason, we also have more to do than simply sit on our porches and admire the hummingbirds and the neighbors. We have to exercise rule in this world.

This introduces the third and last of our scripture lessons for this morning, from Genesis 1:26–28. Listen for the Word of God in it.

> Then God said, "Let us make man in our image, after our likeness; and let them have dominion over the fish of the sea, and over the birds of the air, and over the cattle, and over all the earth, and over every creeping thing that creeps upon the earth." So God created man in his own image, in the image of God he created him; male and female he created them. And God blessed them, and God said to them, "Be fruitful and multiply, and fill the earth and subdue it; and have dominion over the fish of the sea and over the birds of the air and over every living thing that moves upon the earth."

Let me read part of verse 26 again—it is a tough one: "Let us make man in our image, after our likeness." God makes that statement about no other creature. But what does it mean? Many theories have been advanced, but *The Good News Bible* solves this famous puzzle simply by translating as follows: "They will be like us and resemble us." Male and female, one and many, human beings "resemble" God. They are, as it were, living, walking icons of God, God's surrogates—not in all respects, to be sure, but specifically to this end: "[that] they [may] have dominion over the fish, the birds, and all animals, domestic and wild, large and small" (v. 26b).

Did you hear that? At the culmination of the works of God, the creature who resembles God is invited to look back over the whole chain of being and there to discern a vocation. God gives to the human creature a job to do, the divine power-of-attorney to rule the earth on God's behalf and as God would do!

But how would God rule the earth if God were to do so directly? Ah, to that question there are beautiful and tender answers. "God created the great sea monsters, all kinds of creatures that live in the water, and all kinds of birds. And God was pleased with what he saw" (Gen. 1:21). Pleased with sea monsters? With Nessie? Just imagine! But that is what the Bible says. God returns to the theme in the discussion with Job: "Look at the monster Behemoth; I created him and I created you. He eats grass like a cow, but what strength there is in his body, and what power there is in his muscles! . . . The most amazing of all my creatures!" (Job 40:15–19). God loves every aspect of the Creation, and even brags about the hippopotamus, if that is what Behemoth is. No wonder the psalmist cries out to every creature of the world by name, "Praise the Lord from the earth, sea monsters and all ocean depths; lightning and hail, snow and clouds, strong winds that obey his command. Praise him, hills and mountains, fruit trees and forests; all animals, tame and wild, reptiles and birds" (Ps. 147:7–10).

That is the spirit in which God would rule. But God doesn't rule the world directly. The king of the universe gives that royal signet ring, the power-of-attorney, to the king's steward. I'm talking about us, friends.

Now, the good steward practices good stewardship. The good steward doesn't waste life and resources, because those things belong to the king and are precious to the king, every one of them. Far from challenging the very existence of life with nuclear, biological, and chemical threats, the good steward is always looking for ways to enlarge life. Want to talk about the creatures below us in the great chain of being? The good steward works to enhance the chance of the bald eagle, the snail darter, and the Chesapeake Bay. Want to talk about our peers, the people of the earth? The good steward knows that people are never simply demons who should be blasted away, and is therefore not content to gaze at them only through the cross hairs of rifle sights. The view is no good, considering how marvelous people made in the image of God really are! No, the good steward will insist on walking across the ground toward them with outstretched hands, hoping to establish normal human relationships with them. The good steward struggles, really struggles, on behalf of fellow humans who are threatened with starvation, exploitation, or toxification. The good steward seeks for the world what God gave it in the beginning—wholesome vitality, right relationships, *shalom.*

Before taking one last step, let me say where we have gotten to right now.

There is God's world, and it is a beauty all right. But God doesn't run it on a day-to-day basis, personally ordering the pain and suffering of this individual creature or that. The world operates according to the ancient orders of creation which have produced the life that teems here and elsewhere. Out of the bubbling bio-mass God is drawing a creature like God's own self, capable of entering into the divine fellowship. Thank you mosquitos, thank you frogs, thank you flounder and trout for helping make this possible! This exquisite creature stands as the veritable link between the creation and the Creator. We have a job to do, a vocation called "dominion." We are to bear rule on the earth on God's behalf. And if we do it properly, the world will be glad and will celebrate our leadership.

Now here is the last daring step which these texts encourage us to take.

God has a brilliant future for us if we will accept it. Far from being bogged down in fear and guilt and the feelings of lowliness and exhaustion that so often afflict us, God wants us really to live while we are alive. There is no waste in God, you know. God is a saver, not a waster. And God wants us to save, not waste our vitality; yes, to maximize it, even to evolve ourselves so that we can assume ever more responsibility in the world.

And you know, we are doing it. With God's permission and using the gifts which God has given us, little by little we are doing it! You men and women of science in this congregation, you doctors, nurses, teachers, and agriculturalists know that. Our colleagues in the world of social science and in theology are busy, too! As knowledge of the world has increased, so has the true scope of the possibilities contained in the God-given mandate to exercise dominion. The ancient psalmist could *see* the stars and cry, "The heavens declare the glory of God, and the firmament shows his handiwork" (Ps. 19:1). But now, in the exercise of the dominion that God has given us, we can see ten thousand, ten million times as far as the psalmist could. We have extended our eyes, even to the ability to go away from the earth and look back at it. Ears? The biblical writers could *hear* intimations of the grandeur of God and could thus disclose God's creative, powerful image in them. "Day to day pours forth speech," they cried, "and night to night declares knowledge." But now, we have enlarged our ears to hear the signals of distant novae. We can hear, we are told, the primal sound of creation itself, the original big bang, still echoing and clamoring out at the edge of space. And if and when the first call comes from another rational being out there somewhere, a plaintive note that will immediately raise severe political and theological questions, we who know that it is God's world will be challenged to cope as God would do, as God's stewards in this place, namely, to rejoice and glory in the new voice, not to be afraid, but to answer back.

Is it too upbeat for you? It's realistic, friends! It is scripture's antidote to despair and self-hatred. When we fall into those feelings and even into the kindred feelings of violence and cruelty, someone will say, "Well, they are only humans after all." That is a view of the place and the purpose of our species in the great order of things which scripture intends to combat. "Hey, we are *human!*" is more like the spirit that scripture encourages in us. And if the view from your porch is anything like the one from ours, then I say that God has given us a glorious opportunity to enter heaven's service as responsible and loving partners in creation, and with God's help, to grow and evolve even further into the fullness of the stature that is within us, even up to the stature of Christ. Then with our help the work of redemption can continue in this world until the day that God makes all things new.

> O God, who did not think it unseemly to make us in your own image and likeness, and who found it right and good to exhibit your image on a cross, enable us, we pray, to face the fact that we can become what you have made us to be only by accepting profound responsibility. To the eel grass and the oyster spat, to the bluebird and the blue crab, to our neighbor's body and to his faith, to the refugee's hunger and to her hopelessness, to the survival of the farms and the cities, for our own daily use of food, drink, gasoline, and money, for our opportunity to become even more of what we are—help us, O God, be joyously responsible. In the name of him who is the image of the invisible God, whom we dare to call our helper and our friend, even Jesus Christ our Lord, we pray. Amen.

23. God's Grief

Charles W. Scriven

Texts: Isaiah 53:3–5; Philippians 2:5–8; Colossians 1:15

IF IT HASN'T happened, it will: one day you will mourn in grief or moan in pain; one day your world, or some important part of it, will shatter like the first window you broke in childhood.

This will happen because you are part of us and we are human, and this is what human beings go through. Maybe you are going through it now; maybe you have already done so. But whenever it happens, the hurt is deep and the wounds are many. Russell Baker, the distinguished columnist of *The New York Times,* writes in his autobiography, *Growing Up,* about the day he learned his father died. Baker was five years old and playing in the woods; he believed his father would soon be coming home from the hospital.

Then his cousins came out to where he was and told him his father was dead. Baker remembers that at first he argued with them, denying their report. But by the time he got home the neighborhood women were already housecleaning and cooking; this was a ritual response to death in the small Virginia

Charles W. Scriven is senior pastor of Sligo Seventh-day Adventist Church in Takoma Park, Maryland. A graduate of Walla Walla College and Andrews University, Scriven was awarded his Ph.D. from the Graduate Theological Union in Berkeley, California, in 1984. He has served as associate professor of theology at Walla Walla College. Scriven's articles have appeared in *Spectrum* and *Signs of the Times.*

town where he grew up, and even though his mother had not yet returned from the hospital, he knew it was true; his father was gone.

That afternoon he was sent to Bessie Scott's house across town, where he cried himself out and for the first time, he tells us, "thought seriously about God."

Baker's father had been only thirty-three, and despite Bessie Scott's assurance that God loves us as his own children, the five-year-old boy did not understand.

Here is how Baker remembers his thoughts: "That afternoon, though I couldn't have phrased it this way then, I decided that God was a lot less interested in people than anybody in Morrisonville was willing to admit. That day I decided that God was not entirely to be trusted."

He continues: "At the age of five I had become a skeptic and began to sense that any happiness that came my way might be the prelude to some grim, cosmic joke."[1]

Grief and pain, I said, leave many wounds. One of them is the blow they strike, or can strike, against our faith. We have been taught that God is all-powerful, and so it seems to us that he is in a position to prevent evil from happening. We have been taught that he is all-good, and so it seems to us that he must want to prevent evil from happening. Yet evil does happen, and when it comes close, piercing our hearts, we can't help wondering why, in *God's* world, it has to be this way. If you have ever doubted God's goodness, or even raised your fist at him in agony and anger, it is surely understandable.

Christian pastors have known this from the beginning and have tried to offer reassuring explanations of why bad things happen in God's world.

One of the most famous is what we may call the *free-will explanation*. God is powerful and good, the explanation goes, and just because of this he has made a world with *persons* in it, creatures with freedom to chose how they will live. Not even an all-powerful God, however, can guarantee that free persons will choose to be good; their freedom entails that they may choose to be evil. So if people suffer it is not because God has failed; it is because human beings have chosen a course of evil that engenders suffering. We may wish God had forestalled evil altogether, but he could only have done so at the price of reducing us to robots.

That's the free-will explanation. But now think back to Russell Baker and his memory of his father's death at thirty-three. Could this explanation begin to undo his distrust of God? I think not, and the reason is that the father's death did not happen as a result of human evil. His father was a diabetic before doctors knew about insulin, and he was doomed from the beginning to early death, not as the victim of some evil human choice, but as the victim of nature itself.

Some of you are, or will be, the tragic victims of nature. Why is nature so unkind? Why death at an early age? Why, besides sickness, the other catastrophes, the famines, the earthquakes, the birth defects? How can a good God preside over all this, anyway?

This brings us to the second of the two most famous explanations of why bad things happen in God's world. It is another means of reassuring sufferers and we may call it the *moral-growth explanation.* It is true, this explanation goes, that pain occurs in the interplay between the world's stuff and the natural laws that govern it. But God has made the world this way, and he has done so precisely in order to provide an environment for moral growth. Only in a world, it is said, where pain can happen is it possible for human beings to learn the virtues, such as self-sacrificing love, that dignify and enrich our existence in the world.

There is a certain plausibility in this. And it does address the sort of doubt Russell Baker felt when he was five; it does help us, that is, to cope with suffering brought about, not by human beings, but by nature. Still, I cannot imagine the five-year-old Russell Baker overcoming his skepticism on the basis of this explanation. I cannot imagine his trusting God because of it.

Let me say why—why, indeed, neither the free-will nor the moral-growth explanation seems completely satisfying. The reason is that in real cases of grief and pain, the wounds run too deep, including the wound to faith. Both explanations serve a purpose, but the sufferer's questions about God cannot be resolved by anything so neat, so tidy.

Sooner or later it dawns on us, moreover, that the amount and degree of suffering in this world are just overwhelming. What about the pain of starving children? What about the victims of sheer atrocities . . . In Central America? In Cambodia? Among the boat people of Vietnam?

The nineteenth-century Russian author Dostoyevski reflects on faith and suffering in his famous story of *The Brothers Karamazov.* At one point the brother Ivan, a skeptic, tells about a poor serf child who at play hit his master's hunting dog with a stone. The outraged master had the child seized and the next morning torn to pieces by hounds before his mother's eyes.

Can such suffering ever be justified? Ivan says no. If that is the price that must be paid in order for God's Kingdom to come, then the price is too high. "We cannot afford to pay so much for admission," Ivan declares. "And therefore I hasten to return my ticket of admission."

Ivan means this: he cannot in good conscience go along with a God who permits this kind of torment. He questions the moral acceptability of a process that submits the innocent to so much suffering.

The story of the child may at first hearing seem farfetched to you. But recall what has happened in our own century in the Nazi concentration camps and you will realize it is not farfetched; even worse evils against children have occurred within the lifetime of many of you.

Eyewitnesses tell us that in the summer of 1944 the Auschwitz gas chamber used for children was out of order. To meet the daily quota of deaths, the Nazis made layer upon layer of wood and gasoline, and lit it; then they lined up the children and simply threw them onto the open flames. Several thousand children died that way—not to mention, of course, the hundreds of thousands who were merely gassed. And these victims had done nothing whatever to offend; they were murdered for no other reason than they were Jews.

How can we accept a God who presides over a world where this can happen? How can we believe that he is good?

Let me say this: I do not believe any answer can silence the questions completely. God has never removed the possibility of doubt. To do so he would have had to remove suffering, for suffering engenders doubt, and always will. Nevertheless, there is something to say on God's behalf, and in order to say it we must turn finally to the passages of Scripture we have read together this morning.

The first, you remember, was Isaiah 53:3-5. The prophet who wrote them was addressing exiles, Jews whom the Babylonians had uprooted from their homeland. They were sufferers; their faith was flagging.

In a dramatic departure from the conventional wisdom in ancient Israel, the prophet imagined the existence of a servant, a new leader of Israel; indeed, a new Israel. And it is the traits of this servant that he describes in verses 3-5: "He was despised and rejected by men, a man of sorrows, and familiar with suffering," says the prophet. "Surely he took up our infirmities and carried out sorrow," he goes on, and then in verse 5 declares, "But he was pierced for our transgressions, he was crushed for our iniquities; the punishment that brought us peace was upon him, and by his wounds we are healed."

To the suffering exiles the prophet affirms the possibility of salvation won *through* suffering. God's wounded servant can—precisely through his wounds—bring healing and establish peace. This is the hope the prophet offers to his people.

The second passage we read together is from Philippians 2. Here we find Paul affirming that Jesus took upon himself, so verse 7 tells us, "the very nature of a servant." He "became obedient unto death—even death on a cross." And in the verses that follow the ones we read, Paul tells us that because of all this, God exalted Jesus "to the highest place" so that one day every knee would bow before him and every tongue confess that he is Lord.

Paul may have actually been thinking of the Servant Song in Isaiah when he described Jesus as having taken upon himself the "nature of a servant." Or he may have been thinking about the servants—literally, slaves—who in Roman society had no rights or privileges. What is clear in either case is this: Jesus was willing to be a sufferer; he was willing to be a victim, and for Paul it is just in virtue of this that he pleased God and became Lord of heaven and earth.

The third passage we read is Colossians 1:15. Speaking of Jesus, the author of this letter declares: "He is the image of the invisible God." The Greek behind the word "image" makes it clear that what the author means is this: Jesus reveals what God is truly like; Jesus is the concrete manifestation of God's own will and way in the world.

Now do you see what all this entails? It entails that *God himself is a suffering servant.* What the Bible is telling us today is that God is not some cold heavenly power distant from our grief and pain. God was actually "in Christ," as Paul tells us in yet another passage, chapter 5 of 2 Corinthians. God actually participated in the suffering of Jesus, and in doing so exhibited the love and willingness to suffer that is the very essence of his being.

Among the survivors of the Nazi holocaust is the Jewish author Elie Wiesel. His book *Night* describes the experience he went through in the concentration camps as a boy barely into his teens. Among the most devastating scenes is his description of a hanging at Buna, a camp near Auschwitz in the south of Poland.

The three victims, one of them a child, had been suspected of blowing up a power station. Now the other inmates were being made to march by the hanging bodies in order to see them at close range and be deterred themselves from acts of resistance. The two adults were dead by the time Wiesel marched by, but the child was still alive, struggling between life and death.

Behind him Wiesel heard a man repeat a question he had asked moments before as the inmates were approaching the gallows: "Where is God now? Where is he?"

Then Wiesel writes: "And I heard a voice within me answer him: 'Where is he? Here he is—He is hanging here on the gallows. . . . ''[2]

For Wiesel, a Jewish boy who at the time was losing the religious vision he grew up with, this was not, I think, an affirmation of faith but a statement of despair. Though Wiesel has since come to believe again, he was at that time a boy whose God was being murdered before his very eyes, a boy whose faith was dying.

But if we consider the remark from the standpoint of what we have read today, it is a stunning and true description. For the Bible has taught us today that wherever suffering occurs, God is there, bearing it with us, a companion who knows and feels our sorrows and out pains. We have seen that our grief is God's grief; he allows no burden to befall us which he does not take upon himself.

In 1978, along with my wife, Marianne, and a choir from the college where she taught music, I visited Auschwitz. It was in the bleak midwinter, and the light banter on the bus ride out from Cracow became dead silence as soon as we walked through the main gate of the camp. Two fences surrounded the red brick barracks and a ghastly crematorium from which, our guide told us, one hundred tons of human ashes had been hauled away for fertilizer.

What we saw stunned us into teary silence: mounds of human hair, piles of luggage, stacks of crutches and artificial limbs, all from the innocent who were gassed and burned in the camp.

Finally we came to the wall of death, solid brick and concrete linking two of the barracks buildings. Against this wall, we were told, some twenty thousand prisoners, mostly the highly educated, had been shot to death at a distance of half a meter. It was there, beside the wreaths of flowers at the base of the wall, that the choir stopped to sing. The piece, which they knew by heart, was Egil Hovland's "The Glory of the Father," based on a text from chapter one of the Gospel of John.

"The Word was made flesh, and dwelt among us," the choir began. The melody was plain and solemn, as in a chant from long ago. The choir sang on: "We beheld the glory of the Father, full of grace and truth." Standing in the sullen cold, I knew that those words declared the Gospel. They still do. We behold the Father when we see the Son, and because the Son suffered with us, we know the Father suffers with us, too. We are not abandoned when we hurt; God makes our grief his own.

NOTES

1. Russell Baker, *Growing Up* (New York: Signet, 1984), pp. 79–81.

2. Elie Wiesel, *Night, Dawn, Day* (New York: Aronson/B'nai B'rith, 1985), pp. 71–72.

24. On Being an Honorary Jew
R. Benjamin Garrison

Scripture: Deuteronomy 6:4–5

THE LATE Pope Pius XII observed that spiritually, we are all Semites. Today we worship in a mode based upon our Jewish heritage. In this sermon I shall pay tribute and assess the contributions made to our faith by our Jewish foreparents. It is significant and symbolic that, as a Protestant minister, I commence by quoting a Catholic bishop claiming that spiritually we are all Jews.

This heritage has been much in evidence to those who have worshiped with any attention this morning. The service began with a choral introit from the Nineteenth Psalm. The opening hymn is the only purely Jewish hymn in our hymnal. Its words date from the fourteenth century and in earlier editions of the hymnal it was more accurately titled "The God of Abraham Praise." The final hymn, "O Lord, Our Fathers Oft Have Told," is a paraphrase of Psalm 40. The anthem was a setting from Isaiah. The unison prayer and the prayers used by the minister in the morning prayers came from the *Hebrew Union Prayerbook.* We used as our creed the historic *Shemá,*

R. Benjamin Garrison is pastor of the Seward United Methodist Church, Seward, Nebraska. He was educated at DePauw, Drew, and Cambridge universities, and he was awarded a doctor of divinity from MacMurray College. Garrison is the author of numerous articles and books, including *Creeds in Collision, Worldly Holiness, Seven Questions Jesus Asked,* and *Are You the Christ?*

"Hear O Israel, the Lord is our God, the Lord is one." The very fact that most of these materials are taken from our hymnal is quiet testimony to the pervasiveness of the Hebrew tradition in our Christian heritage.

From the Jews we receive the Ten Commandments. (I could almost feel the hush that came across the congregation as this charter of our faith and morality was read.) Even persons who own no religious allegiance are indebted to this warrant, or sanction, for morality. From the Jewish prophets we have gained lofty and—whether we like it or not—sometimes revolutionary insights into the nature of life. Our Lord, remember always, was born of their bone and came from their community.

Supremely, their God is our God. Tarry with me as we look at this latter gift, namely the God they gave us, a gift that makes us all spiritual Semites.

I

We proudly proclaim that ours is a Jewish faith because we believe in one God. Today we take this for granted. Time was, however, when people treated their gods as we do our electrical appliances: a different one for each purpose. So monotheism was a perfectly amazing discovery in that time. At the time when "Hear, O Israel, the Lord is our God, the Lord is one" was proclaimed, much of the world took a different attitude toward their gods.

> Did it rain? Some goddess was washing her hair.
> Did one wish a son? One then made a sacrifice to
> the goddess of fertility.
> Were the crops poor? The agricultural gods were
> displeased with the farmer.
> Did one's swine take sick and die? They had an
> evil spirit.
> Were one's enemies at the gates? Then invoke a
> four-star general god.

In this midst of this very lottery of gods it took a man with a good deal of brains and spine to stand up and say, as David did in the psalm:

> Pagan idols are mere gold and silver
> made by the hands of men,
> with mouths, but they never speak;
> with eyes but they cannot see;
> with ears but they cannot hear;
> with no breath on their lips.
> So be it with their makers,
> with all who trust in them.
>
> (Ps. 115:4–8)

Nor was it easy for this God to gain recognition beyond the rigid national boundaries that had been drawn up for gods in those days. They had a kind of Old Testament McCarran Immigration Act. When you moved from one land to another, you did not just get a transfer of membership from one church to another but from one god to another. And you had jolly well better take the loyalty oath if you wanted in. Remember how Ruth said to her mother-in-law, as they were going off to a strange country, "Your God shall be my God." She was changing regions and so assumed she had also to change gods. This was because it was commonly assumed that a god's domain was limited to one province or kingdom. Thus those brokenhearted Jews far off in a strange land cried, "How shall we sing the Lord's song in a strange land?" We would not find this difficult, but they, though they believed in this God intensely, thought that he was now far away from them, for they were in another province.

Furthermore, these jurisdictional agreements made by the International Union of Heavenly Managers, Inc., were taken quite seriously. The Hebrews in exile saw no great contradiction in worshiping the fertility goddess. When Jeremiah protested, they didn't like it a bit. They were in a different political province, and they cautioned their preacher to keep his nose out of politics—an argument I have some vague memory of having heard elsewhere! Jeremiah was worried because of what this was doing in the life of his people but even more because of what it seemed to do to God. He knew that God (Yahweh) was being judged (or misjudged) on the basis of the way they served him. This is the story of God's life, God's continual plight. If Sunday's worship has no discernible effect on Monday's work or Tuesday's vote, then it is very easy for people to conclude that the god involved isn't much of a god. It would seem that the better logic would be that it is the human beings who are deficient, but this is not the way people view it. People unfortunately conclude that God is no good if God's people are not. The cleverest way to deny God is not to deny but to belittle: the Greek dramatist Euripides did not believe in the gods, but he was too smart to tell the public that. That would have affected box-office sales. So what did he do? He wrote plays in which the gods acted like fools. He did not need to deny them if he could belittle them.

Nevertheless, in the midst of this Jewish people there were always those who wanted to remind them that there was one God and that therefore they should act like it. If this faith in one God were false, then, they thought, it did not matter much how they acted. The Hebrews called these persons prophets. So the *Shemá* which we used as our creed this morning is a blaring trumpet at midnight, a glaring light in the middle of the darkness, "Hear, O Israel, the Lord is our God, the Lord is one."

If you are to get some picture of that kind of trumpet call, I invite you to think about where your ancestors were at the time, particularly those of you who pride yourself on your proper Anglo-Saxon, northern European stock. I do not know about *your* ancestors, but I know where mine were. When those prophets said, "Hear, O Israel, the Lord is our God, the Lord is one," my ancestors were still swinging stone axes and worshiping wooden gods, roasting raw meat on forked sticks over crude northern European fires. Yet over at the far end of the Mediterranean, the Jews had found another light that would burn and burn and burn until a twentieth-century pope could say, "Spiritually we are all Jews."

II

Second, I proudly proclaim that we are Jews because we affirm that this one God has revealed himself in history, concretely in events. Remember the film of several years ago, Cecil B. DeMille's Cinemascope presentation, *The Ten Commandments.* About the only thing that DeMille managed to leave out of that picture was the main point. I know that a lot of people who saw the picture will never bother to read the book. But the question is, What did you see? What you saw was the cause of enlightened religion set back at least twenty years. Some of you wouldn't sit under my preaching for two successive Sundays if we treated the Bible that literally. Yet many of you watching that movie left the theater or turned off your TV feeling that you had been treated to something special. You had—something especially misleading. Long ago it was the scholarly fashion to talk of these things as the mighty acts of Moses. In latter days the scholars have learned to speak more accurately of the mighty acts of *God.* Nevertheless, you could have seen that entire picture and never have been reminded of God at all. What you saw were the magical machinations of a Hebrew Houdini. God was not there, except for the so-called voice of God, which sounded to me as if somebody in Forest Lawn Cemetery had put on an old 78-rpm phonograph at 33 1/3. Then there was that marvelously educated lightning which came out and chiseled the Hebrew law into the stone tablets, and then conveniently translated it into English. You could have seen the entire movie and never had the idea that what we are talking about are the mighty acts of God, that in the author's original version God confronts humans in events.

Grant that this people's history is a very complex one. This is because the Hebrew Scriptures are not an orderly journal of socially respectable happenings. They are the amazingly candid, and at times embarrassingly detailed, chronicle of a people who did not hesitate to air their dirty robes in public. Somebody has said that if the Jews had played football, the rules would have been in the Old Testament. The point is, however, that all these events are meaningless without the biblical point of view. They are simply one more example of a little ancient history. The biblical point of view is that God has revealed the divine will concretely, in events.

This is because one cannot readily worship an abstract God. One can study an abstract God, but one cannot worship him, or it. The old aphorism, "The Greeks had a word for it," is an understatement. The Greeks had many words for God. They had long, bearded words like *omnipresent*; polysyllabic words like *omniscient*; words which have no counterpart in the Hebrew vocabulary because they have no counterpart in the Hebrew experience of God.

The Hebrews' experience of God was graphic, pictorial, touchable, practical, everyday. So when they wanted to speak of the creative power of God, they spoke of the finger of the Lord. (One can almost see God fingerpainting, as a child would.) When they wanted to speak of the uplifting, sustaining power of God, they spoke of the hand of God. When they wanted to talk about the might of God, they spoke of the arm of the Lord. Any Jew who had ever tied a halter on a camel in the desert or played games around the tents or lifted a burden knew what was meant. They did not know what was meant by omnipotent, but they knew a God who had delivered his people, their fathers. And so they knew.

One evening a friend of mine was looking over my bookshelves for something to read. I handed him a book on the Old Testament, or what I prefer to call the Hebrew Scriptures. He looked at me as if I had just given him an obsolete version of the Omaha telephone directory. He said, "I don't go for that Old Testament stuff." But you see, the Old Testament and the New Testament are not bound together for the convenience of the bookseller. They are bound together because they *belong* together. Christians who talk about the New Testament being the fulfillment of the Old Testament are talking nonsense unless they know enough about the Old Testament to know what it is that is being fulfilled. The older book is very earthy: Abraham having supper with God; Job arguing with God as if God were a quarrelsome old wife. The Bible is earthy and everyday because the Hebrews recognized that only in the concrete encounter of events does God become real to us. For this reason, then, among others, ours is a Jewish faith.

III

Finally, I proudly proclaim that I am a Jew not only because I believe in one God encountered in human events, but because I belong to a community, called apart for service, a chosen people.

Much misunderstanding, even among the Jews, has been caused by this notion of being called apart as a chosen people (just as, by the way, there have been many misconceptions on the part of Christians about the idea of predestination). The basic idea at the heart of both is the same: it is that whatever we have and whatever the reasons for our having it, it cannot be that we deserve it. Listen to Deuteronomy:

> The Lord did not set His love upon you or
> choose you because you were more in number
> than any other people, for you were fewest of
> all people, but because the Lord loved you.

If you cut out the center of that sentence and take away all the negative statements, you have a sentence that would drive any teacher of English to despair, because what it really says is, "God loves you . . . because God loves you." God won't say why. We *can't* say why. God just does, so we are to act like it.

While this choosing confers upon us some special privilege, it also bestows upon us some special responsibilities. Israel (the Jewish people) and the new Israel (the Christian church) are chosen for only one reason: chosen to serve, chosen to sacrifice. Along with a chosen people goes a chosen task. One of the Greek words for church, *ekklesia,* from which we get words like ecclesiastical, means those who are called together, called together for service.

So God's chosen people, whether in eastern Nebraska or in East Africa, are a community of accountable people, accountable to God. Somebody has said that, in its briefest form, the Hebrew Christian religion means the idea and challenge of the One—the one God and the one thing needful: "I will be your God and you will be my people."

This chosen community, however, is a community of accountable individuals. True monotheism—hear me now—is not simply the bare belief that there is one God. Rather it is the belief that all of life belongs to God. Here is the idea of stewardship, once more and for always. The Jew measured out his good grain in the knowledge that it has come from the hand of God, not from the Seward County Co-op. We teach our pupils better if we recognize that both pupils and teachers sit at the feet of him from whom all truth comes. We rear our children best if we recognize that they are God's children. I am responsible for the world around me because I am responsible to the God beyond me.

Then this which, though not my main point, is not alien to my main point: W. N. Ewer has a quatrain which says

How odd
of God
to choose
the Jews.

To this someone has added,

But not so odd
As those who choose
The Jewish God
And spurn the
Jews.[1]

When one thinks—if one can bear to think of it—of the six million Jews who were cremated by a so-called Christian nation; when one recalls that Karl Marx sought Christian baptism in order to protect himself and his family from the indignities of the Christian church against the Jews; when one reads the bitter, vitriolic ink that Marx subsequently poured out against the Christian church; when one recalls the ghettoes to which the Jew has been confined and the jibes to which he has been subjected (like the condescending phrase "Jew him down"); and then when one places all of this over against this marvelous spiritual legacy which we have nevertheless received, one can only cry out, "God be merciful to us Christians."

I said to a young Christian woman who was contemplating a Jewish marriage that about 75 percent of that time I have more in common with my rabbi brothers and sisters than with my fundamentalist Christian brothers. (The latter, I strongly suspect, would change that percentage to something close to 100 percent.) I went on to say to her that the 25 percent I do not share in common with my Jewish friends is for me utterly irrevocable and unique. I cannot give it up. Nevertheless, this day I stand here to say that I am proud, happy, and grateful for that 75 percent that I have received from my Jewish foreparents and contemporaries.

When I spoke at a statewide conference of United Methodists and Jews in Florida some time ago, I introduced an idea of Dean Krister Stendahl, then of Harvard. He suggested that Jewish and Christian brothers and sisters might helpfully and hopefully bestow the titles "Honorary Jew" and "Honorary Christian" upon one another. This would recognize a givenness about being a Jew, or about being a Christian, a givenness that we can never fully share. It would also recognize, however, that much that is imperishable and imperative, for both of us, can be offered for our mutual enrichment. You can imagine how moved I was when, at the close of my address, my Jewish counterpart keynoter arose and said, "Brother Benjamin, I welcome you as an honorary Jew."

You may recall that moving passage in John Hersey's novel of wartime Poland, *The Wall.* An old rabbi makes his way out of the ghetto in Warsaw at the risk of his life, furtively traveling along the darkened streets, going to a cemetery at the edge of the city and there burying his Torah, or Law, so that it will not be desecrated by the German soldiers who will soon arrive to kill him.

I am very sure that only a Jew can really understand this: understand, I mean, taking the Bible and risking your life to bury it in some place so that it will not fall into hands that do not love God's law.

I think, though, I understand it a little. I seem to see there a man who knew God, forbidding yet forbearing, severe in judgments yet fatherly in love. I seem to see too a God who has really encountered a man, really and concretely, in the synagogue but also in the marketplace and ultimately in the gas chamber. I see a man who found his manhood by being a part of a people who are called apart for splendid witness even when they are despised and rejected.

The Christian faith is a healthier religion today because it lives under the constant cross-questioning of the Jewish faith, as, I dare say, Judaism is healthier because of Christianity's cross-questioning.

I see a person who makes me proud to say, with the Holy Father of Rome, spiritually we are all Jews.

That is why I am glad and proud and humbled to be an honorary Jew.

NOTE

1. *The Silver Treasury of Light Verse.* ed. Oscar Williams (New York: New American Library, 1957).

25. Onward, Christian Soldiers?

David J. Bailey

Scripture: Ephesians 6:10–20

THERE IS ONE issue that has surfaced to rouse more controversy within the Christian church this year than all other issues. Dare I say that this issue has even had church people up in arms? The issue is not, as it usually is, the church's official position on Nicaragua or South Africa or abortion or the World Council of Churches, though it may have something to do with several of those issues. The issue is that a committee working on a new hymnbook for the United Methodist Church decided to leave the hymn "Onward, Christian Soldiers" out of that new hymnbook, because the language is too militaristic. After that announcement, more than four thousand letters and phone calls were received by the committee, many violently condemning their decision. Hostile articles were written in newspapers across the country. In the paper this week was an article saying that the committee has decided to meet to reconsider its decision and will probably reverse its course.

I'm addressing this topic today while it is still raging because the issues involved are important. Also, some of the

---

David J. Bailey is pastor of the West Avenue Presbyterian Church in Gastonia, North Carolina. A graduate of Davidson College and Columbia Theological Seminary, he is a cowinner of the 1982 Lyman and Myki Morley Prize in Biblical Scholarship from Columbia Seminary.

same kinds of battles are probably going to take place in the Presbyterian Church, which has a committee that is just getting started on its task of compiling a new hymnbook for the reunited Presbyterian Church.

So who is right here? Are we Christian soldiers, marching as to war, or aren't we? In administering the sacrament of infant baptism this morning, have we inducted a new soldier into the army? In order not to keep you in suspense, I'm going to tell you at the very beginning that while I think both sides are right in some of their major points, I think the hymn ought to stay in the book if people want to sing it that much.

"Onward, Christian Soldiers" is one of a number of hymns in our book that use militaristic language. It is not one of my personal favorites, but that has to do more with the pounding tune than with the words. But a couple of my favorite hymns have militaristic language: "A Mighty Fortress Is Our God" and "Soldiers of Christ, Arise."

What must be remembered is that the militaristic language in these hymns is symbolic. "Marching *as to* war" is what the hymn says, not "marching *off to* war." The point is being made in these hymns that the Christian life is not always a waltz through the rose garden, but is more often an out-and-out battle against sin, against evil, against hatred, against oppression. For this battle the Christian needs to be prepared, just as a soldier needs to be prepared for a military battle. The Christian needs to be dedicated to the cause, to have the necessary weapons, and to be protected with the appropriate armor in order to be victorious in the battle. I believe that is a very accurate and appropriate analogy for the Christian life, and I have no objection to our singing in such terms as long as we understand what we are and are not saying by it.

But that is where the thorn was for the Methodist hymnal committee. They are right that too often in history Christians have been all too willing to take up arms and march off to war, believing that they were upholding the side of truth, of the church, indeed of Christ himself. In the twelfth century the crusaders marched off to war with the infidels, the Moslems, with the cross of Jesus going on before on their banners. In the sixteenth and seventeenth centuries, Christians fought bitter and bloody wars against one another, each side believing that Christ the royal master was leading them against their foes, forward into battle. Hitler convinced much of the German Christian population that part of the Christian's call was to exterminate all Jews.

Even today—even in America—there are many Christians who see no conflict between the Christian emphasis on justice and compassion *for* all and the militaristic emphasis on power and domination *over* all. They sing, "Leave no unguarded place, no weakness of the soul," and begin devising a Star Wars defense program thinking it will leave no unguarded place. They sing, "And take, to arm you for the fight, the panoply of God," and think of a glorious diversified nuclear arsenal—with submarines, planes, rockets, and ships. They sing, "From strength to strength go on; wrestle, and fight, and pray; tread all the powers of darkness down, and win the well-fought day," and they plot out strategies for world domination.[1]

Perhaps I overstate my case, but that is, I think, what the committee was getting at. These hymns stress power and strength and glorious victories in vicious battles. They say nothing about being willing to suffer for others, about being willing to be a servant for others, about sacrificing your own interests for the good of another, about giving your life so another may live.

But no hymn carries the entire weight of the gospel by itself. Each tells a part of the story, and only in using them all at various times do we get the full richness of the gospel in song. We need the personal, pietistic hymns, because each person has his or her own individual relationship with Christ; but we also need the hymns that stress the corporate life of the church community, because we are the body of Christ working together. We need the sorrowful hymns of confession, because we are all sinners; but we also need the triumphant hymns of victory and forgiveness because of the gifts of forgiveness and salvation. We need the hymns that exhort us to battle, because the powers of darkness are many and powerful; but we also need the hymns that remind us that we are to suffer for others and to be servants of all. Only by combining them all do we find balance in our spiritual lives. If we sing only one kind of hymn, we become one-sided Christians and get off-balance. That is why we use such a wide variety of hymns, with different themes and different tempos.

I do not believe we need to be in the business of censoring our hymnbook, any more than we should be censoring our libraries. What we should be doing is studying the words and the implications of the songs so that we know what they are saying. Maybe because of the conflict the Methodists are experiencing, we will all be educated about the real meaning and importance of these so-called "militaristic" hymns so that we will know what they do and do not say.

So—have we inducted a new soldier into the army today? Well, in a spiritual sense, yes. Her parents have returned her to God and asked him to be her divine protector. In addition, her parents and you, the members of this congregation, have pledged this day to help provide her with the training and weapons that she will need in order to be victorious in the battles that lie ahead of her.

What will she need to be victorious? Paul says it best in the words that are echoed in our "militaristic" hymns. She will need the belt of truth buckled around her waist. She needs the breastplate of righteousness and the shield of faith to protect her from the arrows of temptation. She needs to have her feet fitted with the gospel of peace as a firm footing. She needs the helmet of salvation and the sword of the Spirit, which is the word of God. Undergirding all of this, she needs prayer—our prayers—as she grows and matures and prepares to take up the battle herself.

Those are the things we all need in order to be victorious: truth, peace, righteousness, faith, salvation, the word of God, and prayer. Those are the weapons we need, not guns, planes, rockets, and submarines, because our battle, Paul says, is not against flesh-and-blood armies and rulers, but against powers of oppression and hatred and evil.

When I sing "Onward, Christian Soldiers," I think not of marching armies but of Martin Luther King, Jr., and thousands of others marching through the South with no weapons but faith and hope and truth and the word of God, bringing down a powerful structure of hatred and oppression, just as Joshua and his marchers brought down the walls of Jericho. I think of black South Africans last week marching to remind the world of the tenth anniversary of the Soweto massacre. I think of Jesus Christ walking, carrying his cross, going up the hill to Calvary. Let us follow, then. "Onward, Christian soldiers, marching as to war, with the cross of Jesus going on before."

NOTE

1. Quotations in this paragraph are from the hymn, "Soldiers of Christ, Arise," words by Charles Wesley (1749), tune by George J. Elvey, 1868. *The Hymnbook* (Philadelphia: 1955), p. 308.

IV. ETHICAL

26. The Other, the Others, and You

Walter J. Burghardt, S.J.

Scripture: Jeremiah 9:23–24

IT'S BEEN A rough year for ethics. A politician, a preacher, and an entrepreneur: a politician whose quest for the presidency was in doubt because he was tarred with womanizing; a preacher who can no longer Praise The Lord because he used blackmail to cover adultery; an entrepreneur who gives all Wall Street the shakes when he confesses to illegal inside trading. And all sorts of shenanigans from nursing homes to the basement of the White House.

Now this is not a jeremiad against the modern world. Despite the half century that separates you and me in age, I shall not abuse your Budweiser time by telling you how good things used to be. They weren't; and even if they were, you wouldn't believe me. But this long winter and this strange spring do raise questions, raise them to a pitch of urgency that touches you intimately because tomorrow you replace the Harts and

Walter John Burghardt was born in 1914 in New York City. He was educated at Woodstock College and the Catholic University of America. Father Burghardt, a Jesuit priest, currently is theologian-in-residence at Georgetown University, and is editor in chief of *Theological Studies.* He has received thirteen honorary degrees from American colleges and universities and is the author of a number of books, most recently *Preaching: The Art and the Craft.* "The Other, the Others, and You" is a baccalaureate sermon given at Colgate University in Hamilton, New York.

Norths, the Bakkers and Boeskys; you will shape our world after I have joined my ancestors. They raise questions about what it means to be human, to be a man or a woman, to be genuinely religious, to be alive in the Judeo-Christian tradition that helped fashion this singular nation of freedom under law.

Let me, then, speak very directly to you. Allow me to tell you simply what I in the winter of existence expect of you in your spring and summer, what I should like to see in you after four years in Hamilton, what I hope for you, and so for our world, as you begin to dance theron, as you start shaping it in your image. My hope for you has three dimensions: first, the Other—capital O; second, the others—small o; third, you yourself.

I

First, the Other—capital O. To an ancient society that prized three possessions above all else—wisdom, power, wealth—the prophet Jeremiah thundered:

> Thus says the Lord: "Let not the wise man
> glory in his wisdom, let not the mighty man
> glory in his might, let not the rich man glory in
> his wealth; but let him who glories glory in this,
> that he understands and knows me, that I am
> the Lord who practice steadfast love, justice,
> and righteousness in the earth; for in these
> things I delight," says the Lord. (Jer. 9:23–24)

Now these words are not writ large over your fourteen hundred acres. The Baptists of 1819 surely had them in mind when they established a seminary here; but the movement from ministry to liberal arts and science has meant a movement from tranquil acceptance of God to a search for God, a struggle, to an atmosphere where atheists and agnostics mingle with fundamentalists and liberal believers, where the Quran enjoys equal official favor with the Prior Testament and the New, where the Mahayana Buddhist need not feel uncomfortable. Here is where God is worshiped and denied, prayed to and ridiculed, debated in class and over foaming mugs—or just ignored. The God of Abraham and the God of Jesus Christ makes himself (or herself) at home here by human persuasion, not by divine right.

And that can be a good thing. I say "can" because not everyone can "take" it. But for those who can, Colgate should be a liberating experience. For here religion is not the Baltimore Catechism, even No. 3; here religion is not a naked Scripture; here faith seeks understanding. Here you wrestle with revelation, wrestle with ideas, wrestle like Jacob with God. And wrestle you must. For if God is, if you exist only because a loving God fashioned you out of nothing but love, then that God wants you to know him. This, as Jeremiah exclaimed, this is your glory: that you know the Lord.

But the wrestling is a sweaty job. If you are a Jew, you wrestle with Auschwitz, with mountains of human bones, with six million men, women, and children gassed into oblivion; and you may be tempted to conclude, as some do, that "God died in Auschwitz." If you are a Christian, any brand or breed, you wrestle with a God who gave his own Son to a bloody death, with a God of several hundred sects competing for souls, with a Christ who promises perplexing paradoxes: life through death, losing all to gain all, blessedness on the poor and the hungry and those who weep, woes on the rich and the fat and the merry. If you are a Catholic Christian, you may well wrestle with a church that claims to know God's mind for you, that breathes down your neck in bedroom and boardroom, that keeps you from love when your marriage is dead, that seems to keep women in second-class slavery.

I assume you are here, in this house of God, because God has somehow touched you, because you love him or fear him or are just plain puzzled by him. No matter. What I hope for you is that you will never cease wrestling with God, for that in itself is a proof of love: you want to know him, know what he is like, what makes him tick, how he can possibly leave his own world the contradiction it is—where we love enough to die for one another, hate enough to kill one another. I hope that by wrestling with God you will discover what I have experienced—discover that your God has never stopped loving you, for in the touching segment from the prophet Isaiah

> Zion said: "The Lord has forsaken me,
> my Lord has forgotten me."
> "Can a woman forget her suckling child,
> that she should have no compassion on the son of her womb?
> Even these may forget,
> yet I will not forget you.
> Behold, I have graven you on the palms of my hands. . . ."
>
> (Isa. 49:14–16a)

I hope that by wrestling with God you will discover that the Lord not only loves you but lives in you, has compassion on you not from outer space but from within your bone and marrow, is more intimate to you than you are to yourself. I hope that by wrestling with God you will experience the joy, the even sensuous pleasure, that comes from being in love—in love with him who made you, who is faithful despite our infidelities, who cares even in our uncaring.

It's worth getting to know God. After all, you're going to have to live with God . . . forever.

II

Second, the others—small o. Over two decades ago, a remarkable rabbi, Abraham Joshua Heschel, wrote an article titled "No Religion Is an Island." Two short paragraphs from that article consistently haunt me:

> To meet a human being is a major challenge to mind and heart. I must recall what I normally forget. A person is not just a specimen called *homo sapiens.* He is all of humanity in one, and whenever one man is hurt we are all injured. The human is a disclosure of the divine, and all men are one in God's care for man. Many

> things on earth are precious, some are holy,
> humanity is holy of holies.
>   To meet a human being is an opportunity to
> sense the image of God, *the presence* of God.
> According to a rabbinical interpretation, the
> Lord said to Moses: "Wherever you see the
> trace of man there I stand before you. . . ."[1]

The image of God, the presence of God, in each woman and man—a thrilling thought. The Other comes alive in the other. Regrettably, the traditional thought clashes with contemporary reality. First-rate sociologists insist that what we are experiencing today is a resurgence of late-nineteenth-century rugged individualism, that in today's America what is of supreme importance is for me to get to the well first before it dries up, that in the last analysis the one reality that matters is myself; here is *numero uno,* here is my ultimate responsibility.[2] The race is to the swift, the shrewd, the savage; and "the devil take the hindmost."

It frightens me, my friends. For religious reasons, to begin with. Both Old Testament and New command us: "You shall love your neighbor as [you love] yourself" (Lev. 19:18; Matt. 22:39). The God of Abraham demanded that the children of Abraham father the fatherless and feed the stranger, not because the orphan and the sojourner deserved it, but because that was the way God had acted toward *them.* In freeing the oppressed, they were mirroring the loving Lord who had delivered *them* from oppression, had freed them from Pharaoh. The Christ of Christians tells us that when we feed the hungry and welcome the stranger, when we clothe the naked and visit the sick and the shackled, we do it to him.

Heschel is right on target: "Humanity is holy of holies." Not humanity as an abstract concept. Heschel's humanity is the flesh and blood seated beside you. Humanity is each person you touch each day. Humanity is the man or women you work with or compete against. Humanity is the color and smell that makes you gag. Humanity is the down-and-out bum and the "bag lady." Humanity is, yes, the Russian peasant and the Iranian ayatollah. Humanity is, God forgive us, the Klaus Barbie who sent forty-one Jewish children, aged three to thirteen, to the gas chambers of Auschwitz. We are commanded, poor humans, to see in each, somehow, the trace of God. Not to condone what criminals do; only to see, beneath the image of God defiled and desecrated, the God who cannot forget them, the God who has graven even them on the palms of his hands.

Here the religious approach is crucial; unless you can see the face of God "wherever you see the trace of man [or woman]," you risk limiting justice to an ethical construct: give to each what is due to each, what each person has a strict right to demand, because he or she is a human being and has rights that can be proven by philosophy or have been written into law.

I am not denigrating philosophy or law. Without philosophers from Aristotle to Whitehead we would be wanting in wisdom; and only in a nation under law can society survive. Nor am I claiming that only if you believe in God can you spend your life for others, lay down your life for the other. History makes a mockery of any such claim; and I suspect that your own Volunteers Colgate has its share of admirable infidels. I do say that if you can add a divine dimension to the purely human, if you can "sense the image of God, the presence of God," in every individual who meets your eye, you will *surely* give to others more than they deserve; you will *surely* not do unto others before they do it unto you; you will *surely* act toward others with the love the Lord God lavished on Israel despite its ceaseless infidelities, the love the Lord God rains on all of us no matter how little deserving of love we prove.

It will not be easy. In medicine you may find it difficult to discern the divine in blood and guts, in meningitis and metastasis. Law may blind you to all save the raw in humankind, all but the rot and the rape in human hearts. Politics has seduced many a good servant with a passion for personal power. And "business as usual" in a computer culture can deafen you to the cries of "the others," those condemned to wallow in the mire of poverty and ignorance. In our age, the age President Reagan has called the era of the entrepreneur, "the other" risks becoming a rival only, a threat, someone who might get to the well before you do.

My hope for you, for your era, is that the human, all that is genuinely human, may increasingly disclose to you the divine, the image of God in every man, women, and child. It's worth getting to love "the others." After all, you're going to have to live with them . . . forever.

III

Third, you. I have already said much about you; let me bring it to a focus, get perilously personal. Last year, when Harvard was celebrating its 350th birthday, its president revealed the top three goals the incoming freshmen had declared: one, money; two, power; three, reputation.[3] I suspect, from sociological research, that much the same goals dominate most college scenes today.

Once again, I shall not launch into a lament. Money, power, and reputation are not ethical evils—not in themselves. Like so much else, they take their morality or immorality from a single-syllable question: Why? With Colgate in your résumé, many of you will make megabucks; some of you will wield influence, from rock'n'roll through E. F. Hutton to the power houses in Washington; and a fair number of you will make headlines or neon lights. Splendid! You have this Jesuit's blessing. But you still have not answered the neuralgic question: Why? Why money, why power, why reputation? To get technical, are these ends for you or means? And if means, means to what?

The robber barons of the nineteenth century had money to burn, and burned their morals to make it. Hitler and Stalin dominated most of Europe, from the Atlantic Ocean to the Caspian Sea, but they dominated only to enslave. The names in today's news are all too often the names of those who have smashed the tablets on which the Ten Commandments were sculpted.

And what of you? You know, you have been impressively privileged. At Colgate your mind has come to know what is true; your senses, to delight in what is beautiful; your will, to love what is good. Not indeed everything, but a fair beginning. You have struggled with ideas: wrestled with philosophers from ancient Greece to modern Britain; parleyed with politicians from the Soviet State and the Middle East, from China and Central America; marveled at matter through a microscope, at galaxies through a telescope; cruised through cultures and societies other than your own; winged your way back millions of years to the very origins of human living. You have fallen in love with beauty: Sappho and Shakespeare, Leonardo da Vinci and Michelangelo, the pyramids of Egypt and the Eiffel Tower, Anna Pavlova and Baryshnikov, Yoda and *Children of a Lesser God*. You have grappled to grasp what it means to be good: in boardroom and bedroom, on Capitol Hill and Wall Street, with nuclear warheads and African apartheid.

The task is not finished; it will never be. But I trust that enough of what is true, beautiful, and good has suffused your spirit to instill a threefold conviction. First: money, wealth, however hard-earned, is a gift to you—a gift from the very God who made it all possible by giving you life and breath, talent and toughness; a gift not to be clutched in hot little hands but to be given, to be shared, to lift the less-gifted from the grime and the grit, to slake their hunger for bread or justice, for peace or freedom, for knowledge or understanding—yes, for God. Second: power is a possession plagued with peril but potent with promise. Not because it satisfies a lust for control, but because it lets you be a servant, lets you minister to your sisters and brothers, lets you imitate the God and Father of us all, whose power is identical with his love, identical with his goodness, identical with his self-giving. Third: reputation, fame, is not yours to ape Narcissus, the mythological youth who fell in love with his own image. Fame allows the other to know you, to know what you are like, and so to lie at your golden gate, like poor Lazarus in the Gospel, and be fed at least with the crumbs from your table (cf. Luke 16:20–21).

Graduates: the more I read about you, the larger is my hope for you. I am thrilled when I read what one of you has written in *The Colgate Scene* about

the commitment and concern for others that is
the driving force behind volunteerism at
Colgate. Students have come to realize that
reaching out and caring for others is a
rewarding experience. They have learned to
value an elderly woman's story and the love in
the touch of a child's hand. And they have
come to appreciate the beauty and dignity
inherent in their fellow man. One can but
wonder at the learning that goes on in college.[4]

For many of you, this will be the heart, the core, of your
lifelong search. For it is "the other" that will disclose the divine to you, "the Other." Disclose the divine where you least
expect it: not so much in the palaces of the powerful as in the
poverty of the powerless. And it is "the other" that will reveal
yourself to you: who you are, what you ought to be, what you
can be. Wed your varied riches—your wealth and power and
fame, your truth and beauty and goodness—wed your varied
riches to the parti-colored poverty that encircles you, and one
day you will know yourself, and you will like what you see. It's
worth getting to know and love yourself. After all, you're going to have to life with yourself . . . forever.

My prayers for you, good friends: may "the Other" show
his face to you in love. May "the others" find in you, and you
in them, a reflection of "the Other." And may you come to see
yourself as an image of "the Other," a delightful mirror of the
Lord who looked on "everything that he had made, and behold, it was very good" (Gen. 1:31).

NOTES

1. Abraham Joshua Heschel, "No Religion Is an Island," *Union
Seminary Quarterly Review* 21 (1965–66): 121.

2. See Robert N. Bellah, "Religion & Power in America Today,"
Commonweal 109, No. 21 (Dec. 3, 1982): 650–55.

3. See *Time* 128, no. 10 (Sept. 8, 1986): 57.

4. Jeff Kaczorowski, "Reaching Out," *The Colgate Scene*, (January
1986): 7.

27. Up Against the Powers that Be

David G. Buttrick

Scripture: Ephesians 6:10–19

SOME YEARS AGO, one of the Protestant denominations was putting together a hymnbook. A committee had to decide which hymns to keep and which to discard. Well, the committee got into an awful fight over "Onward Christian Soldiers." Some said the hymn was loved and had to be included, while others claimed it was militaristic and ought to be dumped. If we have trouble with our hymns, what on earth are we going to do with the Bible? The Bible is filled with warfare. Almost every book of the Old Testament tells of battles, and the New Testament is not much better. Listen: "Put on the whole armor of God," cries Ephesians, and then goes on to talk of shield and buckler, helmet and sword. Why is it that whenever we want to describe the Christian life, we end up using military metaphors? "Put on," says Ephesians, "Put on the whole armor of God!"

David G. Buttrick was born in 1927 in New York City. His graduate work includes a degree from Union Theological Seminary in New York and doctoral study at the Garrett Institute of Theology and Northwestern University. He is an ordained Presbyterian minister currently serving as professor of homiletics and liturgics at the Divinity School at Vanderbilt University in Nashville, Tennessee. His extensive writings include the text *Homiletic.*

I

Well, if you're going to live for God in the twentieth century, you're in for a fight. Living for God these days is nothing less than combat. Oh, we're not involved in a little arm wrestling; no, our warfare is something straight out of Starship *Galactica*. The forces we're up against are huge: "We wrestle not against blood and flesh, but principalities and powers and world rulers." Think of it, a handful of believers up against General Motors, the Pentagon, an American eagle, a Russian bear, and in the words of a famous senator, "the best congress money can buy!" Do you remember the story of John Steinbeck's sharecropper? He wanted to know who had foreclosed his farm. It wasn't the local banker because he was responsible to a home office; and it wasn't the home office because they had a board of directors; and it wasn't the board of directors because after all there were thousands of stockholders. Conclusion: nobody was guilty, because everybody was guilty. The system was guilty. "We wrestle not against flesh and blood, but principalities and powers and rulers of the world." Fact is, if you want to keep faith in the twentieth century you're in for a fight.

Of course, *the actual enemy is unseen.* The actual enemy is invisible, and bigger than we know. For the real enemy is in our minds, in the common mind of our age. We've all been brainwashed, haven't we? We can't seem to think without a twist in our thinking. Suppose you want to urge folk to live lives of simple poverty in a needy world; can they hear you? Not a chance. They've seen too many pictures of Volvos and stereos, of stainless steel kitchens and fire-lit family rooms. Or suppose you want to stand up for "peace on earth" in a nuclear age, how can you cut through the slogans? "Keep America strong." "Never bargain from weakness." "Winning isn't everyhing; it's the only thing!" The real enemy is ideas, ideas that invade our minds and subtly take over. There was a wonderful cartoon in *The New Yorker*. It showed a plump housewife talking to her four-star-general husband: "Tell me again, dear," she asked, "how big an army will we need to live at peace with the whole world?" We laugh, but not loudly, for we know that mind-set writes our defense budgets and, incidentally, elects presidents. "Principalities and powers": the real enemy is unseen and bigger than we know. Listen, if you want to live for God in the twentieth century, you're in for a fight.

II

Now it's time to be honest. *Our cause, the Christian cause, is absolutely hopeless.* We are too few and the enemy too great. So almost anyone who dares wait for kingdom come in our kind of world is bound to be filled with exotic despair; the situation is hopeless. We Christians are outnumbered and, almost always, out maneuvered. Did you see the poster that showed up in some churches a few years ago? It showed a tiny little clapboard church surrounded: an X-rated drive-in theater, a munitions factory across the street, and miles of concrete freeway crammed with cars. Two church members stood on the front steps, one saying to another: "Do you ever get the feeling that we're losing ground?" Well, it's more than a feeling, isn't it? Here we Christians are, less than 45 percent of the nation, less than 10 percent of the world, dropping pennies in a mission basket, up against The System! You don't have to be Jimmy the Greek to figure the odds. A Bible study circle up against the corporate wealth of Wall Street; a sweet sermon on sacrifice versus a million-dollar advertising campaign bought and paid for by the Mobil Oil Company. "Do you ever get the feeling that we're losing ground?" Good heavens, by all odds, we haven't got a chance! Be honest; our Christian cause *is* absolutely hopeless.

Except. *Except that it happens to be God's cause.* "Shalom," peace, is God's cause; reconciliation is God's cause; justice is God's cause. Contrary to public opinion, God is not on the side of the bigger battalions; God is on the side of the poor, of pennies in a mission basket; God is on the side of those who long with longing lives for freedom. And, in the Bible, God's cause triumphs! Remember old Isaiah's vision: the swords will be beaten into plowshares, and the lion will bed down with the lamb. Perhaps someday in God's good purpose the eagle will waltz with the bear, and fat-cat Americans share holy bread with skeletal kids of Biafra. It shall be! For who can withstand the will of our God? Nor armies that once clanked around the cross on Calvary, nor public opinion that cried, "Crucify him!" nor frightened religion that, to protect its hold on human minds, branded Jesus Christ a heretic. But if Christ was raised by the power of God, will not peace and justice be raised? It's guaranteed by the promise of God. This conversation was overheard in a supermarket: a woman, pointing to a book rack, said, "I couldn't finish the book; it was too depressing." The reply was: "Gee, you should always turn to the end of the story." What's the end of God's story? A world where everyone lolls at peace in their own vineyard, a fine, free world where folk can party together—"The song of them that triumph, the shout of them that feast." God's world doesn't end with a whimper, but with choiring angels and the Lamb upon the throne. God's cause will be!

III

Well, *meanwhile back here on the battlefield, how do we fight?* How can we take on the "powers that be"? We are given one weapon, only one. "Take up the sword," says Ephesians, "which is the word of God." Think of it, we are to go up against the powers that be with nothing more than a word. Doesn't sound like much, does it, in a world where words are tarnished? After all, advertisements use words, and party platforms use words, and it was an American president who labeled the MX missile system "the peacekeeper." There's a euphemism for you! What good is a word when words are so easily twisted around? No good at all, unless it is the impudent, guileless Word of our God! Do you know the wonderful story that came out of the Czech underground after the Russian takeover? To tout their victory, the Communist Party scheduled a great parade—lumbering tanks, trucked-in missiles, battalions of lockstepped soldiers. Suddenly, in the midst of the parade, there was a little blue pickup truck weaving in and out, disrupting the parade, with a six-foot sign on it reading, "For God's sake, why?" Perhaps that's a clue. God's word in all its impudent glory must be spoken to the powers that be, asking, Why? Why? to a bulging defense budget when there are street people huddled in doorways. Why? to our high standard of living when most of the world has a mighty high standard of dying. Why? to the stainless steel kitchen and the fire-lit family room. Why? The impudent Word of God questions our world and can pierce its heart. Think of it, our only weapon, the sword of the Spirit which is the Word of God.

Time for confession: *we have been silent.* The pulpit has been tame and the pew timid. We Christians have been speechless. Perhaps the Catholic Church is still trying to prove it's an all-American option, while the Protestants are trying to hold onto the cash. Perhaps. So in our century, a Catholic cardinal blessed a battleship, while a Protestant evangelist criss-crossed Alabama six times during the height of the civil rights controversy and never once mentioned the subject of race—there's discreet Christianity for you! Fact is, nowadays, the church is running flat-out scared, trying to hold on to public approval in a crumbling age. Think of a Christian community whose bravest utterance during the past few years has been a bumper sticker, reading, "I found it!" Look, is there anything worse than the strange strangulated sense of "I should have spoken"? To live on, knowing that we missed the moment when we should have spoken. So, can we confess? We have been silent, a "silent majority" church. We should have spoken.

Now, guess what: *maybe it is time to speak to our churches.* Maybe it is time for *us* to speak with our churches, to stab away the slumbering Christian conscience of the land with the sharp Word of God. Oh, there's no room for self-righteousness: we speak as people who should have spoken to a people who should have listened. But maybe now's the time to speak out, like Amos standing in front of the suburban church in Bethel, or Jeremiah bumbling up the Temple steps in Jerusalem to meet churchgoers face to face. A few years ago a multi-million-dollar church was built in an eastern city, "New England Colonial" of course. The day of dedication had been set but not all the furnishings had arrived. The chancel was empty: no pulpit or table, no tapestry for the back wall. When worshipers gathered for the dedication, they found that someone had snuck into the building at night and, with a wide brush, had painted in big black letters on the bare wall, "Stop the killing, Feed the poor, Sincerely yours, Jesus Christ." Well, do you sense our strange calling in a blasé world, in a world that will go along with anything for a tank full of gas and an I.R.A.? Somehow we are called to speak, to shake awake God's people with the strong word of Christ. Now, now it is time for us to speak to the churches.

Here we are, 1987. Do you ever get the feeling we're losing ground? Not against blood and flesh, but against principalities and powers and the rulers of our age. Listen, all you need tucked in your arsenal is a word. "The Prince of Darkness grim, we'll tremble not for him, one little word will slay him." Dear friends, the word is Jesus Christ. There is no other word worth speaking. The word is Jesus Christ.

28. The Fight of the Day
Carl F. H. Henry

Scripture: Romans 13:11–14

THE APOSTLE Paul is concerned lest we be asleep when we ought to be on guard duty. We have a fight on our hands, he says, and we need to be awake and primed for it. Phillips Modern English Version paraphrases his comments in Romans 13:11–14:

> The present time is of the highest
> importance—it is time to wake up to the
> reality. The night is nearly over, the day has
> almost dawned. Every day brings God's
> salvation nearer than the day in which we took
> the first step of faith. Let us therefore fling
> away the things that men do in the dark, let us
> arm ourselves for the fight of the day. . . . Let
> us be Christ's men from head to foot, and give
> no chance to the flesh to have its fling.

On my first night in Keruzawa, Japan, I had no idea that I was in an earthquake zone until a midnight jolt awakened me to reality. The tremor didn't register topmost on the Richter

---

Carl F. H. Henry was born in 1913 in New York City. He was educated at Wheaton College, Northern Baptist Theological Seminary, and Boston University, where he received his doctorate. A former editor of *Christianity Today* and lecturer-at-large for World Vision, Dr. Henry currently is visiting professor at Trinity Evangelical Divinity School. He is the author and editor of many books and has written a six-volume work entitled *God: Revelation and Authority.*

scale, but its severity reminded me not to take tomorrow for granted. So these words of the apostle, in the middle of the epistle to the Romans, stab us awake and shock us alive to the invisible realities of the spiritual world, lest we be entrapped in a sinful, slumbering society.

I. American Culture Is Sinking toward Sunset

At the opening of the epistle, Paul unveils God's anger over the depths of Gentile rebellion. Three times we hear that dreadful refrain, *"God gave them over."* We read that, because of their persistent wickedness, God "gave them over to the *sinful desires* of their hearts" (1:24, NIV), that God "gave them over to *shameful lusts*" (1:26), and that God "gave them over to a *depraved mind*" (1:28).

Exegetes have long noted a progression here: desires, lusts, mind-set. As the channel of sin runs ever deeper, God's compensatory judgment moves ever closer to man's final abandonment and inescapable doom. The first chapter closes in fact with a warning of doomsday ahead for those who, in their own consciences, know that all who live wickedly deserve God's death penalty, yet who, nonetheless, defy God and even encourage others to do so (1:32).

I have a heavy heart about America. American culture seems to me to be sinking toward sunset. I do not, like some, call America the epicenter of evil in the world. But we have fallen far from the lofty ideals for which this land came into being. I do not intend to spend most of my time reciting a catalogue of vices. Yet our country seems more and more to act out of traditional character. To be sure, there is a godly remnant—not simply a tiny band but a goodly number—for which we may be grateful. But it is surely not America at her best when we chart the massacre of a million fetuses a year, the flight from the monogamous family, the two and a half million persons trapped in illegal drugs and alcohol (our country now has a larger drug problem than any other industrialized nation in the world), the normalizing of deviant sexual behavior (in the Washington-Baltimore area alone there are now estimated to be 250,000 homosexuals), the proliferation of AIDS to twenty-five thousand persons, more than half of whom have already died.

What is underway is a redefinition of the good life. This redefinition not only perverts the word *good* but perverts the term *life* as well. What is *good* is corrupted into whatever gratifies one's personal desires, whatever promotes self-interest even at the expense of the dignity and worth of others. In that fantasy-world of sinful desires, shameful lusts and a depraved mind, adultery and homosexuality are good, coveting and stealing are good, violence and terrorism are good.

Worse yet, such perversion of the good is connected with what is called *the life*. All that the Bible means by life—spiritual life, moral life, eternal life, a life fit for eternity—is emptied into an existence fit only for beasts and brutes.

"They gave up God," says Paul, "and therefore God gave them up—to be playthings of their own foul desires in dishonoring their own bodies." They "deliberately forfeited the truth of God and accepted a lie, paying homage and giving service to the creature instead of the Creator, who alone is worthy to be worshiped for ever and ever. God therefore handed them over to disgraceful passions" (Rom. 1:24–27, MEV).

Western society is experiencing a great cultural upheaval. More and more, the wicked subculture comes to open cultural manifestation. More and more the unmentionables become the parlance of our day. More and more profanity and vulgarity find expression through the mass media. The sludge of a sick society is rising to the top and, sad to say, the stench does not offend even some public leaders. Our nation increasingly trips the worst ratings on God's Richter scale of fully deserved moral judgment.

God who shook the earth at Sinai, God who shook the earth at Calvary, God who is a consuming fire, warns of one more shaking, that final and decisive shaking: "Yet once more will I make to tremble not the earth only, but also the heaven." This means, as the author of Hebrews says, that "in this final 'shaking' all that is impermanent will be removed . . . and only the unshakable things will remain" (Heb. 12:27, MEV). The world will be asleep when doomsday comes, Peter warns, banking its life on the premise that "everything continues exactly as it has always been since the world began" (2 Pet. 3:4). "But the Day of the Lord will come," he emphasizes, "and the earth and all that is in it will be laid bare" (2 Pet. 3:10).

When that great meltdown comes, where will you be? Trapped in Sodom? In the bleak twilight of a decadent culture, where will you be? Overtaken, like Lot, looking back at the citadels of sin? "Wake up!" says Paul; "wake up!" American culture is sinking toward sunset.

II. Christian Believers Are Stretching toward Sunrise

The remarkable thing about Paul's exhortation to awaken from sleep is that it is addressed to Christians. It apprises them not of encroaching doom but of daybreak at hand, of the imminent sunrise, of the full dawning of God's Kingdom. "Let us arm ourselves for the fight of the day," he writes, "[and] be Christ's men from head to foot."

Christians have duties in the cultural upheaval around us. God has not told us to build an ark or to escape the flood waters by taking to the hills. If there is hope for America, it will come through our vigorous proclamation and application of the Christian message.

The early Christians knew the fierceness of the battle. They knew Gentile wickedness at its worst; it was the moving spirit of the society in which they were reached for the gospel. "You were spiritually dead through your sins and failures, all the time that you followed this world's ideas of living and obeyed the evil ruler of the spiritual realm. . . . We all lived like that in the past," writes Paul, "and followed the desires and imaginings of our lower nature, being in fact under the wrath of God by nature, like everyone else. . . . We were dead in our sins" (Eph. 2:2–3, MEV).

Don't for a moment forget that we ourselves were dug

from the dregs of a decadent society. When recently I wrote *Confessions of a Theologian* it had a double exposure—first, on the world from which Christ rescues even those who become theologians and pastors and deacons, and second, on the world to which Christ lifted me, the spiritual world to which he lifts prostitutes and drug addicts and homosexuals and other redeemed sinners, even those whose worst sin is pride and self-righteousness.

The risen Christ is in the moving and lifting business. How high has Christ lifted you?

It is one thing to run away from sin; it is yet another to hoist a flag for faith. "Fling away the things that men do in the dark," exhorts Paul, and "give no chance to the flesh to have its fling. . . . Be Christ's men from head to foot. . . . Let us arm ourselves for the fight of the day." God wants your whole armory. He wants your mind. He wants your will. He wants your heart—the whole self. "Christ in you" is Paul's great theme in the Colossian letter. Where your feet go, does Christ walk with you? Where your mind reaches, is the mind of Christ yours also? In whatever your will embraces, is Christ's will astride your own?

During the days of the youth counterculture a lad went door to door asking, "Does Jesus Christ live here?" Taken aback, one housewife replied, "My husband's a deacon!" The lad answered, "That's not what I asked: does Jesus Christ live here?"

American culture is sinking toward sunset, but Christians are reaching toward sunrise.

III. We Are Warriors with a Mission in the World

Christian duty requires of us more than personal piety and devotion, important as that is. It's not enough to say no when the culture holds that fornication is morally acceptable and that we may abort the fetus if it's unwanted or take hallucinatory drugs if we are minded to do so.

Are you aware of the cultural challenges we face? Or are

you yourself debilitated by the shoddy secular values of our time?

The fight of the day—are you aware of what that entails?

In the battle between good and evil, are you armed and engaged in "the fight of the day"?

In the battle for the minds of men, are you armed and engaged in "the fight of the day"?

In the battle for the will of humanity, are you armed and engaged in "the fight of the day"?

In the exhibition of a Christian mind-set, are you armed and engaged in "the fight of the day"?

In the deployment of Christian countermoves, are you armed and engaged in "the fight of the day"?

Just as there are depths of depravity in human life, so too are there degrees of dedication. And just as God progressively abandons the renegades to their rebellion, so too does he reward the righteous in their spiritual renewal. When ancient Rome fell it was the godly Christian remnant that walked head high into the future. When medieval Christianity compromised its biblical heritage, the Protestant Reformation emerged to bring great blessing to Europe and the world. When the post-Enlightenment era spawned an antibiblical mind-set, the eighteenth-century evangelical awakening in England spared that nation the travesty and grief of the French Revolution. What will be the final verdict on the evangelical confrontation of today's radically secular humanism and resurgent paganism? We are on the threshold of the decade of destiny, in the last generation before we leave the twentieth century behind, at the end of one century and the beginning of another. What spiritual situation do we bequeath not only to those who follow us, but to our contemporaries as well?

Christian duty requires courageous participation at the frontiers of public concern—education, mass media, politics, law, literature and the arts, labor and economics, and the whole realm of cultural pursuits. The real arena in which we are to work and witness and win others over is the world, or we have ceased to be light, salt, leaven. We need to do more than to sponsor a *Christian subculture*. We need *Christian counterculture* that sets itself alongside the secular rivals and publishes openly the difference that belief in God and his Christ makes in the arenas of thought and action. We need *Christian countermoves* that commend a new climate, countermoves that penetrate the public realm. To live Christianly involves taking a stand for God that calls this world's caesars to account before the sovereign Lord of the universe, that calls this world's sages to account before the wisdom that begins with fear of the Lord, that calls this world's journalists to account before the greatest story ever told. We must strive to reclaim this cosmos for its rightful owner, God, who has title to the cattle on a thousand hills, and for Christ who says to the lost multitudes, "I made you; I died for you; I ransomed you."

What does that imply for the liberal arts and the sciences? What does it imply for the mass media? What are its consequences for the political realm? What does it imply in the debate over human freedom and justice and rights?

We may not know all the answers, but we know some absolutes at least, and that puts us head and shoulders above the relativists, and the woods are full of relativists today. Each of us must find his or her proper station and platform in "the fight of the day." We must use our God-given talent to reflect the truth and justice of God into the world of public affairs. Everywhere around us is strewn the philosophical wreckage of those who rely only on the voice of conscience, on social utility, on aesthetic gratification, on majority consensus—on everything but a sure Word of God. If you are still wavering between the God of the ages and the spirit of the age, listen to Paul's warning summons. American culture is sinking toward sunset; Christian believers are stretching toward sunrise; we are warriors with a mission in the world. Have you enlisted, winsomely and courageously, in what Paul calls "the fight of the day"?

29. This Age and That Age
Allan M. Parrent

Scripture: The sons of this age marry and are given in marriage, but those who are accounted worthy to attain to that age and to the resurrection from the dead neither marry nor are given in marriage.
—Luke 20:27–38

IN THE COLD European winter of 1947, Reinhold Niebuhr returned to Edinburgh, the scene of his famous Gifford Lectures, to give another series of lectures. In that grim postwar period in Britain, rigid rationing was still in effect. Everything was in short supply, including electricity. The hall in which Niebuhr spoke was without heat or light. Special permission was received to use one light bulb at the speaker's podium. Niebuhr, having just left the optimism and energetic idealism of victorious and unscathed America, began his address by saying to the dour Scots in the audience: "I now understand the difference between the cultural optimism of your country and mine—I don't have to persuade you that this is not the Kingdom of God."

That story illustrates in a small way Niebuhr's constant effort to distinguish, though never to separate, this world and

Allan Mitchell Parrent, a native of Frankfort, Kentucky, was born in 1930. He received degrees from Georgetown College and Vanderbilt University and his doctorate from Duke University. Dr. Parrent, an Episcopalian, currently is professor of Christian ethics, associate dean for academic affairs and vice-president at Virginia Theological Seminary in Alexandria, Virginia. He writes and speaks frequently on various ethical issues, with a particular focus on nuclear arms control and national defense.

the next, human history and the time beyond history, the imperfection and moral ambiguity of even the best of human achievements and the perfection that we may glimpse but never realize this side of history. As Jesus made clear to the Sadducees in today's lesson, there is a difference between "this age" and "that age."

We who live between the times, who have a foot in each age, must live with the constant temptation to eliminate that difference. We are constantly tempted to project our highest this-worldly ideals onto heaven, to assume that the perfect Kingdom of God is basically an improved version of the earthly kingdom we know, and then to seek to transplant that perfect Kingdom of God here. It is an understandable and high-minded temptation to realize the hope of the ages in all its fullness now, through our own efforts, because we know precisely its intended form and shape.

But when we reduce "that age" to the familiar terms of our own experience, when we read into that veiled future the same conditions of time and space and social arrangements that provide the framework of our earthly existence in "this age," we tread on dangerous ground. For it is then that we are most likely to reduce the Kingdom of God to some humanly devised, achievable scheme for organizing the human community, and then set out to achieve it, eliminating those who would dare get in the way of so righteous a goal. Such self-assured efforts to substitute our own immanent and achievable kingdom of God for the promised and hoped-for transcendent kingdom are not only dangerous for the well-being of human community, they also represent the opposite of that trust illustrated by Job's proclamation, "I know that my redeemer lives, and at last he will stand upon the earth."

Jesus' words to the Sadducees' devious question about marriage in the Resurrection highlight the tension between the now and the not yet of human existence. Paul spoke in the same way about the two ages. We as Christians do live in two ages, or between two ages. They interact with each other, but they are not to be equated. When the present order is mistaken for the new creation to which we are to aspire, or when it is assumed that it can be made into that new creation through human action and social restructuring, we have created bad theology and laid the groundwork for potentially disastrous social and political policies. It is such Sadducean confusions that allow human communities to assume, for example, that war can be eliminated simply by signing a Kellogg-Briand Pact declaring that tragic human activity to be forever outlawed. It is through similar confusion that human communities can come to believe with a Lenin, for example, that the perfect future can be born on earth as soon as several million of the wrong sorts of people are eliminated.

As Niebuhr told his Edinburgh audience, perhaps unnecessarily, this is not the Kingdom of God. In the Resurrection we will neither marry nor be given in marriage. But in this age God has knit the solitary into families for our own well-being and survival. We establish legal procedures and social conventions to govern and protect the institution of marriage which is so necessary for human flourishing in this world. In the Resurrection, we will have no reason to fear economic exploitation or military aggression perpetrated by one group or another. But in this age those are legitimate fears. The virtue of prudence dictates, and the love of neighbor demands, that economic and political structures be maintained to allay those fears and to protect vulnerable neighbors against exploitation and aggression. In the Resurrection, seminaries (which doubtless will be the one human institution that will continue to exist) will not have to concern themselves with stolen library books and missing reserve books. But in this age rules and procedures are necessary to minimize such losses and to enhance the freedom of all would-be library users in this Christian but still very human community. When that issue came up a few weeks ago at a luncheon meeting, a seminary administrator quipped that 80 percent of administration is dealing with the consequences of original sin. We might debate the percentage, but the point is well taken.

In John Hough's novel, *The Conduct of the Game*, the protagonist Lee Malcolm is a rather aimless young man, drifting through life with no clear purpose. One day he is asked to umpire a baseball game. In the first inning he settles a dispute. He suddenly realizes that he has both power and authority and that without it the game would devolve into a brawl. He says later of the game:

> It is mine to ruin or to make right—the
> difference between noise and music, between a
> free-for-all and the pretty game of baseball. I
> never understood, till that moment, what good
> umpiring means to the game. Baseball can be
> thrilling and it can be beautiful—but only if
> the umpiring is good.

For the words "baseball" and "umpiring" we might substitute "life" and "rules."

The Christian faith calls us to seek the Kingdom of God and his righteousness, not to assume that it is already present in its fullness or to trust in ourselves to make it so. It calls us to put our ultimate trust in God, not in the pristine amiability, the total unselfishness, or the Pelagian goodwill of either ourselves or our fellow human beings, nice people though we all may be. While that does not sit well with the more idealistic sentiments which we all have and must not lose, it is true to lived human experience and, I believe, to the tension of the two ages of which both Jesus and Paul spoke.

There is a "Masterpiece Theatre" production entitled "Paradise Postponed," a poignant story of an Anglican cleric who, in the words of that lovely English hymn, sought to "build Jerusalem in England's green and pleasant land." After his death one of his sons, lamenting his late father's idealistic beliefs, says:

> The trouble with our father's paradise is that it
> keeps getting put off, doesn't it? The promised
> land is always just around the corner. All we
> seem to get is paradise postponed.

The son's analysis rings true to all of us who have had our particular paradises postponed. But that analysis is also dangerous. It is dangerous because it can lead to despair on the one hand or to fanaticism on the other. It can lead to a total resignation to what is a despairing attitude of "what's the use?" Or it can lead to a total fanatical commitment to forcing a reluctant humankind around that last corner to paradise, whatever the human cost. These are indeed the twin dangers of the Sadducean thinking portrayed in the Gospel lesson, despair and fanaticism.

But the Gospel offers us a way through these twin dangers. Despair is the fate of those who know something about sin but nothing about redemption. Fanaticism is the fate of those who know something about redemption but not enough about sin. Through the life, death, and resurrection of Christ we as Christians know something about both. In the Eucharist we acknowledge both, confessing our sin and giving thanks for our redemption. We declare our anticipation of the promised Resurrection and express our thanks that we have been made heirs, through hope, of God's eternal kingdom.

It is the hope in the Resurrection that frees us to involve ourselves in the necessary but always imperfect structures that order our common life in this age. It is the assurance that at the last day God will bring us into the joy of his eternal kingdom, that frees us to work toward a just and humane society in this age, and to do so without succumbing to despair over a paradise postponed or to fanaticism for an imagined paradise just around the corner.

30. The Sure Sign of Status
Mark Trotter

Text: Philippians 2:1–11; Luke 14:1, 7–14

SOMEONE gave me a book entitled *The Second Book of Insults.* It's a funny book. Since it's the "second" book, I assume there was a first book, and that that book was popular enough to deserve a sequel. The category of humor called insults or put-downs must be encyclopedic. Somewhere, I'm sure, there is already a third book of insults.

I notice that there are more English authors cited in *The Second Book of Insults* than people from any other country or nationality. I'm not sure why that is, except maybe there are few societies as formally structured as English society, especially in the nineteenth century, from which most of these citations come. In that society, everybody had a place in the society's hierarchy, everybody was conscious of where they stood in relation to everybody else. In that kind of society somebody is going to stand apart and poke fun at it. And the put-down is one way of doing it. It humbles the proud and knocks the mighty from their seats.

Actually, it's no different in American society. We don't have royalty or social class, no dukes or duchesses or earls or ladies, but we do have a hierarchical society built on some-

Mark Trotter was born in 1934 in Hollywood, California. He received his education at Occidental College and Boston University. He has served as senior minister of the First United Methodist Church in San Diego, California, since 1976 and is the author of *Grace All the Way Home.*

thing else. I suspect it's probably money that determines aristocracy in America.

At any rate, the English are the masters of the put-down. And two of the best wielders of the cutting remark were George Bernard Shaw and Winston Churchill. They were absolute artists at it.

Once Shaw was invited to tea by a woman who was one of those nuisances who like to collect celebrities and drop their names. She sent Shaw her card that read: "Lady So-and-So will be at home Thursday between 4:00 and 6:00." Shaw returned the card with this notation: "Mr. Bernard Shaw, likewise."

Then there's the famous exchange between Churchill and Lady Astor who said, "Mr. Churchill, if I were your wife I'd poison your tea." Churchill said, "Madame, if I were your husband, I'd drink it."

They are masters, Shaw and Churchill, of the fine art of insult. So when you have an anecdote that includes them both, it is called a collector's item. It's like a World Series' pitchers' duel, a classic encounter between two greats, and here it is. Shaw sent two tickets for his new play to Churchill with this note: "These are two tickets for the opening night of my new play, one for you and one for a friend, if you have one." Churchill sent the tickets back with this note: "I cannot attend the opening night. Send two tickets for the next night, if there is one."

They are masters. They are really good. I have to watch myself because I have a weakness for the put-down. I have to restrain my instinct to pounce on some unsuspecting prey with a put-down. I did it once, quite innocently, I thought, for a laugh. I learned later from that person how much what I had said had hurt him. I didn't intend for it to hurt. Or did I?

I rationalize my propensity for the put-down by saying I was raised in a large family. There were six children in the family in which I was raised. Usually, in large families, there is competition among the siblings, and the competition in our family was sublimated into humor, barbed humor. You'd come home, try to boast of something that you'd done that day, and you'd be put down to size, immediately. It was fun, I think. Lots of laughs, anyway. I can recall some guest brought to dinner by a member of the family. This person, the only child in their family, sat there and stared, either in awe or in terror, intimidated by the verbal duel across the supper table. Some of them never came back.

So I thought to myself, this habit of putting people down is simply the result of my childhood. Some children grow up "streetwise." They know how to survive on the street. I grew up "tablewise." I knew how to hold my own at the family table. But I'm older now, and it's occurred to me that I should have outgrown that. I should have put away childish things when I became a man. But I haven't, not completely. None of us has. Not so that we can resist temptation to reach into the quiver of insults to ambush some unsuspecting person.

Why do we do that? Why does insult remain the source of so much humor? Some people make a whole career out of insulting other people. We pay them to do that; we go listen to them. Why do we enjoy it?

Well, I think the reason is that we are preoccupied with our status in the world. Not just our status as siblings in a family, but when we grow up, our status with other people. We worry about where we stand, what other people think about us, how we measure up. We don't outgrow our anxiety about who we are. We take it with us, wherever we go, always wondering, how am I doing? Always worrying about getting ahead of somebody else. Always hoping to be acceptable to those people above us, and keeping a safe distance from those we consider to be lower.

It can become an obsession, like Jay Gatsby staring at the green light across the bay on the dock of the rich and the beautiful people, wanting more than anything else to be one of them. It's pitiful what we will do to improve our status in this world, the money we will spend, the things that we will sacrifice, the people that we will hurt to get ahead. All for status.

And I wish I could tell you that in religion it's different, that religion is the answer to this human frailty. But it isn't.

Might as well be honest about that. It gallops right along through the field of religion.

Some years ago, in *San Diego Magazine*, I think it was, that bellwether of status in San Diego, was printed a list of churches that the smart people go to. Smart, not as in intelligence, but smart as in *chic.* I read it anxiously. I think they listed ten or twelve churches on that list, where all the smart people go. Do you want to know where First United Methodist Church was on that list? You're dying to know where it is. We weren't on it! That means that you belong to a no-account church. In fact, there were no United Methodist Churches at all on that list. Methodists, evidently, still haven't shaken off their humble origins. Though, I suspect, we're working on it.

You see, religion is infected with the same disease. You find it everywhere. It's called snobbery, status consciousness. In fact, Jesus condemned that characteristic of the religious more severely and more frequently than anything else. There is even a word for it that comes out of the New Testament: "pharisaism." It refers to the tendency of the religious to use religion as a means of elevating themselves and putting others down.

Now listen to our text, from the Gospel of Luke. Jesus is the guest at a fancy dinner. His host is a ruler and a Pharisee. That means that this supper party would have been covered by *San Diego Magazine*. It's that kind of party, had that kind of guest list. The host was a ruler, a prominent man, a Pharisee. He moved in the right circles in that town. He invited some friends of his to come over for dinner to see firsthand, up close, what this Nazarene was really like. Jesus was a celebrity by now, famous as a preacher, had notoriety as a healer, perhaps even as a miracle worker. Everybody there at that event had heard of his preaching, although probably none of them had ever heard him preach. It was a nice affair. In the backyard, catered, overlooking the Sea of Galilee.

After the meal, the host gave a most gracious introduction of Jesus, then asked him to say a few words. This is what he said: "I notice the way you maneuvered for the positions at this dinner. You can get away with that here. But I tell you this, when you are invited to a marriage feast, do not sit down at a place of honor, lest a more eminent person arrives and the host has to come over to you, in front of everybody, and say, 'Give your place to this man.' Instead, when you are invited, go and sit at the lowest place so that when the host comes, he may say to you, 'Friend, go on up higher.' For everyone who exalts himself will be humbled and he who humbles himself will be exalted."

It's another judgment parable. The opening sentence gives it away. "When you are invited to a marriage feast . . ." That's the clue. One of the metaphors for the Messiah was "bridegroom," the Kingdom the "marriage feast." So there are lots of parables that Jesus told about bridegrooms, and about bridesmaids who wait for the bridegroom to come, and about the wedding feast; who's invited, where they sit, who comes and who doesn't. This is one of those Kingdom parables. They all give us a glimpse of the end. It's like fast-forwarding the tape to the end of the movie so you can see how it comes out. It says, What you think counts now isn't going to count then. All this jockeying for position, this conspicuous consumption, this over achievement, this accumulation of righteousness. None of that's going to count. What's going to count there is humility. Those who take the lowest seats at the banquet, they'll be moved up higher. And those who rush in, confident of their status, demanding the best seats—at the end when the bridegroom comes, they may just be asked kindly to move over to the table near the kitchen door.

Because nobody knows what's going to happen in the end. Nobody knows who will be saved. Nobody knows who is going to be accounted righteous. But there's a clue. In fact, this is probably the best piece of evidence you can find. There is only one thing that you can count on, and that is that those who will be first in the Kingdom are those who are humble now. "For everyone who exalts himself will be humbled, and he who humbles himself will be exalted."

We turn to Paul's letter to the Philippians, our Epistle lesson. "Have this mind among yourselves, what you have in Christ Jesus, who, though he was in the form of God did not count equality with God a thing to be grasped, but emptied himself, taking the form of a servant." The church at Philippi was having a church fight. People were putting each other down, insulting each other, boasting about how they were better than each other. Paul's answer to petty fights was to hold them up to the greatest act in the history of the world, as if to say, Christ humbled himself to save the world, why can't you humble yourself enough to end an argument? Christ did not wait for you to come to him; he came to you, took on your flesh, lived your life; and you sit there smugly, self-righteously, waiting for the one who has offended you to come crawling for forgiveness. Christ humbled himself as a servant, but you refuse to humble yourself to the likes of these. And being found in human form, he became obedient unto death, even death upon the cross, that you may live. And you won't sacrifice your pride to say the word that will bring new life to the person who is dying to hear it from you.

Paul had a way of writing like that. He takes the petty things that we do and reveals them for what they are by holding them up to the greatest thing that God has done. It's his way of saying that we are supposed to live the way that Jesus lived. We are supposed to work at it. And Jesus didn't care a whit about status. You talk about status; he was the Son of God. But he did not count equality with God a thing to be grasped, but emptied himself, humbled himself for our sake.

He came to do away with status and with everything else that gets in the way of our relationship with God and with our neighbor. In fact, wherever he found status separating people, he defied it. He did something outrageous in order to shock people, like forgiving sinners, or hugging outcasts, just so he could hear the clucking of the Pharisees. Because he knew that, in the end, those things don't count. Not in the Kingdom of God, they don't. That's what he came to reveal. Before God we are all alike. So have this mind in you which you have in Christ Jesus.

Well, it's easier said than done, which means we still have to work at it. Even at church we are still on our way. We still haven't arrived. We are still tempted to elevate ourselves the easy way, by putting other people down. Like the Philippians, we need help.

And to help myself, I try to remember this. It's apt for me because it's an anecdote about preaching, but I think you can identify with it, too. It's an incident out of the life of Harry Emerson Fosdick, one of the greatest preachers in American history. He preached at Riverside Church in New York City for so many years. The church, incidentally, was built for him by John D. Rockefeller when Fosdick was censured by an earlier congregation. Fosdick preached at Riverside Church, and went across the street to teach preaching to seminarians at Union Theological Seminary.

Now preaching classes are dens of lions. That's where seminarians bare their fangs. I remember my experience in seminary preaching class. You were assigned to a section with eight or ten people in it, and you had to preach twice during the semester to those eight or ten colleagues. After which, they got to criticize your sermon. Well, you take your turn, prepare the sermon. You're all ready to go, thinking that you have probably written a minor classic. You're thinking already about publishing. You come out of that class feeling like changing your vocation.

It was the same format there at Union. Fosdick met with every section. Most professors don't do that. Graduate assistants get the humble job of listening to the stream of mediocre and poor preaching. But Fosdick, one of the greatest preachers of all time, emptied himself of his status and met with all of them. He gave of himself to every student. When some poor student finished preaching the sermon, Fosdick would turn to the others in the section and say, "What can we say to Mr. Jones that will be of help to him?"

I think it was something of that spirit that Jesus was talking about when he said, "We are to be humble." It's consistent with his example of humbling himself to be the servant of others, going to them and saying that word that would enable them to find the lives that God had created them to live. What can we way to persons that will be helpful to them

That's what I try to remember, especially when I am tempted to say something that will call attention to me at the expense of somebody else. I try to remember I don't need to do that anymore. I know who I am. I am a child of God, for whom Christ died. I'm already somebody, by grace. I don't need to prove it anymore. I'm somebody.

But that's not all. Because being somebody is not being Christian. Not yet. According to Philippians, we are not Christians just by receiving what Christ gives us; we become Christians by doing what Christ did for others. He humbled himself. This is how you do it. You remember in all situations, even when someone else has the spotlight, "What can I say to this person that will be helpful?"

Because, "Whoever exalts himself will be humbled, and he who humbles himself will be exalted."

31. No Quick Fix
Judith L. Weidman

THE CHRISTIAN calendar is a funny thing. Just three months ago we were in the throes of Christmas. That's a time of such hope and expectation. Which of us isn't hooked by the birth of a baby? Which of us doesn't participate with fairly willing abandon in the commercial display of love and generosity at that time of the year?

Yet the scene shifts suddenly and dramatically. Jesus has grown up; he's been in ministry. The world will never be the same, but it won't come easily or cheaply. Before the final triumph there will be denial, pain, and death.

This is the part of the story we don't handle very well. We are now officially in Lent—that forty-day period leading up to Easter. Our Orthodox and Roman Catholic friends place great emphasis on fasting and penance during this season. In the Protestant tradition, if we think of it at all, it's likely to be a time of study. Our crosses are empty, after all. We prefer to focus on the power of the Easter story.

But I'm not so sure that we haven't been shortchanged a bit. As anyone who's done much living knows, life doesn't come in neat packages. Things happen to us that we think we

Judith Lynne Weidman was born in 1941 in Savanna, Illinois. She holds degrees from DePauw University and Duke Divinity School. A Methodist, Dr. Weidman is editor/director of the Religious News Service in New York City. She has edited three books and in 1987 was named United Methodist Communicator of the Year.

don't deserve: a mate walks out on us, we're passed over for an important assignment.

There are things we can't explain—like the death of a child who darts out in front of a car in pursuit of a baseball. A helicopter crashes—three are killed; one lives and wonders why.

There are injustices that will never be set right in our lifetime—not by the might of our armies, not even by the church. We simply live, for example, with the knowledge that two-thirds of the world's population goes to sleep hungry every night. We're not only not in command of that situation; most of us can't even imagine what that's really like.

So I want to suggest that unless we understand the meaning of the cross, we really have nothing on which to peg much of our lives.

I've had an unusual opportunity in the last six months which has helped clarify a lot of my thinking about this issue. I want to share that with you this morning. Come with me to the Women's Prison in Nashville, Tennessee.

I got involved at the prison through a church and community worker of the United Methodist Church. One day last summer she said to me, "Judy, I'd like to talk to you sometime about doing some volunteer work at the women's prison." I smiled and said, "Oh, is that right?" But underneath I was thinking, "Oh God, not me."

I could think of a dozen excuses: I travel a lot in my work, so I really wouldn't be able to be a very faithful member. I'm a writer, not a group process person. And to give up Sunday afternoons? That's asking a lot.

Fortunately she just let me babble on, and as my words echoed back upon me, I had to say, "I'll give it a try."

I went that first Sunday accompanied by all the stereotypes. I figured it would be a dirty, noisy, crowded place with surly guards pacing up and down in front of cells filled with life's outcasts awaiting execution.

Instead what I found were some bright, attractive, articulate—yes, Christian—women. Not all of them fit this description, of course, but an amazing number in our group do. The facility, while devoid of aesthetic niceties and overcrowded, is modern and reasonably well maintained.

So initially I was relieved that the state wasn't running a hellhole, at least not at this prison.

But soon I was drawn beneath the surface of people's lives and began a journey that has taught me something about the cross. Lent will never again pass without my notice—or careless resolution to give up candy bars.

Let me tell you first about Betty. Betty is a tall, willowy woman. Jet-black hair, sparking eyes, flawless complexion. You believe it when you learn she was a model. Her vocabulary and poise give you advance notice that she's had some college. Her beautiful clothes prepare you for the fact that she married into one of Middle Tennessee's most prominent families. Why is Betty in prison? Because she robbed a bank.

Then there is Sarah. Sarah is a preacher's wife who is in prison for writing bad checks. She met the man of her dreams when she was sixteen and got married a year later.

Things proceeded on schedule with career and family— three children eventually. Sarah's world opened up somewhat unexpectedly, however, when she enrolled at a branch of the New York State University system to take some nursing courses.

But her husband, who was suffering from some allergies, wanted to get back down South. Sarah gave up her nursing course and went with him very reluctantly.

A small church opened up in South Carolina, but what Sarah's husband really wanted to be was a traveling evangelist. So they opened up a small restaurant just across the state line in North Carolina to provide an income for the family while he got started in his ministry. The restaurant wasn't much of a success, but she did successfully organize a choir of poor children from the neighborhood. She wanted them to look as good as they sounded, so she went to a local fabric shop and wrote her first bad check. That was in 1974.

Her husband made that check good, but that wasn't to be the end of it.

He got a larger church in South Carolina—one with a parsonage—so Sarah became an on-site preacher's wife. Soon there was another choir, with sixty young people. They elected officers and opened a checking account in the hope of someday having enough money to buy their own robes. Sarah's name went on the checks, as well as the name of the young girl who had been elected secretary of the group.

Meanwhile, the church had an anniversary celebration, and Sarah was determined to make her husband look good. Good, as it turned out, came to $1,400 worth of flowers and food—all written on the youth choir account. Following the anniversary, Sarah went to New York to visit family and friends, and her husband was off to another evangelistic mission. So when the bank couldn't reach Sarah or her husband about the bad checks, they called the young person whose name was also on the check.

You can imagine the rest of this part of the story. Sarah got four years' probation, and her husband got sent to another church—this time in Tennessee. Again, reluctantly, she followed her husband. But ironically, in leaving South Carolina she broke a condition of her parole and soon was back in jail in South Carolina where a judge ordered a psychiatric evaluation. That turned out to be a way to work off her time, but little else seems to have come of it.

Back in Tennessee she turned, she said in desperation, to a "faith advisor." I take it the woman read palms or cards, something of that nature. The woman not only captured Sarah's imagination but her pocketbook. More bad checks.

And throughout all this time Sarah was always on the go and always writing bad checks. The beginning of the end came when she walked into a welfare office in New Jersey and tried to get food stamps. Somehow she was spotted and arrested and brought back to Tennessee. She sat in jail without bond because they said it wouldn't do any good to let her out. By that time there were warrants out for her arrest in eight other counties in Tennessee.

In the midst of all of this, her mother and sister started proceedings to get custody of the children. Ironically, they didn't succeed. The judge chose to interpret Sarah's attempt to get food stamps for her children in New Jersey as a responsible act of motherhood.

But for the moment it didn't matter. Sarah, of course, left them behind when she was taken to the women's prison in Nashville.

Then there's Louise. I don't know why Louise went to prison; she never told me. But she did show me her scar. During the time she was in the county jail in Memphis waiting for her trial, she had to have surgery. It required an incision from the middle of her front to the middle of her back. Four days after the surgery, the judge ordered her back to jail. When she got there, no preparation had been made for her arrival, so temporarily she was put in the holding tank. There were two drunks in there. One knocked her off the cot she was lying on; the other urinated on her. At this point, Louise became hysterical—and finally got the attention she needed.

What do I do with these stories after I get home on Sunday afternoon? What about the Bettys and Sarahs and Louises of this world?

One of the frustrations of prison work is the presence of a lot of groups preaching what I call the quick-fix gospel. Just get things right with Jesus, and everything will be OK. In the ultimate sense, of course, that's true, but it's irresponsible when it glosses over the tough realities. Just last Sunday Betty said, "I'm scared to death to get out of here. I'm a divorced woman with a small child and a prison record. What man is going to want me? I'm soiled property."

I resent the quick-fix crowd who think life is going to be easy for Betty. And yet I realize my own tendencies to want to set things right—get them a job, give them a book to read, arrange for some counseling. I hope some of this does help. But I also know that a lot of things at the prison can't be fixed, aren't fair, and don't make sense.

On the surface there isn't any reason why Betty, who had everything, would rob a bank. Sarah is due to get out on parole soon, but her eight months in prison undoubtedly haven't broken a pattern of behavior that is of very long standing and has a very complicated pathology.

And when I think of Louise in that holding tank with the drunks, I think of another "criminal," who suffered indignities on the cross. In fact, the only way I can make sense of my Sunday afternoons at the prison is to know that in the cross we have a place to peg a lot of what we see and experience in life that hurts, that limits, that alienates, that just doesn't make sense—and won't go away.

In many ways the cross is the perfect paradigm for prison life. The cross tells us something about ordinary physical need like thirst. In the cross we see concern for a mother left behind. The cross has a word about forgiveness for undeserved injustice. The cross screams with abandonment. The cross reveals death as the ultimate earthly reality.

While *our* lives may be less dramatic and *our* mistakes less culpable, we all need the assurance nevertheless that *our* dark nights of the soul have been received in the cross. That religion isn't just the easy belief that comes when things are going well. That at the very core of our faith there is a place to peg everything from our individual loneliness to our corporate fear of a nuclear holocaust.

We are able to make these assertions, of course, because of the absolutely audacious claim of the Christian community that it was God who hung on that cross, God who bled and got thirsty. Martin Luther speaks of this as the "scandal" of God's subjection to shame, defeat, and death in the person of Jesus on the cross. But it is in this event and because of this event that we have the assurance that God knows our suffering first-hand, that no part of the human experience falls outside God's grasp and understanding.

We are in fact an Easter people. We live in faith and hope; we live with the assurance of victory. But in our haste to get to Easter, there is no way around the cross.

32. Reaching into the Future
Charles H. Bayer

Text: Thy Kingdom come, Thy will be done on earth as it is in
heaven.—Matthew 6:10

I HAVE SELDOM thought of prayer as a dangerous activity.
After having been reared to live a very careful, safe life, the
older I get the more dangerous things I find myself doing. I
hit my fifth decade riding a motorcycle—an altogether fool-
hardy pursuit! After seeing a couple of people scraped off the
highway after going south when their bike went north, I abandoned that avocation before the odds caught up with me. But
the next summer I found myself crawling over a snowfield
high in the Rockies where everything taller than two feet had
been charred by lightning—and there I stood, five foot ten, in
the midst of a violent electrical storm. That's dangerous! But
prayer? You've got to be kidding!

Of all the prayers that appear harmless, the safest is the
comforting, warm, ubiquitous formula we call the Lord's
Prayer. We can say it in our sleep—and probably often do.
Who can get into trouble with that one?

You can, my friend—and so can I! It is a dangerous prayer.
Take a hard look at the central petition around which all the
rest of the prayer revolves: "Thy Kingdom come, Thy will be

Charles Henry Bayer is pastor of First Christian Church, St. Joseph,
Missouri. A graduate of Phillips University and its Graduate Seminary
in Enid, Oklahoma, he has been adjunct professor of preaching and
public worship at Chicago Theological Seminary. Bayer is also the
political columnist for the *St. Joseph Gazette* and has written many
articles and several books.

done on earth as it is in heaven." What we are asking God to produce is a revolution! We are asking that our society replicate the heavenly Kingdom. Before we pray, we better know what this Kingdom of heaven is like, lest its coming catch us unaware.

John appeared in the wilderness scandalizing those who came out to hear him. "Repent, for the Kingdom of Heaven is at hand," he bellowed (Matt. 3:2). After him came Jesus, who described the Kingdom John had heralded. The Kingdom Jesus talked about looked nothing like the kingdoms of this world.

Consider how things are under God's sovereign rule. Who are the blessed? The poor in spirit, or as Luke has it, "the poor," the mourners, the meek, those who hunger and thirst for what is right, the merciful, the pure in heart, the peacemakers, the persecuted.

Where God reigns, if you are struck on one cheek you turn the other. If someone asks for your coat you give him your shirt as well. If anyone has two shirts, one of them is shared with someone who has none. I'm quite sure I don't like that one. I haven't counted recently but I probably have thirty shirts! In the Kingdom you love your enemies and pray for those who would do you in.

It only gets worse in the parables. It is the son who wished his father dead, so he could get his inheritance early, who ends up the hero in Jesus' best-known story. It is a Samaritan who is to be respected for his compassion. Tax collectors and sinners enter the Kingdom before the pious and upright. Lazarus, the beggar, rests in Abraham's bosom, while the rich man at whose gates he had begged languishes in torment. Those who work one hour are paid the same as those who work twelve. What kind of economic order is that?

In the Kingdom nobody is forced to live in poverty. Everyone is treated with dignity, no matter the amount of their productive work. The last go first and the first last. The nobodies get places of honor at the feasts. In story after story, women have the important roles. Women! What in heaven's name is going on here? That's the point. What is going is in heaven's name. That's just how things are in the Kingdom.

If we are poor, powerless, and oppressed, all of this probably sounds like very good news. Indeed, "the poor heard him gladly." But the opposite is true. We in the United States are but 7 percent of the world's population and we consume 40 percent of the world's goods. We are overfed, overgadgeted, overindulged. And what is more, we are spending ourselves into oblivion to insure things stay that way. Defense, we call it. And in the Kingdom we get in last if we get in at all.

It is unimaginable that in heaven anyone goes hungry. Does this mean that if the Kingdom arrives in the here and now *we* may not eat as well? If everyone is entitled to decent medical care, how will we obtain the superior medical care to which we have become accustomed? There are, after all, just so many resources available. If the two-thirds of the human race that lives in the Third World gets the same size slice of the pie we do, it stands to reason our slice is going to get much smaller.

Why, this Kingdom of Heaven business sounds like a communist plot. Communism, however, cannot deliver such a utopian society—and neither can we. This is not Marxist talk, it is Kingdom of God talk. Jesus is describing how things will be when the final reign of God is established. That's how things are in heaven, but saints be praised, not how things are on earth.

We are therefore perfectly safe to read these texts—to jump up and down on our ten verses of Scripture every week—but we are in little danger of being confronted with the Kingdom Jesus described, as long as it stays in some heavenly realm. Just the moment, however, we utter that revolutionary prayer—"Thy Kingdom come, Thy will be done on earth as it is in heaven," we are pleading with God to establish right here the very reality we fear! What if our prayer were suddenly answered?

What is more, the church is called to be the bridge that connects the world in which we live to the Kingdom for which we pray. As such the church invites the revolution that the coming of the Kingdom would surely bring. The church demonstrates the reality of that which is only in God's future.

Not that our prayers or our work bring in the Kingdom. That task is God's and God's alone. Ours is a proximate, not an ultimate task. As liberation theologians put it, we have been given a project. We do not establish the Kingdom, but we live as if the Kingdom were already in our midst. We look in the Bible to see what God's will is. We pray for it. And then we reach into God's future and seize a chunk of it which we bring back into the present. We provide a demonstration project, a preview of things to come. We invade the principalities and powers of this present age with a foretaste of the Kingdom. We plant the leaven of the Kingdom in the doughy lump of our society.

The church is a beachhead of the Kingdom, etched out on the inhospitable shores of this world. As citizens of this new order we proclaim, by the way we live, that God not only will win the final victory, but that the victory has already been accomplished in the Resurrection of Christ.

Our task is evangelistic. Mind you, evangelism has nothing to do with finding people as much as possible as we are, convincing them they are already our kind of people, and providing for them a comfortable environment in which they can feel better about themselves. Evangelism is the proclamation and the demonstration of the coming Kingdom of God.

The church says by what it is and what it does: "Do you want to see how things will be when God finally brings the Kingdom? We will show you. We have reached into God's future, and brought back a chunk of it, and here it is. O yes, it is imperfect, it makes compromises, it is fragmented, it is staffed by sinful people, but here is a shadowed image of what it will be like when God's rule is fully established."

But first we do a very dangerous thing—we pray for it. "Thy Kingdom come. . . ." As our prayer is answered we become the first landing party of God's heavenly invasion. As such, we stand in a different relationship to this world than do those in captivity to the powers and principalities currently occupying it. We are not under their control. We have been made alive in Christ; reborn. We have shared in his death and been raised in his likeness. We are buried with him in baptism, and raised with him in newness of life. And now we live as witnesses to the Resurrection.

What of the old order that still appears to be in control? It has been defeated! "[Christ] has disarmed the principalities and powers and made a public example of them, triumphing over them" (Col. 2:12–14).

Here is the ultimate good news of the gospel. The principalities and powers have been rendered harmless. They have no authority any more. The era of the Kingdom has dawned. God's ultimate disarmament program is already in place. Note the active verb. It is not that God pleaded with, convinced, cajoled, appeased them. God did not initiate a petition drive, or engage in an educational effort. God simply has taken the weapons out of their hands.

We no longer need to cooperate with the principalities and powers as if they were still in command. We do not stumble over our words, trying to explain why we yet appear to be under the control of oppressive economic and political forces which dismantle the hopes of masses of God's children. We live and work as if God's kingdom were already fully present regardless of the spasms and death throes of the old order. We refuse to bow before or pay lip service to gods that have already been defeated.

Are you ready to pray? No, not polite cautious words uttered by the proper before a deity too remote to hear or respond. Are you ready to offer revolutionary words, trusting God will answer—has already answered, before we utter a sound? Are you ready to reach into the future and seize a chunk of that reality which will one day bring justice and peace to this earth, and live it out in the here and now? Are you ready to demonstrate in the here and now the era of the Kingdom in which everyone will sit under his vine and her fig tree and none shall make them afraid; the day when swords will be beaten into plowshares and spears into pruning hooks; the day when the earth will be filled with the knowledge of the Lord as the waters cover the sea; the day when God shall be acknowledged King of Kings and Lord of Lords and shall reign for ever and ever?

I'm not certain I'm ready. My life, as yours, has been seduced by the way things are in this present age. Yet God does not depend on our readiness. Thy Kingdom will come by God's initiative and when God decides. And we shall be part of it only by grace.

Ready or not, we must pray, knowing that the answer to our prayer may change all the comfortable rules by which we have lived. We will come to God's table, receive God's gifts, and tremble as we utter that revolutionary prayer, "Thy Kingdom come. . . ."

If you are ready, then tremble as you come to the most dangerous words you may ever utter: "Thy Kingdom come. . . ."

33. The Righteous and the Good

James N. McCutcheon

> While we were yet helpless, at the right time Christ died for the
> ungodly. Why, one will hardly die for a righteous man—though
> perhaps for a good man one will dare to die.—Romans 5:6–7

I

THE RIGHTEOUS, as that term is generally understood
among us, are people who usually can be relied upon not to
steal, not to lie, not to murder, not to commit adultery. They
take great satisfaction in keeping the law, both of church and
state; and they are inclined to be very hard on those who do
not. But they all too frequently don't extend themselves beyond what the law requires to gratuitous acts of compassion,
charity, and love. The priest and the Levite, in Jesus' parable
of "The Good Samaritan," were seriously righteous people.
But they left a wounded stranger to die in a roadside ditch,
passing by on "the other side," essentially because the law did
not require them to care for him, and it would have put them
at personal risk to have done so (Luke 10:33–37).

James N. McCutcheon is senior minister of Wayzata Community
Church (United Church of Christ) in Wayzata, Minnesota. McCutcheon was educated at Yale University, Union Theological Seminary,
and Harvard University, from which he received the S.T.M. in New
Testament in 1960. He has served pastorates in Pittsfield and Worces-
ter, Massachusetts, and in Kalamazoo, Michigan. In the Korean War
he served with the United States Navy and was twice cited for bravery.
McCutcheon has written articles and sermons for professional journals
and is the author of *The Pastoral Ministry.*

The good are a different sort. They customarily act in response to what kindness requires; and, as a result, they are not always found among those the world deems righteous. Sometimes they are even called "do-gooders," a term not usually intended to convey approval. For often, in their doing of good, they seriously disturb the normal order of society with consequences that are not without costs. "The Good Employer," in Jesus' parable of the same name, was such a person. To the great annoyance of his peers, as well as the majority of his own employees, this gentleman paid some day laborers, hired late in the afternoon, exactly the same wages as others who had worked the entire day, necessarily sacrificing righteousness for goodness, because he did not want any family, within his power to help, to go to bed hungry (Matt. 20:1–16).

Now, the human race, in its more enlightened moments, has always thought better of the good than of the righteous. This is to say that most people, whenever they are reasonably free from insecurity and worry, tend to support not the law and order of the "scribes and Pharisees" but rather the efforts of those who do good for its own sake alone. Which is what lies, at bottom, behind Paul's observation to the Romans: "Why, one will hardly die for a righteous man—though perhaps for a good man one will dare to die." (Rom. 5:7).

But, unfortunately, times are not always secure and worry-free for any of us. Whenever they aren't, compassion, charity, and love tend to dry up. And it is just at those moments that we all too frequently fall back upon keeping the bare letter of the law and doing only what its righteousness demands. That is why we Christians need to keep constant watch over what we are about with our righteousness. We must be certain that in our legitimate longings for law and order, fairness and justice, humanity's higher responsibility for doing good is not forgotten. For life without righteousness may be existence without shape or meaning. But life without goodness is priests "passing by on the other side," the rich getting indigestion while the poor go to bed hungry, and, in the end, a world that isn't worth living in, for anybody!

Fiorello LaGuardia was mayor of New York City during the worst days of the Great Depression and through all of World War II. Fearless, incorruptible, egotistical, champion of the people, "the Little Flower," as the adoring citizens of New York called him, made sure, for over twenty years, that no one in the greatest city on earth ever lost sight of the difference between being righteous and doing good, or the importance, before anything else, of being human.

He used to ride the New York City fire trucks, raid speakeasies with the police department, take entire orphanages to the baseball games, and, whenever the New York newspapers were on strike (which was often in my youth), he used to go on radio and read the Sunday "funnies" to the kids.

In any case, one bitter cold winter's night in 1935, the mayor turned up in a night court that served the poorest ward in the city, dismissed the judge for the evening, and took over the bench himself. A short while into that court session, a tattered old lady was brought before him, charged with stealing a loaf of bread. She told LaGuardia that her daughter's husband had deserted her, her daughter was sick, and her grandchildren were starving. But the shopkeeper, from whom the bread was stolen, refused to drop the charges. "It's a bad neighborhood, Your Honor," the man told the mayor. "She's got to be punished to teach other people around here a lesson."

LaGuardia sighed. He turned to the woman. "I've got to punish you," he said. "The law makes no exceptions—$10.00 or ten days in jail." But the mayor was already reaching into his pocket, even as he pronounced sentence; and, having extracted a bill, he tossed it into his famous sombrero with these words:

> Here's the $10.00 fine which I now remit; and
> furthermore I'm going to fine everyone in this
> courtroom fifty cents for living in a town where
> a person has to steal bread so that her
> grandchildren can eat. Mr. Bailiff, collect the
> fines and give them to the defendant.

So the following day the New York City newspapers reported that $47.50 was turned over to a bewildered old lady who had stolen a loaf of bread to feed her starving grandchildren, fifty cents of that amount being contributed by the red-faced grocery store owner, while some seventy petty criminals, people with traffic violations, and New York City policemen, each of whom had just paid fifty cents for the privilege of doing so, gave their mayor a standing ovation.

II

But as important as it is to respect the limits of righteousness and, as much as may be possible, to do good, they don't add up to the virtue being Christian demands. "Christ died for the ungodly," Paul writes! "Why one will hardly die for a righteous man—though perhaps for a good man one will dare to die!" But "Christ died for the ungodly!"

And, of course, he did. Christ died not only for the "sins of the world" in general (John 1:29). He also died for a particular "ungodly" person, a murderer, robber, and anarchist, named Jesus Barabbas, whom all people, of every circumstance and race, equally loathed and deemed worthy of death (Mt. 27:15–26). But then, when you think about all of his previous life, who he served and what he did for them, was not Jesus' willingness to give himself up and even die for "the ungodly" the core of everything he did to save us? What about all those tax collectors, prostitutes, lepers, adulterers, schizophrenics, and other "ungodly" people for whom Jesus violated the Sabbath regulations against healing, ignored the Levitical regulations against sitting down at table with sinners, and finally, in protest against a religious system that prevented poor people from worshiping God, drove the moneychangers out of the Jerusalem Temple?

Jesus once told a delegation of the righteous and the good, who waited upon him to protest the idea that doing God's will required people to be as concerned as he was about "the ungodly": "Those who are well have no need of a physician, only those who are sick" (Luke 5:31). Yes, indeed! The soul of righteousness and the heart of doing good, at least as Jesus lived them out among us, is finally nothing more than helping all people, but particularly the poor, the outcast, the distressed, and the "ungodly" find the "abundant life" (John 10:10) and become the people God had in mind when they were created.

Six years ago, Christine Sparks published her marvelous biography of Joseph Merrick, *The Elephant Man*. Now Merrick was a victim of neurofibromatosis, a disease for which there is no known cure, and which invariably ends in hideous disfiguration, pain, and premature death. And in late nineteenth-century London, where Merrick grew up, the horror of neurofibromatosis was considerably compounded by a widespread, though erroneous, assumption that this disorder began with some sort of moral lapse, for which either the victim or his parents were responsible.

In any case, Joseph Merrick was discovered by Dr. Frederick Treves while Merrick was working as a freak in the sideshow of a second-rate traveling circus. At the time, Merrick was barely able to speak, horribly deformed in body, hideous to look upon, forced to go about wearing a mask when not on display, and so crushed by the laughter of indifferent circus patrons that he had withdrawn almost completely within himself. He was also, when Dr. Treves took him into his personal care, not yet twenty-three years old and had but four more years to live.

Dr. Treves managed to get Joseph Merrick permanent accommodations at the prestigious London Hospital, where Treves worked as senior surgeon and lecturer in anatomy. Under the physician's care and through the efforts of many who took an interest in him, the real Joseph Merrick gradually began to shine through the "ungodly" body in which he was encased. Other people took note of what was happening. There was a story about the "elephant man" in the *Times of London*. Soon afterward, the Prince and Princess of Wales paid him a visit. Money was collected to provide Merrick with books, a tutor, and craft lessons. And Madge Kendall entered his life.

Madge Kendall was one of the finest actresses and the most beautiful women of her generation. She discovered the "elephant man" through friends, was deeply moved by his plight, and determined that she herself must try to help him. So she made an appointment to visit him. Upon arriving, she presented Merrick with a copy of the complete works of William Shakespeare. The young man took the book in his hands. Tears welled up in his eyes. Without a word, he began fumbling through the volume until he came to *Romeo and Juliet.* And then occurred what Christine Sparks insists was the event that precipitated Merrick's redemption.

Slowly, hesitatingly, in his high, squeaky, broken voice, the young man began to read aloud: "See! how she leans her cheek upon her hand: O! that I were a glove upon that hand, that I might touch that cheek." Madge Kendall slipped into a chair beside him and began to respond from memory with Juliet's lines. And so, as the afternoon shadows lengthened across the pages of the book, the two of them sat there, side by side, reciting to each other, until they had completed the whole second act of *Romeo and Juliet.* Then, Madge Kendall stretched out her hand and took the young man's withered fingers in her own. Leaning over, she kissed his swollen, leathery cheek. And finally, ever so gently, she said to him: "Why, Mr. Merrick, you're not an Elephant Man at all. . . . Oh no! You are Romeo."

It may be enough, for the long run, to know that "while we were yet sinners Christ died for us" (Rom. 5:8). But if, in the short run, the salvation God sent Jesus Christ to give us is to soften this cruel and broken world, then you and I, and other Christians like us, will have to do good and uphold righteousness in ways that will help not only decent people but all people—even the "ungodly"—to find the "abundant life" and become the people God had in mind when he created them! Amen.

34. Suppose God Is Black

Mervyn A. Warren

> When a Samaritan woman came to draw water, Jesus said to her,
> "Will you give me a drink?" (His disciples had gone into the town to
> buy food.) The Samaritan woman said to him, "You are a Jew and I
> am a Samaritan woman. How can you ask me for a drink?" (For Jews
> do not associate with Samaritans.)—John 4:7–9, NIV

SEASONED by a strenuous stint as attorney general of the
United States and solemnized by the assassination of his brother, President John F. Kennedy, the senator visited South Africa in 1966. Upon his return home from that Christian nation,
he reported having seen a form of "love to God" but scant evidence of "love to man." Senator Robert F. Kennedy confirmed what the world already knew: apartheid rigidly
separates the races in South Africa. At that time, the Afri-
kaners' practice of "apartness" meant the segregation of three
million whites from twelve million blacks, and of each of those
groups from 2.2 million mixed-blood (or "colored") people.

It was like a broken record to hear the senator report that
if your skin is black in South Africa you cannot participate in
the political process, and you cannot vote. If your skin is black,
you are restricted to jobs for which no whites are available. If

---

Mervyn A. Warren is chairman of the department of Religion at
Oakwood College in Huntsville, Alabama. Warren pursued his education at Oakwood College, the Seventh-day Adventist Seminary at
Andrews University, Michigan State University (from which he received a Ph.D. in 1966), and Vanderbilt Divinity School. He is the
author of *Black Preaching: Truth and Soul* and *God Made Known*. He and
his wife are the parents of three children.

your skin is black, your wages are from 10 percent to 40 percent of those paid a white person for the same work. You are forbidden to own land except in one small area; you live with your family only if the government approves; and the government will spend one-tenth as much to educate your child as it spends to educate a white child. If your skin is black, you are by law an inferior from birth to death and are totally segregated even at most church services.

When a certain white South African gentleman struck up a conversation with the senator and argued that the black person's inferior role is based on the Bible, Kennedy raised a most confoundingly profound question for modern Christians everywhere to ponder—especially in the Western world. "What if we go to heaven," he posed, "and we, all our lives, have treated the Negro as an inferior, and God is there, and we look up and he is not white? What then is our response? *Suppose God is black?*" Silence.

I should like to break the distrubing silence of this unanswered question by raising it again today, some twenty years later. Imagine, if you will, that by some heavensent vision, some special revelation, in addition to knowing that God is "love" (John 3:16) and that God is "just" (1 John 1:9) and that he is "powerful" and "perfect" and all those grand and glorious attributes, you discovered that God is also "black"! How would your latest finding affect your worship?

Does the idea of a black God encourage your Christian commitment or dampen your innermost spirit? Would you, as a black person, take the blackness of Deity as your special ticket of privilege in spiritual matters? Or, as a white person, would you suddenly awaken to some realization that your conversion to the abundant life is a mistake, that your belief in the God of Abraham, Isaac, and Jacob is suddenly leaning out of kilter, that you misread the divine signals and, therefore, like the apostle Peter, you are now going fishing (John 21:3) and it will be a long, long vacation? Suppose God is black! Does the thought of a black God draw you—whatever your race—to a closer relationship to Yahweh or does it spell grounds for spiritual divorce, and God can keep the alimony?

I submit that raising the question of the blackness of God today is closely akin to, if not the same as, asking in Jesus' day: "Is God a Samaritan?" "Suppose God is Samaritan!" For the conversation in our biblical text (John 4) suggests more than a tug-of-war between two conceptualizations of God. "Our fathers worshiped," says the woman of Samaria, "in this mountain." The *Samaritan* God! "And ye say," she continues, "that in Jerusalem is the place where men ought to worship." The *Jewish* God! Jesus knew all too well the titanic tensions that tested their times. A "great gulf fixed" separated Samaritan and Jew, an "apartness" or antipathy whose waters were first fed by a historical conquest of the Northern Kingdom of Israel in 722 B.C. by the Assyrian kings Tiglath-pileser III and Sargon II. Captured Israelites intermarrying with heathen nations gave birth to the Samaritans, a race with an amalgamated bloodstream. Though racial relatives, Samaritans and Jews bore in their bodies clear scars of genetic as well as religious differences—a tradition that spawned their long-lasting family feud.

What may we learn from this encounter between Jesus and the woman of Samaria? Does their conversation speak at all to you and me in our quest to know God in modern racial times? Can persistent and complex inquiries about race and God forage answers from a simple long-ago, dust-covered interchange by Jacob's well? Let us pause there for the next little while and recapture a dramatic scenario of resolve, redress, race, and reverence.

I

"Now he had to go through Samaria" (John 4:4, NIV). Traveling from Judea into Galilee as Jesus and his disciples were doing this hot sunshiny day, some very straitlaced Jews would take the long and tedious detour around to the east across the Jordan River in order to avoid certain defilement when passing through the nation of despised Samaritans. But in spite of the fact that social intercourse with these people was condemned, Jesus casts ceremonial caution to the wind, places people above policy, and resolves to "go through Samaria"— not around, but through. The pattern is set. Although the nature of the human condition demands law and order for members of society to live together in appropriate harmony, when policies demean persons and violate the dignity of human personality, then the "Jesus through Samaria" principle offers the challenge of placing persons above policy in the name of a higher moral law of personhood under God, after which all human laws are invited to pattern themselves. Anything less in our day is reminiscent of the Dred Scott decision by the U.S. Supreme Court in 1857, which said the black slave in America was less than a person. Anything less in our day smacks of the Hitler-Nazi obsession which says that Jews, Slavs, and other minority groups are inferior if not less than human. Anything less in our day borders on depersonalization and attempts to bypass rather than go through Samaria.

II

"So he came to a town in Samaria called Sychar, near the plot of ground Jacob had given to his son Joseph. Jacob's well was there, and Jesus, tired as he was from the journey, sat down by the well" (John 4:5–6, NIV).

January 31, 1960. North Carolina A & T College. Greensboro. Ezell Blair, Jr., Joseph McNeill, and two other fellow students decide to seek redress for one of them having been denied service at the lunch counter of a Greyhound bus terminal. The next day, they go the local Woolworth five-and-dime store, sit down at the lunch counter reserved for white customers only, and remain for over two hours after having been refused service. Following a repeat of this day after day, these black students are joined by sympathetic white students from Women's College, Duke University, and Wake Forest as well as black students from Teachers College Winston-Salem. Within about two weeks, the spirit spreads not only to other North Carolina cities but also to South Carolina, Tennessee, and Virginia. And the rest is history. The first "sit-in demonstrations," right? Wrong! The movement really began back about A.D. 28 when the Lord of liberation "sat down by the well" in Sychar and challenged sacred custom by asking a Samaritan woman for a drink of water. And this, in spite of the following *Mishnah*-based dictum: "He that eats the bread of the Samaritans is like the one that eats the flesh of swine."

I am declaring today that in every age the church has the clear prophetic role of providing conscience and compass for society. To fulfill effectually her prophetic function often means, however, taking the gospel beyond its stained-glass enclosure and placing it beside a well—the well of courthouse steps, the well of housing authorities, the well of employers and government officials, the well of the real world. Our foremost example in modern times is Martin Luther King, Jr., who took his cues principally from Jesus, Henry David Thoreau, and Mohandas K. Gandhi, and dared to seek redress through nonviolent direct action to bring down the walls of partition separating members of the human family. I can hear him even now proclaiming in clarion tones that "non- cooperation with evil is as much a moral responsibility as is cooperation with good." Prior to the 1863 Emancipation Proclamation, one Ellen White wrote to her church community regarding how they should relate Christian responsibility to unjust civil law:

> When the laws of men conflict with the word
> and law of God, we are to obey the latter,
> whatever the consequences may be. The law of
> our land requiring us to deliver a slave to his
> master, we are not to obey; and we must abide
> the consequences of violating this law. The
> slave is not the property of any man. God is his
> rightful master, and man has no right to take
> God's workmanship into his hands, and claim
> him as his own.

If you miss the moral ethic of redress here, it is the nonviolent challenge to change dehumanizing laws without dehumanizing the oppressor and without impairing one's convenant relation with God. And it is ultimately God to whom Jesus would lead the Samaritan woman when, with tact born of divine love, he asks rather than offers a favor. As love begets love, trust begets trust. The request from Jesus, "Give me a drink," really prefigures a solemn invitation for the woman to give God her heart in a covenant relationship and forever thereafter take fresh draughts of the water of life eternal from the deep well of salvation.

III

The woman says: "Our fathers worshiped on this mountain, but you Jews claim that the place where we must worship is in Jerusalem" (John 4:20, NIV).

Like the beauty of a landscape at the breaking of dawn, it soon becomes manifest that in holding conversation with the woman, Jesus is sociable in order to save, and turns on a light in a dark place. Responding to her quip about race ("You are a Jew and I am a Samaritan"), Jesus leads her from the known to the unknown, from the seen to the unseen, from the earthly to the heavenly, from the well of Syçhar to the way of salvation, from Jesus the man to Jesus the Messiah! "If you knew the gift of God and who it is that asks you for a drink," Jesus assures, "you would have asked him and he would have given you living water" (John 4:10, NIV). That which began as a simple human request for a drink now turns into a whole different matter with spiritual import, a salvation initiative. Moveover, the woman's query about racial identity is met by an opportunity to become acquainted with divine identity. Never think for a moment that Jesus is ignoring her question. He is, rather, leading her to a much larger answer. To be sure, race has also become very pivotal to our living and loving and laboring. So much about us runs along racial contours—where we live, where we work, what schools we choose, whom we marry, where we recreate and, yes, even where we worship. We sooner or later realize that sustained efforts against racial injustice notwithstanding, we still see through a glass darkly and must pray, work, and hope for the final and best solution to come from God—hopefully through us, of course, but certainly from God. One South African colored pastor recently testified in a despairing note to the complexities of apartheid in his homeland: "The only thing that can possibly save us is the imminent return of Christ. We need for him to come quickly." Christ does come in various ways. There is a sense in which he has no hands or feet but ours, and yet in another sense he comes personally in the *parousia.*

To the woman of Samaria, Jesus comes; peels back her light, bantering exterior and zeros in on her deepest need. Verses 11 through 19 catalog so graphically her journey from "You are a *Jew*" to "You are a *prophet.*" But the journey does not end here. It continues on just around the conversational bend to a realization that he is also the *Messiah* (John 4:25, 26, 29). For the moment, however, there remains a racial observation to ponder. "Our fathers worshiped on this mountain," says the woman, "but you Jews claim that the place . . . is in Jerusalem" (John 4:20, NIV). Now that's a sense of history for you, and all races must have it. Jesus neither put down her history nor praised his own, but respected both. Samaritan history, Jewish history, black history, European history, Hispanic history, American history—all deserve to be known, shared, and celebrated in their special context, because it is not race but racism that frustrates brotherhood and denies fatherhood.

Racism raised its ugly head and continued the oppression of blacks during slavery in America and perpetuated subsequent discrimination against black citizens for over a hundred years. Thus it has become necessary that America's largest minority overcome not only society's finagling of laws against them but also the church's misapplication of the Bible in support of that society. One response by blacks to American racism is the building of a hermeneutic that discovers a God in Scripture who identifies with the oppressed, affirms their sonship and daughtership, liberates them from oppression, judges their oppressor, and at least in this sense, is a black God. Not a racist God, mind you, but a racial God in that he personally makes the oppression of any group (and any individual person) his own divine project for liberation. "The Spirit of the Lord is on me; therefore he has anointed me to preach good news to the poor. He has sent me to proclaim freedom for the prisoners and recovery of sight for the blind, to release the oppressed, to proclaim the year of the Lord's favor" (Luke 4:18–19, NIV).

So God identifies with the poor, the prisoners, the blind, and the oppressed in their present existential situations, and that alone should veto any satisfied complacency with such human conditions as they are. A time is coming, Jesus promises the woman, when neither this mountain (Mount Gerizim) nor Jerusalem will be the place. Something better than the present awaits you. Let us together move toward it. Good, better, best; never let it rest; until our good is better, and our better is best. Could it be that you and I in the 1980s may be prone to forget that that which often looms large and formidable to us in our racist clime and time must never presume to escape the eye of God? History and present have their very important place, but more important is destiny. Even as a higher level of worship awaits the Samaritan woman, a higher level of Christian living awaits us in this world and the world to come— if we are listening to Jesus. Working for a better future brings the future to now.

IV

Jesus says: "True worshipers will worship the Father in spirit and truth, for they are the kind of worshipers the Father seeks. God is spirit" (John 4:23–24, NIV). Need we remind ourselves that worship is corporate, yet ever so personal? Indeed, I would say it begins first with the individual and then proceeds to the group or the church where liturgy and ritual and setting play great importance. In either case, whether with man or multitude, female or flock, true communion with heaven is not confined to form and ceremony, holy mountain and sacred temple. The God-plus-human encounter is first of all a personal experience where, human effort notwithstanding, God takes the initiative, yes, "the Father seeks." And the worship experience to which God desires to lead the Samaritan woman and, of course, you and me is one of "spirit and truth," *en pneumati kai aletheia,* which I interpret to mean reverential worship "in all sincerity" or worship "with the highest faculties of emotions and mind." The bottom line, shall we say, is God re-seen, man remade.

I trust I am not redundant when I say that extremes on both sides of the proverbial battle between emotion and reason must be avoided and kept at bay from our worship. Especially as in corporate worship some church congregations burn up in emotionalism while others freeze in formalism. Perhaps the practical meaning of Christ-and-culture can help us here inasmuch as church congregations are frequently characterized and determined by race as much as, if not more than, other societal divisions. This brings us back to a reality of race in religion, because religious exclusivity that can be identified according to a particular race runs the imminent danger of presupposing a racist deity. Whereby if my race bears certain characteristics generally observed as consistent or even to a degree "unique," then my particular racial qualities may be construed as a true reflection of my God. If God is like my race-uniqueness, then God must be unlike other racial groups. It follows then that when I see an artist's conception of Christ, the divine Son of God, I expect it to reflect *my* race. Should he be sketched or painted to look other than my kind, my race pride feels threatened.

The other side of the coin reflects that our reverence for God contemplates our respect for all his creatures. If God behind the human Jesus is perceived by the Chinese as being Chinese or by the Indian as being Indian, and the perception is mere psychology and not theology, is any harm done? At least such an effort toward divine relatedness is leagues away from the southern white American who claimed God as a charter member of the Ku Klux Klan and the White Citizens' Council.

It all seems so idolatrous, does it not, like attempting to re-create God in one's own racial image, and all the more so since John says earlier on in his Gospel: "No man has ever seen God" (John 1:18a, NIV). God is what he is whether we decide it or not. For all that it means to know that God identifies with me in my situations of need, just as important a question might be would I *prefer* a God who reveals himself to me as a *white* God or would I *prefer* him as a *black* God? Suppose God is black! There are persons whom the notion of a black God sets on top of the world with their toes dangling in stardust. Others are torn asunder or tossed on the sea of human emotions, driven to an avalanche of death. *Must* God be Samaritan or *must* he be Jew, or *must* he be white or black, before I receive him into my life and worship him "in spirit and in truth"? Is it possible, for you, that God could have the *wrong* color?

35. Crossing Over to the Promise

Hal Missiourie Warheim

Text: Joshua 1:1–11

> Be strong and courageous;
> don't be afraid and don't give up hope;
> because the Lord God is with us
> wherever we go.
>
> (Josh. 1:9)

The Purpose

I, Joshua, have assembled you here today to prepare you for tomorrow. For tomorrow we will be leaving this place on the edge of the wilderness where we have wandered for many years and soon we will cross over the river of time into the land of the future. We are going there in quest of our promise and, because there will be perils to face and battles to be fought, I want you to

---

Hal Missiourie Warheim is professor of Christianity and Society at Louisville Presbyterian Theological Seminary in Louisville, Kentucky. An ordained minister of the United Church of Christ and a member of the Kentucky Bar, Warheim graduated from Elmhurst College and Eden Theological Seminary, and earned a law degree from the University of Louisville in 1978. Since 1962, Warheim has taught in his seminary's department of Christianity and society, which he describes as "a dialogical and practical field built upon the disciplines of ethics, sociology, law, and politics that aims to equip Christian leaders to minister faithfully and influentially to modern communities and culture."

be strong and courageous;
don't be afraid and don't give up hope;
because the Lord God is with us
wherever we go.

The Promise

We human beings are people with a promise. Spun out of spirit and stardust, we were created with a dream; a potential destiny in which our deepest human hungers for security, society, self-actualization and significance are to be satisfied; a time and place in this world where peace and justice and love govern the political, economic, religious, sexual, and social affairs of our whole human family; the promise of a paradise for people, our people, all people.

This promise has been our power and our Polaris throughout our long hard pilgrimage on this planet. From our birth in the primeval ocean, our evolution as *homo sapiens,* we have struggled to construct customs and civilizations that would embody this dream. Over the centuries we have called it by many names: the Age of Aquarius, the Great Society, the Rule of the Proletariat, the Kingdom of Heaven, the City of God, among others. And we have tried to build it by a variety of means: totalitarian discipline, democratic consensus, progressive education, welfare programs, laissez-faire competition, religious conversion, among others.

Sometimes, in significant ways, we have come close. Sometimes, on a colossal scale, we have failed. But, always, somehow, we have been resurrected and energized by a new vision of our promise, and we have made ever-new beginnings to actualize our potential and to make this dream of a paradise for all people come true.

This promise, often blurred and betrayed, is our purpose for being in existence. This promise, always costly but worth any price, is our greatest gift from our Creator. This promise, elusive yet alluring, can and must be our future.

Therefore, as we prepare today to cross over into tomorrow, I, Joshua, want to remind you of why we are going and of
the promise which is at stake. So

> be strong and courageous;
> don't be afraid and don't give up hope;
> because the Lord God is with us
> wherever we go.

The Perils

This quest for our promise will not be made without peril.
Evil, in a variety of forms, is pervasive, powerful, and persistent; it attempts to pervert and destroy every good thing that
exists and it has succeeded so far in preventing us from claiming the promise for which we were created. Therefore, let us
not deceive ourselves: there will be some perilous situations
and conditions in the future that will frighten and discourage
us if we let them.

We are already well aware of some of these threats to our
promise because we have battled with them in the present and
the past: poverty, racism, disease, political oppression, illiter-
acy, militarism, and war. And there are others we have only
heard about from our scouts who have spied on the future
with their long-range forecasts of probable things to come: a
polluted planet, mass hunger, global domination by transna-
tional corporations, nuclear winter. And, of course, there is always the possibility of being ambushed in the future by events
that no one can imagine.

Looking out across the frontiers into the twenty-first century at the size and strength of the problems we must face,
some of our people have panicked and want to go back to what
they imagine were "good old days" and "old-fashioned ways":
Bible times or ancient Athens, Puritan America or pre-Viet-
nam. Life then was more satisfying, they think; the promise
was more important in the traditions of the past.

Some others among us are in despair about the third millenium. They no longer believe in the promise because their dreams have been crushed or because they have learned to be contented with cheap counterfeits. They want to stop here in the modern world and stabilize the status quo against any significant change toward the past or the future. "We're living in the Promised Land," they sing. "This is as good as it gets," they try to convince one another. "O Billy," says a mother to her little boy in an Opryland commercial, "this is what we've always dreamed of!"

We must empathize with those who live in fear and without hope in the future; those who want to retreat and those who just want to dig in. Even the heroic souls among us feel their doubt and dismay.

But we can't go back. Even if our nostalgic memories of better times were accurate, the gates to the past are slammed shut forever. There is no way to return, not even through the black hole of insanity.

And we can't stay here. Not just because the modern world isn't the promised paradise for most of humanity, or even because it is an obsolete piece of social machinery that is wantonly wasteful of human lives and is leaking human blood from every joint and seam. We can't stay here because time cannot be stopped nor can any status quo be stabilized for long without its inherent evils perverting and destroying it. We can't stay here because the future is streaming into the present and there is no way to contain its frothy new wine in the brittle wineskins of our past and present traditions.

There is only one thing to do and only one way to go: we must cross over and live toward our promise in the future and we must be prepared to struggle with the perilous problems that would prevent this actualization of our dream.

So, as we get ready to move out of here in the direction of tomorrow with all its threats, I, Joshua, nevertheless, expect you to

> be strong and courageous;
> don't be afraid and don't give up hope;

because the Lord God is with us
wherever we go.

The Plan

Now, here is our plan. All of us can begin to practice these tactics immediately so we can use them expertly as we cross over into the future. Remember that the progressive conquest of our problems and the ultimate realization of our promise depend significantly upon our commitment to act out these strategic behaviors in the appropriate circumstances. These tactics are the means compatible with our ends.

First, we will invade the future in quest of our promise with a new inclusive identity; we will call ourselves by a new name: Human Being. And this new name will indicate to whom we belong, where our fundamental loyalties lie, and whose best interests we will always serve. No longer will we think of ourselves primarily in traditional tribal categories that divide the human family and fuel normal disputes and conflict into holy wars: Afrikaner, heterosexual, Marxist, Democrat, German, fundamentalist, Roman Catholic, Moslem, Christian, Jew. From now on we will take our identity first and mainly from our future rather than from our past; we will name ourselves not for what we have been but for whom we can become. We will march toward our promise identified with the whole human race and flying the rainbow banner of humanity.

Second, we will move into our promised future by affirming all of our sisters and brothers in the human family as equals. We will leave behind us in this place the evil idea that there are people who because of their race, nationality, religious affiliation, occupation, physical appearance, age, sexual identity, and family heritage are to be regarded as superior or inferior in their claims to the goods and services, opportunities and responsibilities needed to participate in the promise. In our churches and communities we will actively assert the equal rights of all people to food, health care, housing, education, political participation, moral employment, leisure, and freedom of conscience. As we close in on the promise, all the members of our human family will be much more equal in wealth, status, power, and the chances to actualize their potential in this world.

Third, when we cross over into tomorrow we will meet the opposition to our promise with peacemaking initiatives. There will be multitudes of people already into the future who will misunderstand and mistrust the dream for humanity that we are pursuing, and they will erect walls of resistance and fortresses of traditions, and send out legions of clever priests and awesome warriors to turn us back, turn us down, turn us off, and turn us in.

This time, however, there will be no holy war and no massacres in the name of Yahweh, national security or any other god; certainly not by us and, hopefully, not of us. Our strategy from today forward will be to draw an impassable line across our human heritage of hatred and hostility, to make friends of those who would regard us as enemies, and to lay claim to our promise by searching for and appealing to mutual best interests, making unilateral moves of trust designed to incite trust, and negotiating our differences to produce win-win solutions.

We will need other tactics as we move forward. Some of these already exist in our present culture and many others will have to be invented by experimentation with new situations.

Whatever must be done to actualize this dream for humanity we must do. Whatever it costs to become the promised people of tomorrow we must pay. But whatever the task and whatever the price, let us

> be strong and courageous;
> don't be afraid and don't give up hope;
> because the Lord God is with us
> wherever we go.

The Power

Finally, I, Joshua, assure you that the Lord God is with us on this quest for our promise. From our conception in the womb of an exploding star, throughout all our wanderings upon this tiny terrestial teardrop, and now as we cross over into a thousand tomorrows, the Lord God is with us. It is the Lord God who gifts us with our promise. It is the Lord God who guides us toward our promise. It is the Lord God who guards our promise against final failure. And wherever we go in pursuit of this promise we will always be within the powerful, protective presence of the Lord God who created the promise for us and put it within us.

Here on the edge of another new century, which is pregnant with potentials for humanity's welfare, the Lord God is called by a number of new and old names: God the Father, Goddess, Life-force, God-in-Christ, Brahman-Atman, Ground of Being, Allah, and many others too numerous to mention. Most, if not all, of these conceptions of the Lord God function as masks for ideologies that promote parochial visions of the promise for certain classes of people and that result in the denial of the promise to certain others. "Gods" are among the chief devices used by nations, races, religions and sexes to steal the promise of humanity for themselves alone and keep the rest of humanity less than human.

There is, however, a Lord God, a God beyond and above all "gods," and the God who gives the promise of actualized human being to all people. This God has no name we know of. But we human beings are creatures of this God and in the depths of our beings we bear the powerful promise of this God. It is a promise beyond and above all the pseudo-promises of sect and class. It is not a promise only for a chosen people composed of white, American, Protestant, heterosexual males, or an elect elite of affluent, First World worshipers of Mars and mammon. It is the promise of the Lord God to all the people, for all the people, and in all the people on the face of the earth.

It is our promise and it is everybody's promise. But, above all, it is the Lord God's promise. The power in the heartbeat of the universe is behind it. The breath of life in all of creation supports it. The jagged, meandering trajectory of human history points in its direction. And beneath all of our ambivalent actions that sometimes help it and sometimes hinder it is our ravenous hunger for it which we must eventually satisfy or die.

The Lord God's promise for humanity cannot be actualized without proper preparation and it can be delayed by malice and mistakes. But with our intense commitment to it and our intelligent cooperation with the Lord God, the God beyond and above all "gods," the promise of a world flowing with milk and honey, the promise of a time filled with righteousness and peace, the promise of all people together in love actualizing their precious human potential, this promise can be kept. Given the threatening alternatives for our future, this promise must be kept. And because it is the Lord God's promise, this promise will be kept. Therefore, I, Joshua, urge you,

> be strong and courageous;
> don't be afaid and don't give up hope;
> because the Lord God is with us
> wherever we go.

V. PASTORAL

36. Learning to Forgive Ourselves

John R. Claypool

Scripture: Galatians 1:11–24

ONE OF the hardest things in the world to do is to forgive another person when that one has wronged you or failed you or in some way let you down. I can think of only one thing harder, really, and that is to forgive yourself when you have miserably failed or grievously sinned. It really does take a special grace to stand in front of a mirror and forgive that person for something you have done or failed to do in the past. I have found it easier to replay the old grievance over and over again than accept the release of forgiveness for myself and get on with it.

I still recall quite vividly one of my first experiences in this area. I was in high school and I was playing football. Like most American males, I had dreamed as a child of being a great athletic hero, but it turned out that I was not fast enough to be a halfback, and in order to play at all, I wound up being the cen-

John Rowan Claypool IV was born in Franklin, Kentucky, in 1930. He has served as pastor of Baptist churches, and he currently is rector of St. Luke's Episcopal Church in Birmingham, Alabama. Dr. Claypool received his education at Mars Hill College, Baylor University, the Southern Baptist Theological Seminary, and the Episcopal Theological Seminary of the Southwest. His book credits include *Tracks of a Fellow Struggler, Stages, Opening Blind Eyes,* and *Glad Reunion,* and his Lyman Beecher Lectures on Preaching at Yale University are contained in *The Preaching Event.*

ter on offense and a linebacker on defense. But one night during my senior year, just before the first half ended, I managed to intercept a pass out in the flat and found myself streaking up the sideline with nothing but daylight between me and the goal line. Suddenly, all of my dreams of being a hero were about to come true, and then right in front of the bleachers on our side of the field, for reasons that I still cannot explain, somehow that football got away from me. I can still see the image of that ball dribbling out of my hands and bouncing onto the ground. Back in those days, it was against the rules to pick up a loose ball and run with it. And so to my great humiliation, there in the open field with no opposing player within twenty yards, I had to recover my own fumble, and with that the first half ended! Needless to say, I became the brunt of unmerciful kidding for days to come. I became known as "glue-fingered Claypool," the guy who could not stand a little success but fell apart in the clutch. And while I tried to take all of this ribbing good-naturedly, inside I died a thousand deaths. You see, I did not want to be a clown out on that field, I wanted to be a star! And it was literally years after this episode before I was able to forgive myself for that mistake. I cannot begin to number the times I relived that sequence of events—right up to the awful moment—and then burned with chagrin at being the kind of person who "goofed up a grand moment" and was not able to "pull it off" in the clutch.

And I imagine that every adult among you can reach back into your memory and recall a similar trauma when you ignobly failed and did that which you wish to God you had not done, or failed to do something you wish to God you had. This raises the question: "What do we do with our burden of regret and remorse, with those feelings of self-loathing that so easily grow out of the botches we have made of things in the past?" This is the issue I want us to deal at this moment. I do not think I need to belabor the point that it is a highly significant one indeed.

I have found that truth is sometimes easier to grasp in personal form rather that abstract concept, so let us look at the story of a person who had much to regret in his life and yet somehow was able to handle it so that he grew as a person rather than being diminished because of failure. I am thinking now of the apostle Paul. In our text from the Galatian letter, he makes reference to what was undoubtedly the greatest single anguish of his life: namely, that one point in time when he had actively persecuted and tried to destroy the very church that he was now trying to build up and enlarge. Saul of Tarsus, as he was known as a young man, had been born into a family of fanatical Jewish people, and he was of the temperament to outdo even his peers in the zealousness of his devotion. Saul regarded Jesus of Nazareth as a misguided imposter and turned with rage on that little bank of people who believed Jesus had been raised from the dead and really was the long-awaited Messiah. Saul intended to wipe this sort of heresy off the face of the earth, and was on just such a mission of destruction to Damascus, when something happened that shook him to his very roots. Here was a religious man—someone who was passionately concerned with being obedient to God— discovering that he was in fact working against that one rather than for him! He was knocked to the ground by a great light, and a voice from heaven said: "Saul, Saul, why are you persecuting me? Why are you kicking against the pricks?" It was an ancient way of saying, "Why are you at cross-purposes with reality, swimming against the very stream of God?" What Saul discovered that day was that Jesus of Nazareth was God's Messiah, and all this time he had been exactly a hundred and eighty degrees off in what he was doing with such fanatical zeal! For an intensely religious person, nothing could be much worse than such a discovery, and there was bound to have followed a deluge of shame and guilt and fear at such a monumental mistake against God. Yet, here is the crucial point— the encounter on the road to Damascus did not end Saul's life of effectiveness, but proved a turning point in making him into an even more creative human being. Saul became more of a person, not less of one, as a result of all this, which leads me to want to delve more deeply into his story and see how an experience of failure and regret turned out to be a time of re-birth and rechanneling into greater authenticity and creativity.

As I have pondered this question, I think the answer lies in two important things that Paul discovered on his way to Damascus. First of all, he discovered that there was something bigger than he was in the world, and second, that that something bigger was a reality of grace and mercy and patience and ingenuity. Both of these discoveries, rightly understood, are momentous indeed.

In recognizing that there was something bigger in the world than he was, Paul was drawn out of that preoccupation with himself that is always such a major component of guilt and remorse and regret. Let me confess that this is a relatively new insight to me. In fact, it was not until my year of study in New Orleans that I began to recognize how much egotism is usually present in an experience of guilt. You see, to dwell excessively on what I have done or failed to do, and to make that the predominent focus of attention, is really another form of pride or self-concern. It is a way of saying that my actions are the most important realities in history, a tendency that my therapist aptly described in the phrase "dark grandiosity." This is the truth behind so much of our guilt. The first thing Paul discovered on the way to Damascus applies directly to this. In his great confrontation with reality, Paul and his actions were placed in proper perspective—what he had done was serious, to be sure, but not of an ultimate nature. He was confronted in all his mistaken zeal, but not written off or rejected totally. "Go into Damascus and wait to be told what to do next," said the heavenly voice. Here was the revelation that there was much more at work in history than Paul and his deeds of violence. There was also God, and the one was not only bigger than Paul, but also one of grace and mercy and patience and ingenuity, and this is what got Paul through the trauma of failure and regret. The focus of concern was effectively shifted from himself to this other and to the incredible willingness of the other to keep on working with Paul in spite of his past. He had set himself squarely over against God, and this was taken seriously and confronted directly. But lo and behold, God's goodness proved bigger and more resourceful than Paul's badness, and his willingness not to obliterate Paul but to continue to work with him was the saving difference.

I am convinced that this is the secret for all of us in our struggle with guilt and remorse. The power to forgive ourselves and reach out to a future that is different from the past is not something we have to come up with on our own. *It is given to us,* exactly as our births were given to us, and on the same terms—because of what God is, not what we are. None of us earns our way into this world at birth, nor do we earn our way into the experience of forgiveness. We are given second and third and God-only-knows-how-many chances on the same terms as we got our first chance at life, namely, without our deserving it; and realizing this stupendous fact is what released us from spending all our energies saying "How bad I am!" to the awe and gratitude of saying "How good God is to give me new chances after I have blown my first one!" We cannot go back and undo or redo any of the past, but the significance it has for us can be altered. Focus on the goodness of God can replace a focus on our badness, and that is what opens the way for us to respond as Paul did and begin to build up at the very places where once we tore down. I love the way this ingenious God set Paul to that very task. This is a vivid illustration of the meaning of repentance, or turning around and acting differently in the future than one did in the past. Repentance is not what we do in order to earn forgiveness; it is what we do because we have been forgiven, and serves as an expression of gratitude rather than an effort to earn. This sequence of forgiveness and then repentance, rather than repentance and then forgiveness, is crucial to keep in mind when any attempt at reparation is undertaken.

Once I heard Ernest Campbell tell of a man in his congregation who came to him a week after his mother's funeral in the clutches of overwhelming guilt and remorse. He confessed to Campbell that he had never really had a good relationship with his mother and as a result had not given her the kind of care in her dying days that she deserved. He was feeling very bad about it, but, of course, she was dead, and there was nothing now that he could do. Campbell shared with him the good news of forgiveness—that there was something bigger in the world than he was and that something bigger was a reality of grace and mercy and patience and ingenuity. He invited him to accept the gift of forgiveness—not because he deserved it but because it was God's nature to give it. But then he said, "I know of an older woman in our congregation who has no children and is very concerned about how she is going to negotiate her last days. Not in order to earn God's forgiveness but as a sign of the fact that you have received this gift, I think it would be wonderful if you would start doing for this woman what you would to God you could do for your own mother but now cannot do." The suggestion made sense to the man and he began to do it. It was a way of concretizing the forgiveness he had experienced and of doing the future differently, not in spite of, but actually because of the past.

My conclusion, then, is that the tangible answer to remorse and guilt is never something that we have to do on our own. How could we ever make up for the sins that we have committed? That would be impossible. No, the crucial shift comes in recognizing that there is something bigger than we are in the world and that something bigger is a reality of grace and mercy and patience and ingenuity. It is what God is willing to do with what we have done that is the answer, and again and again with Paul and countless others like him, it is clear that his goodness is bigger than our badness. Our sins and mistakes are taken seriously. Paul was confronted directly and told he was one hundred and eighty degrees off course. But after the confrontation was the work: "Go into Damascus and wait to be told what to do next." Lo and behold, God still had a future for Paul in spite of his past! He had not been overwhelmed or defeated utterly by Paul's misdeeds. Remember, God is bigger than we are and can do incredibly ingenious things with the messes we have made of our lives. He was able to take a persecutor of the church and transform him into its most effective leader. What cannot that kind of merciful ingenuity yet do with any of our lives? That is the note on which I choose to end. To be sure, all of us adults are persons of sorrow, acquainted with guilt. We all have shadows and skeletons in our backgrounds. But listen, there is something bigger in this world than we are, and that something bigger is full of grace and mercy and patience and ingenuity. The moment the focus of your life shifts from your badness to his goodness and the question becomes not "What have I done?" but "What can he do?," release from remorse can happen; miracle of miracles, you can forgive yourself because you are forgiven, accept yourself because you are accepted, and begin to start building up at the very places you once tore down. There is a grace to help in every time of trouble. That grace is the secret to being able to forgive ourselves. Trust it, brothers and sisters; shift the focus of your life from your failure to his gracious ability to bring success out of your failures. That is where the hope is: when the circle of self-concern grows smaller, the circle of divine forgiveness grows larger. Then one can swallow up the other: persecutors become apostles. What cannot such a one do if invited in and given a chance?

37. The Seasons of Life
A. Leonard Griffith

For everything there is a season. . . . — Ecclesiastes 3:1

ONE ADVANTAGE of living in Canada is that we enjoy four distinct seasons, each with its own beauty, and we all have our favorite. We may welcome the spring, when the ice breaks on the rivers and lakes and the sap flows from the trees and the whole earth comes to life again. We may prefer the long, warm, lazy days of summer. Perhaps we like the autumn best, with its vivid colors and the scrunch of fallen leaves beneath our feet. We may even enjoy the winter, when a white blanket of snow covers the earth and sparkles like a thousand gems in the sunlight.

Today I want to speak about the seasons of *life*—its spring, summer, autumn and winter. That's not exactly what the author of Ecclesiastes had in mind when he wrote, "For everything there is a season." By the word *season* he meant *the right time*, as indicated in the verses that follow:

For everything there is a season, and a time for every matter under heaven;
a time to be born, and a time to die;
a time to plant, and a time to pluck up what is planted . . .

Arthur Leonard Griffith was born in 1920 in England. He was educated at Wesley College, Dublin, Ireland, McGill University, and the United Theological College, Montreal, Canada. An ordained minister in the United Church of Canada, he served on the staff at St. Paul's Church in Toronto. His books include *What Is a Christian?* and *From Sunday to Sunday,* his autobiography.

Ecclesiastes is not a cheerful book. In fact, it's really quite cynical; a yawn, a tired sigh from an oriental rocking chair. The writer, who has been around and tried everything, asks the question, "Is life worth living?" and he states a number of convictions that add up to a negative answer. "Emptiness! Emptiness! All is emptiness!" Yes, he was a cynic right enough.

Yet he was also very wise, or else his book would not be included in the Wisdom Writings of the Old Testament; and there are several passages where his wisdom seems to overcome his cynicism. One of them is this familiar passage in the third chapter, that was made into a popular song. The New English Bible translates it,

For everything its season, and for every activity under heaven its time:
a time to be born and a time to die;
a time to plant and a time to uproot;
a time to kill and a time to heal;
a time to pull down and a time to build up;
a time to weep and a time to laugh;
a time for mourning and a time for dancing;
a time to scatter stones and a time to gather them;
a time to embrace and a time to refrain from embracing;
a time to seek and a time to lose;
a time to keep and a time to throw away;
a time to tear and a time to mend;
a time for silence and a time for speech;
a time to love and a time to hate;
a time for war and a time for peace.

On the surface there doesn't seem to be much religion in that passage; it doesn't even mention the name of God. Yet the more deeply we think about it, the more it strengthens our faith in God's providence. The writer is telling us that *God has appointed a season, a right time for every activity in life, and that the way of wisdom is to accept God's schedule and order our lives according to his plan.*

I

That is my proposition, the big truth that I want you to consider today. It suggests that life does have seasons, with values, priorities, attitudes, activities, and lifestyle appropriate to each one. In each stage or period certain needs have to be met, certain tasks fulfilled, certain problems faced. That is how God has ordered our journey from the cradle to the grave. That is the normal process of physical and psychological growth. Our life moves forward and matures like the seasons of the year.

First comes *spring,* that begins with birth and continues through childhood and youth. Our babies are in the early spring, they are like buds on the trees which have not yet begun to open, and they have to be tended carefully. For a long time they will be wholly dependent on their parents. They are scarcely conscious of themselves as individuals. That will come with adolescence, but even then they will still be growing. They may mature in their bodies, but their minds and characters will not be fully formed, and they will need all the understanding and help we can give them. There is wisdom in the words that one adolescent addressed to his parents: "Please don't be impatient. God isn't finished with me yet."

Summer, the longest season, lasts through the middle years of life. That's a time for all sorts of wonderful things—getting married, having babies, building a career. It's also a time when we become tired and anxious as we bear the burden and heat of the day. Someone has said that between the golden years of youth and the golden years of maturity come the nickle-plated years of middle age when we do all the work, make all the decisions, and pay all the taxes. Yet it's still the most productive and satisfying season of life. That's when our education pays off, and the job opportunities open for us, and we make our mark in the world, and our children are the greatest delight. The middle years are like a long summer afternoon.

Autumn, the later middle years that reach into the early part of retirement, should be a time of beauty and leisure.

That's the season when we don't have to be on the make any more, because a new generation has come along to take our place and do our work in the world. That's when we can slow down and relax and begin to reap the harvest of our early planting. Our grandchildren have arrived, and we don't have to bring them up, only enjoy them. I used to tell my family that some year I should like to take a holiday during Indian summer, those warm days in autumn when church life is at its busiest. They always replied, "If you'll just be patient for a few years you can have a holiday every Indian Summer." How right they were!

After autumn comes *winter*. Older people don't go out very much in the winter. If they can't afford Florida they stay indoors and try to keep warm. They are in the winter of life and they can feel it in their bones. The birds have migrated, the leaves are off the trees, the roses buried under the snow, and the whole earth seems dead. Soon they will die, perhaps peacefully, perhaps painfully. They can appreciate Sir Winston Churchill, who in his old age described the winter of life as "the surly advance of decrepitude."

II

Those are the seasons of life as God has planned them; and if we live on the basis of the Bible wisdom we shall be willing to move from one to another, making the adjustment as we do with the seasons of the year. That is God's purpose for us, but unfortunately some people fight against God's purpose. They are not willing to move and mature with the seasons. Biologically they get older but emotionally they lock themselves into a particular season and refuse to advance beyond it.

Some lock themselves into the springtime of childhood. There is something within every person that wishes to remain a child, and the desire may become so dominant that a person refuses to grow up. We see it in a youth who won't leave his parents' home but remains dependent on them well into his adult years. We see it in the professional student who graduates from university and keeps coming back for more and more advanced degrees. We see it in Mr. Skimpole, a character in Charles Dickens' novel, *Bleak House.* Although a grown man with wife and children, he steadfastly refuses to accept responsibility but sponges on his friends and keeps telling everyone, "You can't expect me to manage my affairs. I don't understand business. I'm just a child." Such people are trying to prolong the springtime of life.

Others try to prolong the summer. In their appearance, activities, values, and lifestyle they do everything possible to disguise their approaching age. They are like "mutton dressed up as lamb." Not just female lambs either. Two million Americans had cosmetic surgery in 1985, one-third of whom were middle-aged men, who probably felt that they had to look ten years younger in order to survive in a youth-oriented business world. I knew a man in Britain who proudly told me that his greatest ambition was always to appear and act at least ten years younger than his age. He succeeded remarkably, kept company with younger women, played tennis with younger men, and did a full day's work long after his friends had retired. He died of a heart attack at age seventy.

Such people are fighting against the providence of God. To all of us God gives the precious gift of life and, in each period, the grace to supply our needs. In the first half of life he gives us the ambition, energy, and opportunity to establish ourselves in a career, master a job, build a home, bring up our children, and make ourselves financially secure. In the second half he surrounds us with other values that broaden our minds, uplift our spirits and bring into operation the talents, interests, and friendships that we may have neglected in our early struggle to succeed. Each half of life has its appropriate psychology; and we cannot carry the psychology of the first half into the second, or we shall become boring, stereotyped, and neurotic. In God's providence each season of life has its own challenge and opportunity; and if we live on the basis of the Bible wisdom we shall accept that arrangement and be willing to move forward and mature from one season to another.

III

Also we shall welcome the opportunities and meet the challenges of the season in which we are living right now. That seems obvious enough, yet two things prevent us from doing it. One of them, as we have already seen, is the temptation to live in the past. Looking back over our lives, we can see that some seasons were more enjoyable, fulfilling, and productive than others; and we are tempted to take those good years and frame them and put them on display in the picture gallery of our thoughts and conversation.

To give a personal example, those of us who served the Canadian church during the post-war "boom" of the forties and fifties would be tempted to look back and say that those were our best years in terms of opportunity, influence, and personal fulfilment. The church was very popular at that time. Everyone went to church or at least supported it from the outside. It was a good time to be a pastor; in fact, if things had been any better they would have been sinful. I remember saying to my wife, after I had preached to a Sunday *evening* congregation of a thousand people, "These are our best years. Let's enjoy them, because we may never see anything like them again." I was right. Those were exciting years for the Canadian church, and we have been trying to recapture their glories ever since. If we keep looking back, however, we shall be turned into a pillar of salt. Whatever the main business of our lives, our best years are never in the past, they are right now; and we must resist the temptation to live in the past or we shall miss the challenge and opportunity of the present.

Also we must resist the temptation to live in the future. There is a negative way of looking at the future which is like looking through binoculars at a distant scene and becoming so enamored of it that we miss the beautiful scenery all around us. An eminent psychologist asked three thousand persons the question, "What are you living for?" He was shocked to find 90 percent simply putting up with the present while they waited for the future, waited for something to happen—for marriage, for a promotion, for the children to grow up and leave home, for someone to die, for retirement—waited for some future season while the present season slipped by unnoticed.

Yet only the present season has been given to us. Wherever we are right now, in whatever season we are living, God has surrounded us with opportunities, challenges, and resources that we have never seen before and may never see again. So the way of wisdom is not to live in the past or wait for the future but to cast down our buckets where we are. That picturesque phrase comes from the story of a sailing ship that was crippled off the coast of South America. Sighting a friendly vessel, it sent up the signal, "Water! Water! We die of thirst!" The answer came back, "Cast down your bucket, where you are." The captain of the distressed vessel thought there must be a mistake, so he repeated the signal and received the same answer. He didn't know that they were just then crossing the Amazon ocean current and that instead of being in salt water they were actually sailing in fresh water. Finally he did what he was told, cast down his bucket, and it came up with fresh, sparkling water from the mouth of the Amazon River. A parable of life!

IV

There is, however, a positive way of looking at the future, and that's one more thing we shall do if we live on the basis of the Bible wisdom. As Christians we shall face the future with a hope that grows out of our faith in the providence and purpose of God revealed in Jesus Christ.

One reason many people refuse to go forward with the seasons is that they are afraid of what lies ahead. Things have been so bad for them in the past that they fear the future can only get worse. Or they are having such a good time right now that they fear the bubble will burst. So they begrudge the passing of time, they try to prolong the present, they wish they could be like Joshua, who stopped the sun in its course. They don't want to grow old and they do everything possible to disguise it. Above all, they don't want to die.

Yet, as the Bible says, there is a time to grow old and die. That's one of the seasons of our life as God has created it. A very old man told me about taking a great-grandchild on his knee. The little fellow said, "Grandpa, I know why you are so old. You just won't die." There is some truth in that. Many older people cling to their adult life because they are not able to see beyond it. For them the approaching winter means the end of life, and they take little comfort in the words of the poet, "If winter comes, can spring be far behind?" Yet the poet spoke the truth if God is true and Jesus is true and the wisdom of the Bible is true. Dietrich Bonhoeffer believed it, martyred in the summer of his life. As the Nazis led him out of the prison camp to be executed, he was heard to say, "This is the end. For me the beginning of life."

That is our Christian hope and it is expressed in an old Dutch fable that I love to tell to children. There were three tulip bulbs named *No, Maybe* and *Yes.* They lived at the bottom of a bulb tin, content to be round and fat and clothed in their silky brown garments. When autumn came, they fell to discussing the destiny of tulip bulbs. *No* said, "I don't think there is any other life for tulip bulbs. Besides, I am satisfied with things as they are." So he rolled over in the corner to sleep the winter away. *Maybe* said, "I am not satisfied with things as they are. I feel that there is a better life than the life I now have. I feel something within me that I must achieve and I believe that I can achieve it." So he squeezed himself and squeezed himself and ended up in a fit of frustration. Then *Yes* said, "I have been told that we can do nothing of ourselves but that the good Lord will fulfill our destiny if we put ourselves in his power." So one day a hand reached down into the bin groping for tulip bulbs. *Yes* gave himself to the hand and was buried in the earth throughout the long winter months. Meanwhile *No* and *Maybe* shrivelled away to nothing, but when spring came, *Yes* burst forth with all the richness and loveliness of new life.

That is our Christian hope, and we celebrate it in the holy

season of Easter which for us comes providentially in the springtime. Easter promises that beyond the winter of this life there is a springtime in eternity. It promises that we have a future, always a future, no matter how old we are. Therefore we shall be willing to move forward with the seasons, making the most of the present but looking forward to the future with hope.

38. Reflections on a Wedding
Roger Lovette

Scripture: Genesis 2:18

YESTERDAY I did something that I have not done in all my days as a minister. Early, before my daughter's wedding began, I slipped into the balcony of the church and listened to the gorgeous Bach chorales being played on the organ. It was a holy moment to see members of this church file in and take their places for our daughter's wedding. I listened to the music fill the church as the ushers quietly walked down the aisle and lit the candles until, finally, the sanctuary was bathed in candlelight. And then, about five minutes before the hour, with a lump in my throat, I made my way back to where my pulpit robe was waiting.

Our first child was getting married and leaving home. Though she had been away at school for five years, this leaving was different. And those of you who have been through the wedding ordeal know all that is involved: the energy, the details, the expense, and the time. Because I have had little else on my mind for the last few weeks, I want to share with you some of my reflections on a wedding.

After the chiming of the hour I came out with my son-in-

Lawrence Roger Lovette was born in 1935 in Columbus, Georgia. He received his education at Samford University, the Southern Baptist Theological Seminary, and Lexington Theological Seminary. Dr. Lovette is senior minister of the First Baptist Church in Clemson, South Carolina. His writings include four books as well as numerous articles in a variety of periodicals.

law-to-be and his best man. The bridal party took their places and finally the music stopped. The first thing I was conscious of was all the faces. Nervously, I opened the old book and began to intone those most solemn of words: "Dearly beloved, we are gathered together. . . ." This was most appropriate.

Marriage is a communal act. It is a gathering of people from all over. The thing that has moved and humbled me in this whole experience is the number of people from whom we have heard. Our daughter received a present from the nurse that helped deliver her in the hospital. She decorated and framed our daughter's wedding invitation and sent it back to her as a gift. In the back of the frame she included a "To Whom This May Concern" letter. The letter recalled that night that Leslie was born and her recollections of the excitement of the new mother and father. Now in her sixties with many problems of her own, that nurse remembered. Two carloads came four hundred miles from a church we served eighteen years ago, bringing presents and memories. Yesterday there was a young lady here with her own family from Washington, D.C. As a college student she used to baby-sit with Leslie. Our son was a ringbearer in her wedding. And as long as I live I do not think I will forget how beautifully this congregation sang Leslie's favorite hymn, "All Creatures of our God and King." Of all the gifts that the bride and groom received, this may have been the best of all.

I would remind you that at these special moments of intersection it matters terribly that we are surrounded. It means a great deal to the family when people take the time and trouble to come together and share in our joy. This is the meaning of the biblical word *fellowship*. We come together to undergird these young people and to encourage their families in this most difficult of transitions.

I blinked back the tears as I looked out at row after row of the beloved community. And it hit me like a thunderbolt: we need each other. I have seen fellowship happen in this special place so many times through the years: funerals, weddings, anniversary celebrations, and communion times. Yesterday you came to stand with us and this is a very real part of marriage. Standing by the family and cheering a young couple on is one of the great gifts that we can give each other.

Marriage is also a sacred occasion. Most of our weddings are held in church, but all weddings are primarily religious occasions. We open the sacred book. We read Scriptures. We sing hymns. We intone the Lord's Prayer and ask God's blessing on what we are about to do.

So much in our culture negates the spiritual dimension of marriage. Brides and their mothers can get so caught up in the trappings that they miss the real occasion. And we moderns love our distractions that hold the holy at arm's length.

Perhaps this is why we have the theme from *The Godfather* used at weddings. If this is a sacred occasion, then surely we can choose something more worshipful than the theme from *Ice Castles*.

Elton Trueblood reminds us that in the convenantal relationship only a strong moral sense can succeed. Physical attractiveness is not enough. He reminds us that in that part of the country that has the highest concentration of physical beauty we find the most marriage failure.[1] The old Hollywood song "Love Will Keep Us Together" is not glue enough.

We believe that marriage is a sacrament. This means that the grace of God shines through what happens when a young man and a young woman stand seriously at the altar. Meaning and purpose in life are found in such an act.

And so we ask for God's blessing. We turn to an old ceremonythat dates back at least to 1559 in Salisbury, England. We lean on symbols: a veil, a white dress, flowers, candlelight, special places for family members, rings, kisses, rice, and festivity.

I always tell young couples about to be married that a strong faith will keep them honest with each other. True faith presents us with a clear view of reality. Marriage is a sacred occasion. What happens at this altar has ultimate consequences.

Marriage is a family time. It is not happenstance that there are special places reserved for the parents of the bride and groom and other members of the family. And in the wedding party yesterday my eighteen-year-old son came down the aisle with his sister on his arm. And we found ourselves surrounded by cousins as bridesmaids and ushers. And from all over, the church was filled with relatives we had not seen in years. This is as it should be.

The father of the bride usually accompanies his daughter. This is our way of saying: we support you in this union. We stand by you and we love you. We will do all in our power to make this marriage work.

The father of the bride usually speaks for both families. He does not give the bride away. She does not belong to him. Our children are not our own, but are gifts from God that make our homes special. But families can help or they can hurt. Small wonder there are special places in the wedding party for relatives.

Marriage is the saying of vows. As we move through the ceremony we know that the most important part of the service is when the couple turns to face each other. This is the heart of the service. "I John, take thee, Mary, to be my wedded wife, to have and to hold from this day forward, for better or for worse, for richer or for poorer, in sickness and in health, to love and to cherish, till death us do part, according to God's holy ordinance; and, thereto, I give thee my faith."

We are known by the vows we live by and the pledges we make. Promise-keeping has taken a beating in our time. Loyalty is up for grabs. People shed commitments and loyalties as often as they change clothes. Everything is disposable and the highways are cluttered with the debris it brings.

The vows we keep are the steel that holds the structure of our lives in place. Carl Sandburg captured this in his autobiographical novel, *Always the Young Strangers.* This is the story of Sandburg's own parents who came to this country as immigrants from Sweden. It is a tale of hard work and rugged existence and fidelity always. Sandburg describes how his mother felt about the vows she had made long ago:

Mama's wedding ring was never lost—was
always on that finger as placed there with
pledges years ago. It was a sign and seal of
something that ran deep and held fast between
the two of them. . . . How they happened to
meet I heard only from my mother. . . . A smile
spread over her face half-bashful and a bright
light came to her blue eyes as she said, "I saw it
was my chance." She was saying this at least
twenty years after the wedding and there had
been hard work always, tough luck at times,
seven children of whom two had died on the
same day—and she had not one regret that she
had jumped at her "chance" when she saw it.[2]

The heart of the wedding is the saying of the vows.

Marriage is an emotional time. Small wonder there are so
many tears at weddings. There are powerful emotions swirl-
ing in the church on any wedding day. Anne Morrow Lind-
berg has captured these feelings in her little book, *Dearly
Beloved.* She breaks down each part of the wedding service and
then pauses to let us see what is going on in the minds of those
who came. The words spoken in the wedding ceremony have a
way of triggering a multitude of feelings from us all.

We all need to be especially sensitive to the parents in such a
time. This is a life-changing time for any family. Things will be
forever different. Children suddenly are adults. We find ourselves getting older. Carlyle Marney expressed it well: "Yesterday she cut her first tooth, today she cut a twelve-year molar,
tomorrow you are ordering an upper plate for yourself."[3]

There is grief in all of this. The colors of our emotions are
mixed in such moments. We are happy and we are sad. Life is
changing. A chapter is closing. Things will be different. No
wonder we bring hankies to weddings.

Marriage is also a hopeful time. A new generation is beginning. Hopefully, there will be grandchildren. And we pray
that these two that stand at the altar with stars in their eyes will

have it better in every way than we had it. We hope that some of the things we have tried to teach them stick. We hope they have learned to love God and find enough faith of their own to make it through whatever it is they will face. We hope, too, that the world will be better because they have lived and loved each other. So this is a hopeful time.

David Mace has said that marriage is like a young couple who have the great ambition to have a beautiful garden of their own. They see it as a place of peace and serenity. They know there will be tall trees and beautiful flowers and lush green lawns and a lake. And the parents, understanding this dream, make it possible for the young couple to have that garden. They give them a piece of vacant land and the title has the couple's name on it.

Mace says that the hope of every parent is that the young couple will not take two deck chairs, place them in the middle of the land and sit down and wait for the garden to happen. Life does not work that way. The young man and woman will have to do a lot of learning. They will discover some things about soil chemistry and what kinds of plants will grow best. They will study the art of arranging and planting. In time, they will discover new skills. And if they devote time and hard work, one day their dream will begin to come true.

Yesterday, finally, after great struggle on my part, the wedding was over. The recessional sounded and the bride and groom made their way out of the candle-lit church into the dazzling sunlight of a different world. I remembered the words I had read earlier from my black book: "It is not good for man to be alone. . . . I will give him a helpmeet."

NOTES

1. Elton Trueblood, *The Common Ventures of Life* (New York: Harper & Row, 1949), p. 59.

2. Carl Sandburg, *Always the Young Strangers* (New York: Harcourt, Brace and Company, Inc., 1952).

3. Carlyle Marney, *Dangerous Fathers, Problem Mothers and Terrible Teens* (Nashville: Abingdon, 1958), p. 14.

39. Of Children and Streets and the Kingdom

Elizabeth Achtemeier

Old Testament Lesson: Zechariah 8:1–8
New Testament Lesson: Matthew 18:1–4

"THY KINGDOM COME, thy will be done, on earth as it is in heaven." We pray every Sunday for God to bring in the Kingdom of Heaven, but I wonder if we really want it. Do we really want the Kingdom of God to come? That is the question. Certainly every time we celebrate the Lord's Supper, we look forward to the coming of that kingdom. In the words of Paul, as often as we eat the bread and drink the cup, we proclaim the Lord's death *Until he comes.* Indeed, the Lord's Supper is understood in the Christian church as a foretaste of that final, messianic banquet in the new age, when God's kingdom will have come in its fullness and God's work with his world will have been brought to completion. But it probably is a real question whether any of us wants to attend that final banquet. At least it is a question whether we want to attend it soon. Jesus taught, in his parables, that the Kingdom of God was like a

---

Elizabeth Rice Achtemeier was born in 1926 in Bartlesville, Oklahoma. She was educated at Stanford University, Union Theological Seminary in New York, and Columbia University, where she received her doctorate. A Presbyterian, Dr. Achtemeier has served as adjunct professor of Bible and homiletics at Union Theological Seminary in Virginia since 1973. She is the author of several books on preaching, including *Creative Preaching, Preaching as Theology and Art,* and, most recently, *Preaching About Family Relationships.*

pearl of great price, or like a treasure uncovered in a field, that was so valuable and so desirable that men were willing to sell everything they had in order to obtain it, but few of us would be willing to make that sacrifice. We are not all that sure that we want the Kingdom of God to come. And the reasons for that are very clear.

In the first place, we are a very comfortable people. We like our life as it is. Despite all the problems that we Americans have with our marriages or money or jobs or families, we really are fairly contented. Polls have occasionally been taken of the American public, in which it has been repeatedly shown that some 60 to 75 percent of us are satisfied with our lives. Preachers, and indeed our writers and artists, are accustomed to painting very gloomy pictures of us. For example, Nathan Scott has said that "At the center of our literature is a narrative of estrangement and alienation: the story told is a tale of our abandonment in some blind lobby, or corridor of time. And in that dark, no thread." But I am not sure such literature is an accurate portrayal of our everyday lives. After all, most of us have families and friends whom we enjoy and jobs that keep us busy and happy and a religious faith that sustains us in the rougher moments. And while we may pray every Sunday for the Kingdom of God to come, we probably would add, "but not yet." "Thy kingdom come, O Lord, but maybe not just now."

Besides, we might well ask, in the second place, have we not achieved here in the United States a way of living that is just about as close to heaven on earth as we are likely to get? For the first time in history, those of us in the Western world have built societies in which most human beings no longer have to worry about the basic necessities of life. Ever since the human race began, its societies have been concerned about one thing—how to stay alive: about where the next meal is coming from, about providing shelter to live in, about having clothes enough to protect themselves against the elements.

Certainly that was true of the inhabitants of Jerusalem, who listened to Zechariah's preaching about the kingdom in gees who had managed to survive the Babylonian destruction of their country in 587 B.C. Some of them had spent years of exile in Babylonia and then had been allowed to return to Palestine. Others, who were among the poorer classes, had been allowed to remain in Palestine all along, and they had simply scraped out a living in that devastated land as best they could. But now, in the year 518 B.C., when this passage in Zechariah was written, all of the inhabitants of Jerusalem were in desperate straits. Their temple was still a burned-out ruin. Their city walls were nothing but rubble. Drought and blight withered their crops, and hunger was rampant. Inflation, caused by a shortage of goods, ate up their meager earnings. They no longer even had a king or a national government. They were just a tiny, impoverished subprovince in the vast Persian Empire. Their life was a matter of grubbing for the basic necessities of life, so it is no wonder that they heard Zechariah gladly when he preached this passage to them about the coming of the Kingdom of God. They needed something better—and that is still true for most of the peoples on this earth. Most peoples need something better, because they still have to worry about simply managing to exist.

But that is no longer true for most of us in the U.S. We no longer worry about getting enough to eat. On the contrary, we worry about getting too fat. We even worry about our dogs and cats getting too fat, so we put them on diets too. We are so free of anxiety about the basic necessities of life that we can just worry about which computer system to buy, or about how many we should plan on for the party Friday night, or about which fast-food chain puts the most beef in its hamburgers. We have pretty well got it made, we think, so who wants to leave all that for some unknown realm called the Kingdom of God? Who wants to give up the good life in America for some ethereal realm in the sky?

And perhaps that is the third reason we do not really want the Kingdom of God to come—because we think of it as some vague realm way off in heaven somewhere, separated from all the good things that we so enjoy in this life.

We have very strange conceptions of the Kingdom of God.

Usually we think of it as a place in heaven where we will go
after we die. And our pictures of the kingdom have been very
much influenced by all those fanciful stories of pearly gates
and angels flying about. We have inherited those pictures
from a hundred different sources: from such literature as *Pilgrim's Progress*, from the art of Reubens and Michelangelo;
from Negro spirituals that sing of golden slippers walking the
golden streets, and from the imagery and symbolism of the Bible itself. We have even put all those pictures into our hymns:
"Holy, holy, holy," runs the second verse of the well-known
hymn, "all the saints adore thee / Casting down their golden
crowns around the glassy sea / Cherubim and seraphim falling
down before thee / Who were, and art, and evermore shalt
be." None of that makes very much sense to us, nor does it
appear too appealing. And so we may pray in the Lord's prayer for God's Kingdom to come, we are not sure we want it.
Seek ye first the kingdom of earth, is our motto, and let heaven take care of itself.

Now certainly, in the Bible, there is a reality to heaven. It is
the dwelling place of God the Father, Son, and Holy Spirit.
And the Bible simply strains at the limits of human language to
describe that dwelling place. But alongside that, our Old Testament lesson from the prophet Zechariah gives us another,
different, supplementary picture of the Kingdom of God. And
it is a picture that participates very much in the realities of this
earth. Let me read it to you again:

> Thus says the Lord: I will return to Zion, and
> will dwell in the midst of Jerusalem, and
> Jerusalem shall be called the faithful city
> ....Old men and old women shall again sit in
> the streets of Jerusalem, each with staff in hand
> for very age. And the streets of the city shall be
> full of boys and girls playing in the squares.

What is the Kingdom of God, according to the prophet
Zechariah? It is a public park! It is a park where old people are
no longer cold and lonely and ill and senile, but participants in

a community. It is a public park where the elderly can sit together and bask in the sun, and talk and laugh over the good old days in full vigor and clear mind and satisfaction of life.

The Kingdom of God is a public park where little children can run and play in its squares, in safety and fun and delight. It is a place where no pervert is waiting to lure one of them away with offers of candy; where no drug pusher is lurking to tempt the older children to try a brightly colored pill. It is a place where no child is abused or unwanted or malnourished, and where there is not even a bully among the group, shoving and taunting the littler ones until they break into tears. The Kingdom of God, says Zechariah, is a public park where the streets are safe for children.

You see, the Kingdom of God, according to the Bible, is not some never-never land in the sweet by-and-by. Most of the Bible really is not very interested in heaven. No, the Kingdom of God is life on this earth—life transformed to accord with the will and purpose of a loving God. The Lord's Prayer does not say, "Thy kingdom come in heaven." It says, "Thy kingdom come on earth, even as it is in heaven." God works to accomplish his will for the earth. He works to fulfill his purpose and intention for human life in the world here and now. He presses on toward the time when this solid, everyday, common land of ours will become the good place that he intended in the beginning for it to be.

And in the light of all that, it is very clear that we do not yet have it made, that we are not yet living in the Kingdom of God—not even here in the U.S.A. For in the Kingdom of God, our streets will be safe for our children. And right now, they are certainly far from being fit places for our little ones. Few parents would send their child into any one of our parks now to play unaccompanied, because our parks are not fit for children. On the streets of Los Angeles, children as young as ten or eleven sell themselves as prostitutes. And as for the streets of the world—well, children scrounge for garbage in the streets of Calcutta and Saigon. Children in northern Ethiopia are dying by the hundreds every day. Children in El Salvador fall victim, with their parents, to the murderous sweeps of death squads.

And since that be true, can we not and must we not daily, earnestly pray, "Thy kingdom come, thy will be done, on earth as it is in heaven"? O Lord, bring in the time when our streets will be fit for our children! For if that time is not coming, then there really is not much point to all that you and I are doing, is there? If Zechariah's vision is not the goal of human history, then there is no purpose to our sojourn on this globe.

The Kingdom of God—a place where little children can play— yes, that is very much a goal for which we pray and yearn and struggle.

Zechariah further tells us in our Old Testament lesson that the kingdom will not have come until our children are also fit for our streets. And that means that you and I have work to do. Now do not misunderstand me. Certainly we human beings, by our own efforts, cannot create the kingdom. Only God can work such a radical transformation of society. But having been given Zechariah's vision of what God's final purpose is for this planet of ours, we can at least say yes to that purpose of good and try to live our lives in accordance with it. And that means we have work to do as parents and grandparents, as teachers and examples and leaders. It is not enough that we accept God's purpose by working in society to make our streets fit for children; we also have to work in our homes and schools and churches to raise children who are fit for our streets.

I shall never forget the story of the group of civic-minded club members who met one day with the juvenile court judge to ask him what the most important thing was that they could do to improve their community. The judge replied in six simple words: "Be at home for your children." Now that is not to disparage all the efforts such groups make to improve conditions in our communities—those efforts must be made and we are deeply indebted to our volunteers. It also is not to ignore the fact that we all have jobs we have to attend to. But is it to emphasize that question that we constantly should be asking ourselves: are we raising children who are fit for our streets?

A child who has not been taught right from wrong is not fit to be loosed on society. A child who has had no discipline is a child without limits on her selfishness. A child who has not been loved and encouraged and praised and hugged is a child who can never love others. And yes, a child who has not been taught that there is a sovereign God to whom he is responsible is a child who will never use his God-given talents wisely and who therefore will have no purpose and meaning for his life. Are we raising children who can contribute to their fellow human beings, who know how to love God and neighbor? Or are we perpetuating the evils of life in the offspring entrusted to us? Those are the questions we always must ask. Are we raising children who are fit to receive the Kingdom of God?

Maybe we can raise such children, good Christians, only if we ourselves are fit. Maybe our children will be ready for the kingdom only if we ourselves, as parents and grandparents and leaders and citizens, are also ready for it.

Our Lord came preaching the Kingdom of God, the New Testament tells us, and in parable after parable he instructed us how to become citizens of it. We cannot earn our way into the Kingdom of God, he said, by our own good deeds and our own fine works. For the kingdom is simply a gift given to all workers, equally, in the vineyard. Nor can we buy our way into God's peaceable realm, no matter how much our liquid capital. We may be able to buy the best clothes and sirloin steak and even a summer place. We may be able to purchase the latest technology and support the strongest military. But we cannot buy that Kingdom of God that Zechariah pictures, with its peace and contentment, its secure joy, and its happy elders and children. Indeed, taught Jesus, it is very hard for a rich person to enter the Kingdom of God at all; for you see, rich people tend to depend on themselves and their wealth, when what we have to do to be citizens of the kingdom—whether we be rich or poor or middle-class—is to depend solely on God and his working in our lives. We have to trust him.

And so it finally comes down, it seems, to that story we

heard for our New Testament lesson, that story in which Jesus took that little child and set him in the midst as an example. It finally comes down to humbly depending on our God as a child depends on his father. For in the Kingdom of God, God is truly king. He rules. He orders life. His will is done. And until we stop trying to be our own gods and goddesses; until we cease making decisions apart from his will given us in the Scriptures; until we stop thinking that anything goes and start asking what God wants; until we quit relying on our own petty strength to live righteous and meaningful and decent lives in this world, we will never be ready to live in the Kingdom of God and neither will our children. It is no wonder that Zechariah can picture that happy public park in his prophecy, because the happiness in that park depends on something else— it depends on the fact that God dwells in the midst of the city and orders and rules its life.

And so you see, if our children are to be fit for the streets of any city, they have to be raised by parents and adults who depend on the will and power of God. They have to be raised by adults who themselves have become humble, as a little child is humble. They have to be guided by parents who can truly pray, "Our Father . . . *thy* kingdom come, *thy* will be done, on earth as it is in heaven."

But if we can truly pray that prayer, good Christians, if we can want God's will for our lives and for the lives of our children, with all hearts and minds and strength, then maybe we and our children will be ready to receive our King and his kingdom that is coming. For the kingdom comes, friends, it surely comes. Make no mistake about it.

It began to come that night when that one Child, who is fit for all streets, in all places and all times, was born in the city of Bethlehem. It began when God himself, incarnate in that child, drew near to us and took up his dwelling in our midst, in fulfillment of Zechariah's promise. It began when that one Child, grown up, died on a cross and was raised by his Father and became the victor over all the evil and violence, all the ugliness and death that haunt our communities. And so we know in Jesus Christ that Zechariah's promise will finally be fully fulfilled, and that our city, and the cities of the world, will become faithful cities. God will dwell in the midst of us, as our Ruler and Father. And old men and old women shall again sit in the park, each with staff in hand for very age. And the streets of our city shall be full of boys and girls, playing in the squares.

O Lord, thy kingdom come—yea, quickly come—on earth as it is in heaven. Amen.

40. Remember Not . . . Remember Me

William H. Willimon

> Remember not the sins of my youth, or my transgressions; according to thy steadfast love remember me, for thy goodness' sake, O Lord!—Psalm 25

AS I WRESTLE with what to say to you each Sunday, only rarely does some word, some phrase leap from the biblical text, grab me by the throat, and demand to be preached. In looking over the assigned lessons for this Sunday, nothing accosted me until, glancing over the psalm for the day, I read this phrase: "Remember not the sins of my youth, or my transgressions; according to thy steadfast love remember me. . . . "

I was hooked. It's too good a text to let pass in a university chapel. "Remember not the sins of my youth." What an evocative phrase! "Remember not the sins of my youth." What are these "sins of youth" for which the psalmist begs divine amnesia?

Sins of my youth! I see a smoke-filled, sleazy dive known as "Sam's Bar and Grill." All-night binges followed by aching

---

William H. Willimon was born in 1946 in Greenville, South Carolina. He is a graduate of Wofford College and Yale Divinity School and received his doctorate at Emory University. Dr. Willimon, a Methodist, is minister to the University and professor of the practice of Christian ministry at Duke University in Durham, North Carolina. He is the author of twenty-six books, including *Sighing for Eden* and *What's Right with the Church,* and is an editor-at-large for *The Christian Century.*

head. Road trips, descents into the hell of God-knows-where. *Animal House* remade in Durham. Encounters in back seats of Chevrolets. At about the age of a Duke sophomore, Saint Augustine, who spent the rest of his life repaying God for debts incurred during youthful degredation, prayed, "O Lord, make me chaste, but not yet!" For this prayer he became patron saint of college students. Sins of youth!

Every year, in the Chapel Choir's annual presentation of *Messiah,* there is that time when the little boy steps forward and sings in soprano about corruption. "He suffered not corruption. He suffered not corruption." Corruption? What right has an eleven-year-old to sing of corruption? Does he know of such a thing? "Come back when you're a sophomore at Duke," I tell him, "and you can sing of corruption with conviction."

Sins of my youth! Speaking at a little college in Iowa, located in a town so small that everything closed down by sunset, "What on earth do students do here for entertainment?" I wondered aloud. My host warned, "Oh preacher, don't ask!"

Every person over ten or twelve has some secret room somewhere, or a trunk hidden away in the attic, a closed casket buried deep in the basement of the soul, closed, dusty, cluttered with dark moments, memories we would as soon forget. And the older you get the more memory you try to put in that room, that trunk, that grave; the older you grow, the more you have to forget. What is remorse but bitter memory? What is guilt but accusing memory?

In my counseling with people, the most frequent sort of suffering I encounter is suffering brought on by memory. What is this nervousness, this sleeplessness, nail biting, tossing and turning, drug taking except a result of the feelings of fear, suspicion, anxiety resulting from memory too painful to bear? We fill our rooms with the trophies, diplomas, rings, photographs, and blue ribbons of good memories. But deeply hidden in the center of our being is where we stuff the memories too painful to remember.

Our first response to undesirable memories is to try to forget them. "Let's agree to forget about it. Let's both act as if this just never happened."

"Why dwell on the past? What's done is done. Let's talk about something more pleasant."

Remember not the sins of my youth. But bad memory unremembered, pushed back into the secret place of ourselves, can do much harm. The unconscious has no digestive tract. It's not as if we can just swallow hard and have our painful past pass from our consciousness and be done with it. We've tried to do that as a nation about past national traumas. We've tried to do it as individuals. When we try to forget the painful memories, we become strangers to ourselves, having cut down our history to pleasant, comfortable size, the stuff of our daydreams rather than our nightmares. Burying our past, says Henri Nouwen, is turning our back on our best teacher.

We wish that our past were over and done with, but it's not done with us, not yet. We're not the escape artists that we wish we were. We chatter, make jokes, turn on the radio, take a drink, try to live only for today. But then there's that face, the casual gesture, the wisp of an old tune, and we remember.

We would to God that we could forget.

A while back I was accosted by an alumnus of my college. We were students together there. Knowing that I was now a trustee of the place he said, "Today's students are irresponsible and a disgrace. Are you aware of what is going on in the dorms at our college? You trustees should tighten the rules, stick by your guns, make them shape up or ship out."

Unfortunately for him, my memory of him had not been dulled by the years. Apparently, I remember his student days better than he. "Tighten the rules? Shape up or ship out? As I recall, when we were students, there were rather rigid rules against dorm visitation by members of the opposite sex."

"Right," he said. "And those rules ought to still be in force."

"But aren't you glad they were not enforced on a certain night in early April 1967, I believe? Or was it April of 1968? When a certain person smuggled in a certain other person of the opposite. . . ."

He wished to God that I had forgot.

In seminary, it never failed. The chief radical on our floor, the person who was always ranting and raving about "rabid fundamentalists" or "stupid conservatives" was himself, almost without fail, a former fundamentalist. He was ranting and raving against his own past, wishing to God to be over and done with his own religious background.

At my high school reunion, with a band belting out oldies but goodies in the background, a former classmate asked, "You weren't always planning on being a preacher, were you? You weren't thinking about that when we were in high school, were you?"

"No," I said, "I wasn't."

"Good," she said. "That at least makes me feel better."

Remember not the sins of my youth.

Remember not, not just the things we did on Saturday night, but also what we did all week. The way we treated our parents. The people, people whose names we can't even recall, whom we hurt in thought, word, and deed; by things done and left undone. Dare we to remember even for a moment, and admit that the ancient, honest words of confession are right? "We have followed too much the desires and devices of our own hearts. There is no health in us. We are not worthy to be called thy children."

We wish to God we could forget.

And the wishing to forget is not over and done with when you're twenty-one. You've just begun to want to forget. If children must yearn for their parents' forgiveness and forgetfulness, how much more ought we parents to seek the forgiveness of our children. Someday every parent looks at his or her grown children and thinks not, "Look at all I have done for them," but "Look at all I have done *to* them." How can there ever be enough forgetfulness to go around?

A student said of his younger sister, in her second year of psychotherapy, chemically dependent, in misery, "If she could only learn to forgive our parents for what they did or didn't do to her. If she could only learn to forgive herself for what she did or didn't do to them." He hoped that the therapist could help her to remember and then to forget.

And if we yearn for the forgetfulness of other people, our parents, our children, how much more ought we to beg for the forgetfulness of God. As another psalm asks, "O Lord, if thou should count our iniquities, Lord, who could stand?"

If God is omniscient, omnipresent, all-knowing, and all-wise, think of the pain God suffers because of us. At least we are human. We are prone to let some things pass. Eventually, many of our wounds heal. Amnesia sets in, and we achieve relative peace. I can't even remember what I had for lunch yesterday, much less whom I offended. But God? If God remembers everything, God must suffer terribly. How can God endure the silence of the universe if God remembers, as vividly as if yesterday, the cries of Hiroshima, Auschwitz, the Battle of Hastings, Waterloo, and last moment's unkind thought or deed of meanness?

Does God have the alleged memory of an elephant? "Smith? Is that E. Smith? Yes, let's see. Gabriel, bring me the file on E. Smith." Lord, who could stand?

Jesus and the woman at the well: she says, "My husband," and Jesus, with divine memory, reminds her, "You've had five husbands, and the man you're living with now, as I recall, is not your husband." She runs to her friends crying, "Come see a man who told me everything I ever did."

So the psalmist cries, "Remember not the sins of my youth, or my transgressions." Forget it. We wish to God that God could forget.

Some day each of us stands before our father, our mother, and looks into their eyes, and sees reflected back our youth, the demands we made, the words we spoke, the ways we disappointed and hurt without even trying, and we silently ask for their forgiveness, their forgetfulness.

Some day, each of us will ask the same forgetfulness of God. Remember not. Will God forget?

Observe our delight in remembering, recalling, recollecting someone else's sordid past. "Smith, is that Smith the banker? Or is that Smith the—if memory serves me—Smith the philanderer?"

"Citizen of the year? Well, I'm not so old that I don't remember the time there was that trouble with the IRS."

We delight in remembering the sins of the youth, middle age, and any other age because our remembrance is a way of putting and keeping others in their place. Pinning them down. Oh, they may try to begin again, start over, make a go of it, but they can never break out of our remembrance, always enslaved. "Joe Smith? Yes, he's the one who, back in 1958, fell from grace."

One day Thomas Aquinas was lecturing to his students on the omnipotence of God. God is all-powerful, all-knowing. "Is there any way in which God is limited?" a student asked the learned Aquinas.

"Yes," he replied. A shocked hush fell upon the classroom. "Yes. God has his limits. Even God almighty cannot make the past not to have been."

Even God almighty cannot wipe out our past. What's done is done. What's done is remembered and what's remembered, even the sins of our long past youth, are forever. Trapped, desolate, doomed to bear this burden forever, we are.

I'll tell you who your real friends are: a friend is someone who knows you, remembers you perhaps better than you know yourself, *but who doesn't remember.* Friends are those who discreetly forget, before whom certain things don't have to be dredged up, recollected. For the sake of love, they forget. A friend is someone who forgets what you've *done* in order never to forget who you *are.*

Remember not the sins of my youth. Remember me. Isn't that what each of us wants from God? That God will love us enough to forget what we have done and left undone, in thought, word, and deed, in order that God might remember us. In scripture, such divine forgetfulness is called *forgiveness.* On our knees, with outstretched hands, that's the mercy for which we beg, the mercy that God will forget in order to remember. "Smith? Is that E. Smith? Gabriel, forget the file. I remember you. I remember you."

Hanging on the cross, one thief mocked Jesus. The other said, "Man, don't you fear God? We're getting what we deserved. This man has done nothing wrong."

And then he said, "Jesus, remember me. . . . "

Remember not the sins . . . remember me. It's our last, deepest prayer.

Two psalms later (27:10), the poet recalls, "If my father or mother forsake me, Lord, you will take me."

"Remember not the sins of my youth, or my transgressions; according to thy steadfast love remember *me!*"

41. Unfinished Business
Howard V. Pendley III

Scripture: Deuteronomy 34:1–12

IN A COMMENTARY on this passage, David Buttrick recalled an etching by a nineteenth-century artist, Sir Frederick
Leighton. It is a picture of Moses, standing on a high rock
ledge overlooking the promised land. When you see the picture, you become aware that we, the viewers, are standing in
the promised land, looking back at Moses. With one eye, Moses seems to be staring ahead, gazing across to Canaan. His
other eye appears to be drooping, as if nodding off into sleep.[1]

You can stand today on a hill overlooking the ancient city
of Jericho, and, if you face eastward towards the Jordan River,
you can see all the way over past the Plains of Moab to the
mountains in the distance. Somewhere over there—nobody
had ever known exactly where—lies the grave of Moses. It is
within sight of—but just beyond— the boundary of the promised land. Moses, who spent the last forty years of his life trying
to forge a nation out of an army of ex-slaves, saw the promised
land, but died without actually reaching the goal he'd been
striving toward for nearly half a century. Like us, Moses had
to learn to deal with unfinished business.

Howard V. Pendley III is pastor of Bedford Baptist Church in
Bedford, Virginia. He pursued his education at Samford University
and Southern Baptist Theological Seminary, from which he received
his Ph.D. in 1976. Pendley has also been a pastor in Bluefield, West
Virginia. He has written articles for *Search* and *Church and State* as
well as materials for Youth Church Training for the Southern Baptist
Sunday School Board.

The reason—or reasons—why Moses was stopped short of the goal are interesting to note in passing, but, for our purposes today, they're not all that important. For one thing, Moses was an old man—a hundred and twenty years old, according to the Scriptures. In addition, the accounts of his life suggest two other reasons why Moses never made it to the promised land. One tradition suggests that Moses was prevented from entering the land because of his presumptuousness in striking a rock to obtain water from it, after God had instructed him merely to speak to it. Elsewhere in Deuteronomy is the suggestion that Moses wasn't allowed to cross the river because of the sins of the Israelites. Either way, the fact remains: the main goal of Moses—that which he'd spent a third of his lifetime trying to reach—was denied him. At his death, it still remained unfinished business.

Three events in recent weeks have turned my thoughts even more than usual toward the unfinished business of life. The first was the tragic explosion at the rubber products manufacturing plant in our own city. One minute, everything was business as usual. Then, in an instant of time, everything changed. Although critical injuries resulted, we may be thankful that, thus far at least, no one has died of his injuries. Even so, it reminds us that in the twinkling of an eye, anybody's business can become unfinished business.

The second event was the unexpected passing of two men who were part of our church family. One day they were with us; the next day they were gone. Again, I was reminded of the fragile string by which all our lives are held, and how quickly all our business can become unfinished business.

The third event was the tragedy of the space shuttle *Challenger*. Handsome, young, gifted, well trained, and exuberant, the seven astronauts lifted off in a spacecraft that represented the most up-to-date, sophisticated technology yet devised by the human race. All the checks, double checks, and triple checks were made. Nothing could possibly go wrong. But the lives of seven courageous men and women were snuffed out in an instant, and whatever business they hadn't already taken care of remained unfinished business.

These three events, together with the experience of Moses on Mount Nebo, do indeed remind us of one of the most characteristic things about human existence: no matter how long or short our lives may be, there is always going to be some unfinished business left at the end of them. The list of those who died with their work apparently unfinished is almost literally inexhaustible.

I think of Wolfgang Amadeus Mozart, who died at age thirty-five. Who knows how much wonderful music died with him?

I think of Abraham Lincoln, who died less than a week after the end of the War between the States, his life cut short by an assassin's bullet. His death had enormously adverse effects on both the reconstruction of our nation and the integration into our national life of the former black slaves and their descendants. More than a century later, we are still paying the price for Lincoln's untimely death.

I think of Martin Luther King, Jr., who awakened the conscience of our nation, and, because of his insistence on the principles of nonviolence, was able to moderate many of the extremes on both sides of the civil rights movement. With his assassination at the early age of thirty-nine, his moderating influence was gone, and a social upheaval that was already painful enough for everybody involved became fraught with even more violence because of the loss of King's leadership.

I think, of course, of Jesus, crucified at about thirty years of age. How many more sermons might have been preached? How many more people were left unhealed? How many broken lives were left to be put back together? How much more did he have left to teach us?

We don't like loose ends, do we? We become uncomfortable when we have to end a thing without being able to feel we have completed it. We're taught, from our earliest years, to finish what we start. Don't put more on your plate than you're going to be able to eat. Don't start music lessons if you don't plan to master your instrument. Don't try out for a sport if you're not willing to stick with it at least until the end of the season. Don't start college unless you mean to graduate. Don't get married if it's not for a lifetime. We're taught that success demands sticking with a task until it's done, and we generally have a low opinion of folks who don't finish what they start. In fact, it's a good rule for life: if a thing isn't worth finishing, it's not worth starting.

But there's another side to the coin, too. None of us ever accomplishes everything we want to accomplish, no matter how long and hard we work at it, and regardless of how committed we are to finishing it. And so, I believe, part of coming to terms with life is learning to come to terms with its loose ends. You see, if we're trying to live successfully, there will never be a time when we reach all our goals. As we achieve one, we will immediately try to find another one. For as long as we live—if we're truly living—there will be some place we want to get to, some river to cross, some mountain to climb. If we're really living, we'll come to the end of life—whenever it is—with some business still unfinished. Permit me to share with you three observations about the unfinished business of life.

To begin with, we can—and need to—reduce the unfinished business of our lives. Of course, there are always going to be some loose ends in our lives, however carefully we plan, and however hard we strive. There's nothing wrong with that. It just means that we're always working toward goals, and that's good. As Robert Browning reminded us in his exquisite poem, "Andrea del Sarto": "Ah, but a man's reach should exceed his grasp / Or what's a heaven for?" Some loose ends can't—and shouldn't be—tied up. But some can. And should.

I'm thinking, for one thing, about the loose ends in our relationships. For most of us—if not all of us—it's perfectly true that if we died this minute, there's somebody in our lives who would have desperately needed to hear something that we desperately needed to say, but hadn't yet said. These are loose ends that we can—and should—tie up. Who is it in your life that needs to hear you say: "I'm sorry," "I love you," "I'm proud of you," "I forgive you," "I need you," "You mean so very much to me," "Please forgive me," "I really appreciate all you've done for me"? To whom do you need to say these words, or words like them? Let me say something to you: do it. Say them. Say them today. Don't let another day pass without saying them. There will never be a better time. There may never be another time. That's some business you can finish.

I'm thinking, too, of some of the things you want and need to do for your own personal enrichment. Things within your reach, with a little effort. I don't know what they are in your life, but I know what they are in mine. Let me ask you: when are you going to do them? Next year? In ten years? When you retire? Do you know that you will still be around when that time comes? Do you know that your health will permit you to do them? Do you know that you will still have with you whoever it is you need to share them with if they are to be truly enjoyable for you? If you want to do something, and if it's within your reach, you don't have to leave that business unfinished.

A second observation: while it's good to finish what we begin, there's a lot to be gained by working toward our goals, whether or not we ultimately reach them. Perhaps you know the story of the two boys who decided to try to dig a hole to China. They dug fervently for a number of days. They played games in the hole. They studied all the bugs they found. After some days, an older boy in the neighborhood came by and asked them what they were doing. "Digging a hole to China," came the reply. The older boy laughed out loud at the answer. "You'll never get to China," he said contemptuously. At that, one of the excavators picked up a container of bugs he'd discovered, and said: "So what if we don't get all the way to China? Look what we found on the way!"

The young boy was wiser than we often are. Quite often, we set goals for ourselves, and, if we don't reach them completely, we feel that we've failed utterly. That's not necessarily so. Of course, there's nothing wrong with setting worthy goals. One might begin college with the hope and expectation that he or she will graduate with a perfect grade-point average. It's a little unrealistic for most of us, but it's certainly a noble aspiration. Now, if our whole purpose is to graduate with all A's, what's going to happen the first time we get a B? We're going to be discouraged. We're going to feel that we've failed. We may even decide to drop out altogether. On the other hand, if our real purpose is to learn something, we can accomplish that—and take pride in our accomplishment—whether or not we graduate summa cum laude.

The same is true in every area of life. Goals are good. But sometimes we may become so preoccupied with the top of the mountain that we completely fail to see the beautiful things all around us on the way up. We need to learn how to celebrate what we experience on the way up. We need to learn how to celebrate those who accompany us on the pilgrimage. We need to learn how to celebrate our progress by looking back once in a while to see how far we've come. We need to learn how to celebrate our struggles on the way up, for they've made us strong enough to get where we are, and through them, we have probably encountered some kindred spirits, friends who have helped us overcome our adversities. All these are things we can celebrate, quite apart from whether or not we ever reach the top of the mountain.

A final observation, and, I think, a most important one: ultimately it is God, and God alone, who makes the determination of how completely we've fulfilled our purpose for being here. To our minds, it's sad that Moses died when he did. So near, and yet so far away! He was allowed to see, but not to touch, the promised land. To us, so goal-oriented, so achievement-oriented as we are, his life was tragically unfulfilled. But notice again what our text says about him: there was never another one like him. Consider all that God had done through him. Nobody ever knew the Lord face-to-face as had Moses.

You see, the Bible has other criteria than we do for evaluating the life of a person. In human judgment, one's life is deemed successful on the basis of human standards: how prominent one becomes, how much power one amasses and exercises, how much material wealth one accumulates. The Bible, in contrast, has only one real criterion for determining the success of the life of a person: conformity to God's will as he makes it known to the individual. By that standard, the life of Moses was successfully completed.

Looking at the life of Jesus from a purely human point of view, we might feel sadness at its brevity. Again, one wonders what he might have accomplished with another twenty, thirty, or forty years. No one knows; and, in fact, it doesn't really make a great deal of difference. What matters is this: the time he had was utterly devoted to God's use and service. He spent his life in total obedience to the will of the Father. And, at the end, with almost his very last breath, he affirmed: "It is finished."

What was finished? Everything he wanted to do in life? Every dream he had for himself? Every goal he'd set for himself? Every good thing he'd have liked the opportunity to do? No, of course not. Even Jesus had some unfinished business. He took care of some of it during the period between his resurrection and his ascension. The Holy Spirit took care of more of it at Pentecost, and continues to take care of it every time God's word comes to a person and finds a lodging place in his or her heart. But something essential *was* accomplished on that first Good Friday; namely, a way was made for persons of every age in the centuries to follow to be forgiven of sin, and to come into the family of God.

If today were your last day, could you affirm, as did Jesus: "It is finished"? Could you truthfully say that you've accomplished what you were put here to accomplish? Could you honestly say that you've tied up what loose ends you could? Could you affirm that you can trust God for the unfinished business that you'd have to leave behind? These are some of the things it means to be a Christian. These are some of the things it means to live abundantly. In fact, these are some of the things it means to live at all. It is this he offers all of us. It is this to which he invites each of us.

NOTE

1. David Buttrick, "Epiphany," *Proclamation 3*, series ed. Elizabeth Achtemeier (Philadelphia: Fortress Press, 1985), p. 56.

42. How to Forgive
Ronald D. Sisk

Text: Matthew 18:21–35

IT'S 7:30 A.M. and you're just pulling onto the freeway on your way to work. You're adjusting the radio on the on ramp, trying to tune out that drivel John Madden passes off as sports commentary, when you suddenly realize you're going thirty-five and you've just pulled over in front of a semi doing sixty. The air brakes squeal. Your ears burn as some guy with twenty-inch biceps disputes your ancestry on his way around. "Boy," you think as your heart slips back down out of your throat, "some people have no tolerance at all." Going up the next hill, the semi begins to have trouble making the grade. You're sailing along at a comfortable fifty-five, checking the part in your hair, as he pulls over in front of you at forty, giving you a better look at chrome-plated mud flaps than you ever wanted to have, as well as the chance to discover whether it really is possible to stand on the brake, change lanes, and lose your religion all at the same time. The day continues in the same vein. That night your brother-in-law calls for the

Ronald D. Sisk is pastor of the Tiburon Baptist Church in Tiburon, California. Sisk is a graduate of the University of Arkansas, New York University, and Southern Baptist Theological Seminary, from which he received a Ph.D. in 1982. He has served as director of program development for the Christian Life Commission of the Southern Baptist Convention, and is the author of several publications of the Christian Life Commission, including *Alcohol Awareness: A Guide for Teenagers and Their Parents* and *Critical Issues: Nuclear Doomsday.*

third time in a year and asks to borrow five hundred dollars to help pay his overdue rent. He's calling you from the cellular phone in his BMW. The text for your bedtime devotional turns out to be "Forgive us our trespasses as we forgive those who trespass against us." However it happens, you and I come face-to-face again and again with what may be the most difficult issue of the Christian life: what does it mean, how is it possible, for you and me to practice forgiveness? How do we forgive?

With Peter, you and I stand before Jesus and ask in all seriousness, "Lord, how often must we forgive?" The answer is, you forgive as often as you are asked. Peter, of course, thought he was being generous. The rabbis were agreed that if someone sinned against you three times you should forgive them. But if they stepped on your toe four times, you could get out your stomping boots and not even God would expect any different. Peter, hearing Jesus' call to practice forgiveness, doubles the rabbis' limit and adds one. "How about if I wait till the eighth time, Jesus? Then can I give the so-and-so what he's got coming to him?" And Jesus answered, "No, you keep on forgiving and keep on and keep on, seventy times seven." Some scholars think what Jesus may have been doing was answering the Old Testament law of revenge as set forth by Lamech in Genesis 4:23–24. Lamech says, "I have slain a man for wounding me, a young man for striking me. If Cain is avenged sevenfold, truly Lamech seventy-sevenfold." Lamech was sort of the Sylvester Stallone of Genesis. At any rate, Jesus' point is neither seventy-seven nor four-hundred ninety; it is that forgiveness has no limit.

Christians are people who forgive. Nothing about you and me is as distinctive to most people outside the church as that we practice forgiveness. Nothing is more difficult to do. Forgiving can be a heavy demand. One of my earliest memories is of the day my uncle Jimmy Wayne Cook died. He had once been my father's best friend. And there had been a falling out. And I remember my father sitting at the kitchen table and saying "No, I would not walk across the street to see the man when he was alive. Nor will I drive five hundred miles to attend his funeral." When you have been hurt, forgiveness is not easy to give. Yet the clear teaching of our Lord is you and I must give it.

We must forgive when we are asked. In some cases, forgiveness is a transaction. It is the proper response of the Christian to a brother's or sister's act of repentance. The temptation, of course, is to sit back and sigh with relief. "Well, that lets me off the hook. She never is going to ask for my forgiveness. I can go on despising her with God's blessing." But Jesus isn't as easy on us as that. Matthew 18:15 says if your brother sins against you, you go to him. In other words, our clear obligation, even if we're in the right, is to be the one to seek reconciliation, to set the record straight, to let the one who's hurt us know how we feel. Your husband can't ask for forgiveness, wives, if he doesn't know what he's done wrong. "What's the matter?" "Oh, nothing, sigh." Husbands, slamming the door on the way out of the house isn't nearly as articulate as you think it is. Stay and talk about it.

At the same time, of course, repentance is part of the transaction. Here's where the issue gets tough. Most of us have been taught, at least unconsciously, that forgiveness is a kind of sticky sentimentality. We read injunctions like "Forgive your brother from your heart" in Matthew 18:35 and "For if you forgive men their trespasses, your heavenly Father also will forgive you; but if you do not forgive men their trespasses, neither will your heavenly Father forgive your trespasses." And we get the idea that a Christian is a kind of doormat for the world, a sort of walking crucifixion, waiting for someone to come along and drive in the nails. Nothing could be further from the truth.

In the comics Flo Capp takes Andy back again and again and again, despite the fact that he never gives the slightest evidence of changing his ways. And that is not Christian forgiveness. That is stupidity. Christian forgiveness takes sin seriously, recognizes sin for the killer it is, demands that it stop, then accepts the offender as though he or she had done nothing wrong. Jesus said "Not every one who says Lord,

Lord, shall enter the kingdom of heaven, but he who does the will of my Father." Forgiveness requires a change in behavior on the part of the one who is being forgiven. Does that mean you and I don't have to forgive the man who borrows from us and doesn't repay? No, you forgive him. You restore the relationship if he asks you, but you do him no favor to lend him money again without at the same time calling him to responsibility.

So what does it mean to forgive someone from your heart? Just this: forgiveness is an act of the will. For Jesus the heart is the center of the human will. It is our disposition; the decisions you and I have made about how we are going to respond to the situations of our lives. In the parable for today, the king has a forgiving heart in the beginning but the unmerciful steward does not.

To forgive from your heart is to come at life having already decided that the answer to "Will you forgive me?" is "Yes!" Let's go back for just a moment to that freeway at 7:30 A.M. You see, the problem for most of us is that you and I understand all too well why that trucker ought to forgive us for carelessly pulling out in front of him. What we have a hard time with is forgiving him when he slows down in front of us. Our problem is the problem of the unmerciful steward. In the end it boils down to motivation.

To forgive from your heart, you have to have a sufficient reason. The reason is our debt. Interpreters have always had a delightful time trying to compare the debt of the unmerciful steward to that of his servant friend. Ten thousand talents was an enormous sum. The entire yearly revenue of the provinces of Judea, Samaria, and Idumea at the time when Jesus spoke amounted to six hundred talents. If you translate the debt into modern money, you come up with something like ten million dollars. The hundred denarii of the second servant, on the other hand, add up altogether to about twenty dollars. To compare them in another way, if you changed the small debt into quarters, they could be carried in one small sack. The large debt would take 8,600 sixty-pound bags. If you set them down three feet apart, they would make a line five miles long.

Obviously, Jesus is being deliberately ridiculous. The steward could never pay back that kind of debt, especially if he had to shake down his fellow servant for a measly twenty bucks.

But you see, my brothers and sisters, that is precisely the point. As long as you and I approach life insisting on our rights, we will never really know what it means to forgive. I once knew a woman whose husband of thirty years was discovered to be having an affair. The affair was ended. He confessed, changed his behavior, and asked her for her forgiveness. And she would not give it. To this day, as far as I know, she is making his life a living hell. And in couseling her we always came to an impasse when I would say, "But aren't we all sinners? Doesn't even he deserve a second chance?" And she would answer, "I never did anything like that to him." All too often you and I define sin as what the other person does.

We forget that sin is what you and I do, too. That we too owe a debt. Take a moment right now, and think back over just the past month in your life. Think about the times you have spoken sharply to your husband or wife or parent or child. Think about the things you've done you really don't want anybody else to know about. The things out of pure selfishness. Remember taking that shortcut at work? Enjoying somebody else's embarrassment of pain? And then multiply this month's failures by twelve for the months of the year and that again by the number of years in your life. And you begin to understand what Jesus meant by giving the unmerciful steward such an enormous, unmanageable debt.

And if we have eyes to see, we begin to understand how it is you and I can forgive those who trespass against us. We can, we must forgive, because we have been forgiven. In *The Merchant of Venice*, William Shakespeare writes:

Though justice be thy plea, consider this,
That in the course of justice, none of us should see salvation.
We do pray for mercy;
And that same prayer doth teach us to render the deeds of mercy.

George Buttrick wrote, "While God stands at the door in mercy and knocks, revenge broods over injuries and magnifies them, and so becomes deaf to God's knocking. Revenge is not sweet; it is burning poison. . . . No life is open to God which bitterly nurses its resentments. Such a life revokes its own pardon." Such a life puts its own judgment above the mercy of God. "Then his lord summoned him and said to him, 'You wicked servant! I forgave you all that debt because you besought me; and should you not have had mercy on your fellow servant, as I had mercy on you?' " In the final analysis, you and I forgive because as long as we refuse to forgive, we get no mercy for ourselves. Because our own need for forgiveness is so great, and because, miracle of miracles, if only we have turned to him, you and I have been, are being, and will be forgiven.

You see, my brothers and sisters, in all the long course of human history, there has been only one man who did not himself owe an unpayable debt. And that day, as you and I nailed him to the tree and his lifeblood poured out on the ground, he prayed "Father, forgive them" before forgiveness was even asked. And so he prays today. And so he will pray tomorrow and tomorrow and tomorrow. "How often shall my brother sin against me and I forgive him?" As often as it takes.

43. A Disciple of Long Standing
Brian L. Harbour

Scripture: Acts 21:16

IF I WERE to ask what you know about the biblical character Paul, most of you could respond in some way. You would say that he was a Pharisee, that he took some missionary journeys, that he wrote some of the books of the New Testament, that he had a dramatic conversion experience on the Damascus Road. All of us know something about the apostle Paul.

The same goes for Simon Peter. Mention his name and we picture a rough fisherman called by Jesus to be a disciple. Peter was loud and agressive. He always had something to say. He tried to walk on water once, but started sinking into the water. He preached at Pentecost and three thousand were saved. His nickname was "Rock." All of us know something about Simon Peter.

To a lesser degree, we could all come up with some information about James and John, and Andrew, and John the Baptist, and Zaccheus. But what would you say if I asked you about the New Testament character named Mnason? Most of you

Brian L. Harbour is pastor of Immanuel Baptist Church in Little Rock, Arkansas. A graduate of Baylor University, from which he received a Ph.D. in 1973, Harbour has also pastored Baptist churches in Texas, Georgia, Mississippi, and Florida. He is the author of seven books, including *Famous Couples of the Bible, From Cover to Cover, A New Look at the Book,* and *Rising Above the Crowd,* and is a frequent contributor to *The Ministers Manual* and to religious periodicals.

would say, "Who?" Yet, here he is in our text for today, a man who, one commentator says, "is immortalized in eight words." Only eight words in the original Greek are written about this man. Yet, what an intriguing picture is painted.

Mnason was a common Greek name. Among the Romans, the name was "Nason." "Jason" was the Jewish rendering of the name. Apparently, Mnason lived in Jerusalem. When Paul returned from his Gentile mission to Jerusalem, at a time when anything that threatened the idea of Jewish exclusiveness was looked on with suspicion, Mnason opened his home to Paul. His willingness to be Paul's host shows Mnason's gracious heart and hospitable spirit and also considerable courage in light of the situation.

Notice the phrase used to describe Mnason in Acts 21:16. The King James Version calls him "an old disciple." The Revised Standard Version refers to him as "an early disciple." The New English Version says that Mnason was one "who had been a believer since the early days." I have selected my title for this message from the rendering of these Greek works in the New American Standard. In this translation, Mnason is described as "a disciple of long standing." Contemplation on that phrase, "a disciple of long standing," brought to mind several sterling truths about the Christian life.

The Value of Maturity

This phrase reminds us first of the value of maturity. The King James Version says Mnason was "an old disciple." The Greek word is best translated with the English word "original." Mnason had been a disciple from the beginning. He had been a believer since the early days of the church. He was, as one translator suggests, "a foundation member of the church."

Why did Luke use that phrase to describe Mnason? Several commentators suggest that Luke's special mention of the fact that Mnason was one of the original Jerusalem disciples indicates that Luke acquired much valuable information about the earlier days of the church from him. Mnason had been around a long time. He had, therefore, a broad base of experience from which to speak concerning the Christian faith. He was a mature believer.

How we need that kind of spiritual maturity in today's church. I am thankful for the blessed children of the church, for their freshness and openness is a constant challenge to the rest of us. I am thankful for the dynamic young people of the church, for their excitement and enthusiasm is contagious in its effect. I am thankful for the young adults of our churches, because their idealism and intensity motivates the rest of us. I am thankful for the middle-aged adults of our churches because their dedication and determination provide the dynamism for our churches. Most of all, I am thankful for our older adult members, those who are "disciples of long standing," because they are the pillars who give stability to our churches.

Some say that they are "over the hill." I say, "If they are, then I hope they will tell us what it's like there so we can live our lives better as we approach the hill."

Some say that they are "has-beens." I say, "If so, then I pray that they will remind us of what has been so we can better prepare for what will be."

Some say they are "just waiting to die." I say, "If so, then I wish they would tell us what they have learned in their confrontation with the arithmetic of life so that we can make things add up better in our lives."

Some say all they can do anymore is to pray. I say, "If that is true, then pray for me and for our church and for the challenges before us."

To those disciples of long standing in our churches today, I have this challenge, "Don't retire from God's work. Don't withdraw from positions of responsibility. Don't hide your light under a bushel. Let it shine, for we need what you have to offer." There is nothing more valuable in the church than spiritual maturity.

The Meaning of Discipleship

A second truth evolves out of that phrase used to describe Mnason. Disciples of long standing are those who have discerned the true meaning of discipleship.

Notice two key facts about this man mnason. He had been a disciple for a long time, and he still was. The text not only calls attention to his long-term standing in the the church. The key fact is that Mnason was still active, still in good standing, still involved after all those years.

Mnason realized that discipleship is not just a one-time decision, but a continuing process, not just a step but a walk. Discipleship does not end when a person walks down the aisle and professes faith in Christ. That's where discipleship begins. The greatest challenge facing many in today's church is to move past the decision for Christ and become a disciple of Christ.

A certain husband was surprised to find his wife at home when he came in from work. "I thought you were taking golf lessons," he said. She responded, "I didn't need any more golf lessons today. I learned how to play yesterday." Some people are like that about their discipleship. When they obtained their discipleship at an earlier age, they set it in their spiritual trophy case. And they have been coasting ever since.

The New Testament makes it very clear, however, that a person does not drift into maturity in the Christian life. A person must discipline himself into maturity.

The Christian life is like a race, and the Bible admonishes us to "press on toward the mark" (Phil. 3:14).

The Christian life is like a battle; and the Bible urges us to "put on the whole armor of God" (Eph. 6:13).

The Christian life is like the physical development of a person from childhood to adulthood; and the Bible challenges us to feed ourselves on the strong meat of God's Word so that we can grow up spiritually (1 Pet. 2:2).

The Christian life is like building a house; and the Bible exhorts us to build, on the foundation that Christ has given us, a spiritual house that will bring honor to God (1 Cor. 3:10).

Every picture of the Christian life in the New Testament reminds us that it is a process that demands continued dedication and constant discipline on our part. Nobody drifts into maturity in the Christian life. Discipline is required. Maturity comes through faithful commitment to these five disciplines: diligent study, regular worship, daily prayer, systematic giving, and personal witnessing. When anyone, through dedication to these disciplines, becomes, like Mnason, a "disciple of long standing," then that person has discovered the true meaning of discipleship.

The Importance of Faithfulness

A third truth about the Christian life evolves from this phrase used to describe Mnason: the importance of faithfulness.

Our text does not tell us much about Mnason. We do not know if he was a deacon in his church. We do not know if he was a Sunday school teacher. We do not know if he ever served on a committee. We do not know if he could preach or sing. His name is immortalized in Holy Scripture for one reason and one reason only: he was faithful to his Lord. With the passing years, over a long period of time, he never quit. He was faithful.

That is the one thing God expects from us. The one thing God demands of us is that we be faithful. Whether we have five talents or two talents or one talent, he wants us to do the best we can with what we have. He wants us to be faithful, nothing more or nothing less than that.

At a track meet in Alabama a few years ago, attention was focused on the mile run because one of the schools had a promising miler who had missed the state record in the mile by only one second the previous week. He was out to break that record in this meet. As the boys came to the starting mark, every eye was riveted on him. He was a tall, good-looking, well-built kid. He looked like an athlete. As the eyes of the crowd swept the lineup of boys, they noticed at the other end of the line another boy who in every way was a sharp contrast to the gifted athlete I just mentioned. He was small of stature. His shoulders were narrow. He was hollow-chested. Even his legs were not straight. Everyone wondered what he was doing in the mile race.

When the race began, the favored athlete pushed off at a torrid pace. Every lap increased the distance between this star miler and the others. Especially, the little fellow steadily fell behind. When the leader came around the final turn, the predicted winner sprinted the last hundred yards. As he broke the tape, a deafening roar went up from the crowd. He had established a new state record.

Only a few others even finished the race. Most of the runners dropped out when they saw they had no chance to win. As the field crew brought out the hurdles to set up for the next race, one of the judges shouted, "Get those hurdles out of the way. This race is not over. Look!" Around the turn came that hollow-chested, spindly legged little boy, panting and staggering to keep going. Everybody in the audience stood silently and watched as he dragged up that last hundred yards and literally fell across the finish line. His face ground into the cinder track. One of the judges turned him over on his back and wiped the blood off his face with a handkerchief. The judge asked him, "Son, why didn't you drop out back there?" Between gasps for breath, the boy answered, "My school had a good miler, but he got sick a couple of days ago and couldn't run. The coach promised to have a man in every event, so he asked me if I'd come and run the mile." "Well, son," the man continued, "why didn't you just drop out? You were almost a lap behind." The boy answered, "Sir, they didn't send me here to win. They didn't send me here to quit. They sent me here to run this mile, and I ran it."

God did not call us as Christians to win. He did not call us as Christians to quit. He commissioned us to run the race. If we run the race he has called us to run, to the best of our ability, and refuse to give up, then someday, each of us will be brought into the presence of our heavenly Father and we will hear him say, "Well done, good and faithful servant." The one thing God wants of us is that we be faithful, nothing more, nothing less, nothing else than that.

44. Homily for Easter Sunday
John J. McCullagh

I REMEMBER a late February evening when a neighbor, passing the field where a few of us had been playing football after school, told me that my father was home after four weeks in hospital. The match was forgotten. The score no longer mattered. My brother and I picked up our coats and, trailing schoolbags, ran breathlessly all the way home. It was one of those memorable moments of childhood joy. The winter days of loneliness, the pain of his parting by ambulance, the reports from the hospital of his serious condition, were all things of the past. He was home, pale and with his breathing a little labored, but spring was in the air and we ran around that country parish well into the night, letting everyone know our good news.

The memory of that night came to my mind when I looked at the story of the resurrection of Christ in these last few days leading up to Easter. Easter Sunday is all about running feet.

John Joseph McCullagh is director of pastoral studies at the Pontifical University in Maynooth, Ireland. A Roman Catholic, McCullagh delivered this Easter Sunday sermon in Ardmore, Derry, Northern Ireland. McCullagh is a graduate of St. Columb's College, Maynooth College, and the New University of Ulster. He has been assistant priest at St. Eugene's Cathedral in Derry and has also served as diocesan advisor in religious education. He is a frequent broadcaster with the BBC radio and television and with RTE radio in Ireland and is the author of *Thoughts for the Changing Seasons* and *Prayer for an Irish Home.*

The breathless Mary Magdelene racing back to tell the apostles that Jesus Christ was no longer in the tomb, the younger John outrunning the older fisherman, Peter, to see for themselves if the story could be true, the disciples in Emmaus leaving the unfinished meal and coming with haste through the night to share their good news and boundless joy.

But tell me, on this Easter Sunday all these years later, can you and I *dare* to hope, *dare* to let ourselves look to better days, *dare* shout with joy, or is it a day for muted alleluias, a day when we would ask Christ for a greater miracle than Resurrection, like the miracle of peace descending with the falling darkness of last night on this land of ours. It must be almost impossible for so many people this morning to find any joy when the Good Friday that is Northern Ireland has left its bloodstains, the crossmark of suffering, the nailprints of bereavement, the calvary of painful memories. It isn't easy to believe in a risen Savior when so many who claim to be his followers can't believe sufficiently in one another.

But maybe the endless Good Friday is our own fault, maybe we have grown accustomed to the cross that is so conspicuous in our own land. Maybe we are beginning to think it is an inevitable part of the image of this province. Since the death of Christ on that hillside all those years ago there has been no need for any man to spill the blood of a brother in the name of God. But the sacrilegious blood of your brother and mine pours down urban gutters or is diluted in the rain on country roads because someone felt that his version of God had to be defended. Wouldn't we all love a little paragraph inserted in the Gospel story just before the passion narrative telling us that all the characters are intended to bear no resemblance to any person, living or dead. We could go on then, comfortable in the thought that it was a regrettable piece of history and thank God that we had no hand or part in it. But the way of the cross runs through our cities, along border roads, while too many of us close our eyes to unending funeral processions and lower our blinds to passing death. Today in the glorious sun of spring, the way of the cross still passes by too many silent shocked spectators who wonder where it will all end.

It ended in Resurrection. Truth could be put in a grave, but it couldn't be kept there. Jesus Christ was not to be found among the dead on the morning of Easter, nor is he to be found there this morning. Why do we go on looking for him in the graveyards of the "them" and "us" mentality when he would want us to unburden our children of the legacy of hate and distrust and build a museum for outworn ideas and meaningless cliches?

Why do we search out the dates of the dead and make them further causes of suffering, when Jesus Christ would want us to look to the future and your possibilities in the years that are left to us? Our Easter day will finally dawn when we begin to believe that at last we have been saved from ourselves because Jesus died and rose to save us. Our Easter day will finally dawn when together we have heaved away the stone of neighborhood mistrust, the boulder of the years of pointless division. Our Easter day will finally dawn when we discover how pitifully small our differences are when we hold them up against the endless lines of refugees searching for new life anywhere. Our Easter day will dawn when we begin to believe that, with the help of God, the Irish miracle is possible, that the slow funeral marches of the past years will give way to the triumphant alleluias.

And Easter is the celebration of that hope. The same Jesus Christ who conquered death can conquer our reluctance if only we give him a chance. In these days Christ is the last hope for us scattered people. Because of him there is reason for new beginning; for he shared with us our life, our death; because he himself became a tragic figure in a world where tragedy is commonplace. Without him the strong would make this earth their paradise and the weak would call it hell. Men would long for death and the grave would be the only ambition for tired generations. Because of this risen Christ and our faith in him and in ourselves in this corner of Christian Ireland, we believe that some day things broken will be fixed, friends parted will be gathered, the scars of old wounds will disappear and with them the memories. City ghettoes will no longer scream their denomination at us, the swords will be turned into ploughshares, the hungry will have their fill, the former things will have passed away.

So, may your step be lighter, and may Easter joy and peace be with you. If pain and disappointment, weariness, or anger lies buried in you this Easter day, may you discover many empty tombs.

VI. DEVOTIONAL

45. An Incredible Payoff
James W. Crawford

Scripture: Matthew 20:1–16

THE *NEW YORKER* carried a little cartoon of a shirtsleeved father slumped in his easy chair, a drink on the side table. He's attempting to relax while being asked by his ten-year-old son: "Say, Pop, where do you stand in the pecking order?" It is precisely that kind of question that was eating alive the little church from which Matthew was writing his Gospel. Matthew's church suffered a serious problem: scrambling for status. Some people were throwing their weight around, trying to secure slots in the pecking order. Others finagled for certain power positions. Everyone was trying to manipulate some reward or another. So Matthew tackles this perplexing issue of what loyal, hardworking Christians really deserve—and what they get; and as usual, Peter plays the heavy.

I

Now what's that passage trying to tell us? It's trying to tell us where the payoff is and where the pecking order lies in the Christian life. How do we approach it? What's the key to unlocking this passage? It sounds so grossly unfair—and it is—

James Winfield Crawford was born in 1936 in Rochester, New York. He was educated at Dartmouth College and Union Theological Seminary in New York. A member of the United Church of Christ, he has served as pastor of the Old South Church in Boston, Massachusetts, since 1974.

unless we reposition ourselves; unless we reorient ourselves, our loyalties, and our day-to-day perceptions of the one over-riding truth behind this parable: the vineyard belongs to Christ. The loving, suffering, reconciling Christ owns the vineyard and pays the wages; not Arthur D. Little, not Citibank, not Yale, not the U.S. Treasury, not the Diocese of Massachusetts, the Conference of Virginia, or other of our organizations where bottom lines are figured, the numbers accrued, the grades recorded, and the rewards commensurate.

In this parable we are confronted with a vineyard: a community founded and existing only to exercise Christ's healing, restorative, transforming ministry among the human family; nothing but the quality and integrity of our service on behalf of others counts. In Christ's vineyard—as contrasted with every other vineyard we know—our degrees and seniority, our years of distinguished service, our titles as president, manager, doctor, dean, senior/junior associate, deacon—in Christ's vineyard these slots in the pecking order become irrelevant to the overriding joy of lives surrendered to the difficult but glorious tasks of healing a torn and suffering humanity. In Christ's vineyard we share in the opportunity to counter the futility of a world already exhausted from striving for success, fighting for turf, and carving out its little niches in human life. To enlist in the effort to bind and reconcile humankind is to be a laborer in Christ's vineyard; and the payoff—the wage—is simply the risk and joy of working side by side, stride for stride, with the crucified and risen Christ in that healing, restorative ministry.

II

But for many of us, that payoff misses the mark—just like Peter. Remember, he puts in his time with Jesus, he takes the brunt of three years in the Galilean countryside, he lives with the resistance, the threats, the mockery, the failure. "Hey, Lord," he asks, "any rewards for our loyalty? What's in this enterprise for us who have been around since the beginning? How about a bonus, a raise in wages; what's in it for me?"

Do you see what's happening? For all of his being near Christ's vineyard, Peter still hacks around bucking for perks. He hooks his identity, his security, to the bonuses, the rating sheets, the report cards, the society columns, the power slots, the proper clubs, the heavy committees, the key pulpits. You know Peter; he wants the low-numbered license plate, the fancy letterhead, the clergy sticker. He's angling for the honorary degree, the prefix "honorable," the title "reverend." In all fairness, of course, he deserves it.

Sound familiar—this world outside Christ's vineyard where offices, titles, residences, and credentials are the quid pro quo of loyal citizenship, refusal to rock the boat, and playing by the rules? Most of our families are familiar with it. Erma Bombeck, bless her poison pen and prophetic heart, knows well our world of ego payoffs and our squeezing from life every last credit. You've heard the attitude before: "They never bought *me* a watch 'til I could tell time." Or, "You got the biggest piece of pie for supper. That means I get to sit by the window the next time we go on vacation." Or, "Betsy's arm cost $500. Since I wasn't stupid enough to break my arm, can I have $500 for a new car?" And reluctant as I am to admit it, my friends, the Crawford household lives a fair piece of its life outside Christ's vineyard; especially around dishwashing time. Talk about perks, quid pro quo's and notches in the pecking order: "Pop, I cleaned out the garage last summer, why can't she do the dishes tonight?" You know the scene. Suffice it to say, the dishes get done amid grumbling references to unfairness, wounded seniority, and suggestions that 40 Taylor Crossway, Brookline, Massachusetts, sounds very like the address of a slave labor camp. "I did my stint. Now what do I get? A night off?"

And our churches are not immune. "I've been around here for years; that office deserves to be mine." "How dare she walk in here and take the place over!" The slot's reserved for seniority and experience.

And in our cities? What eats this city up? Well, partly, Boston reflects a series of migrations with each era's majority grabbing special privileges for itself under the rubric: "I'm the majority, so I get to run things." "I own property, so you'd better consult me." "I came over on the *Mayflower;* you'd better invite me." "I'm a special case. Look at all I've done. Give me what I deserve."

It's awful, isn't it: this incessant scrambling for the payoffs outside Christ's vineyard—the world Peter and you and I live in most of the time.

III

Enter Matthew and his stunning parable! He's got an alternative. Matthew offers us a different kind of reality, dissolving pecking orders and merit systems. He's saying that to spend ourselves in turning the human race into the human family for Christ's sake, engenders a unique but marvelous reward. The commitment of our lives to Christ's new creation, whether it be in Sandwich, New Hampshire, or Boston, Massachusetts, or Washington, D.C., is to be engaged in a work of such nobility and grace we can describe it only as Matthew does: "a touch of heaven." When and if we come late to join others in their servant tasks in the vineyard, or course, we receive the same wages they do. And what are they? The gifts of courage, joy, and hope embracing us, particularly when the challenge is tough but the cause is just. Early birds will not begrudge latecomers. If the early birds are working in Christ's vineyard, they'll ask: "Where have you been? What took you so long to get here? It's about time you arrived!" And those among us who arrive late, what can we say, but: "Where has this been all my life? Why didn't I come sooner? Why didn't someone tell me this solidarity with the world of justice and peace makes working in the midday heat feel like the cool of the evening? Indeed, show me the needs. Where can I help? What needs justice? Send me to the trenches. Where can I serve next? Lord, where lies your toughest task? Just be with me as I take it on. That's all I ask." You know as well as I that when you work with someone you love and who loves you, you can't get enough of it.

Do you see how the service of Christ pays off? Not as Peter wanted it: as Senior Disciple, Galilean Volunteer of the Year, Dr. Rock—you name it. No, the payoff came for him and it comes for us whenever we stumble into Christ's vineyard: at dawn, at noon, at sunset, at midnight. And it consists simply of the peace and joy, the strength and power, the release and friendship—yes, friendship—of the suffering and risen Christ, sustaining, beckoning, and standing shoulder to shoulder with us through the heat of the day.

My soul, what a payoff—for you, for me, for our churches, for those who wish to climb on board at any time! What a reward: the solidarity, the camaraderie, the joy of serving Jesus Christ! Who could ask for more?

46. Time and Proximity
Peter J. Gomes

Seek the Lord while he may be found, call upon him while he is near.—Isaiah 55:6

THE SEASON of Advent is upon us all once again, creeping in as it does between holidays that we know and understand and love. It is the strange indigestible filler between Thanksgiving and Christmas. Once again, we are called by the church to go through the motions, at least, of the keeping of Advent: we light the candles, we recognize the movement from darkness to light, and, as children, we open the doors of our Advent calendars, which implies some progress, some motion, some movement toward the real event, that great day of confirmed expectations: Christmas. Yet most of us, even here in our enlightened community, remain confused by all of this—a little annoyed—and greatly confused. We know that there must be more to Advent than liturgical shopping days to Christmas. We know that ought to be the case. But what "more" really is there? In Lent, we know we are supposed to be penitent, and, even if we are not penitent, we know we are acting contrary to the expectations of the season, and there is even some strength and security in that. But what of Advent?

Peter John Gomes was born in 1942 in Boston, Massachusetts. He was educated at Bates College and Harvard Divinity School, where he received his doctorate. A Baptist, Dr. Gomes has served since 1974 as minister of the Harvard Memorial Church and Plummer Professor of Christian Morals at Harvard University. He is the author of several books and was recognized in 1980 by *Time* as one of the outstanding preachers in the United States.

What are its expectations of us and for us? What expectations ought we to have? How ought we to cope with them or the lack of them? Now you need not remember all of those questions because I'm not proposing to answer them all this morning; it is just to set the sermon in motion.

There is the matter of impatience which confronts us with these questions: human impatience, understandable, rational, experiential impatience, the sort that you and I all know only too well. Human impatience, what in Boston traffic terms we might call the yellow light syndrome: in the rest of the automobile world, the yellow light means slow down and caution; in Boston, however, as we all know, it means hurry up and race lest you get caught at the red light. There is the impatience factor where speed is a fascinating, even exciting substitute for direction: as the punkster on the electric skateboard out here in Harvard Square might have said, "We don't know where we are going, but we'll get there faster than anybody else." And so they will. And so there is this desire to "get on with it." It affects how we eat: where else in the world would there be an industry devoted to what is called "fast food"? Our conversations and reports are punctuated with phrases about "the bottom line," which means get to the point, and quickly. We cultivate every opportunity to save time, and indulge our impatience: electric toothbrushes, automatic bank tellers, and that most absurd of needless delusions, the airplane telephone, where, as the advertisement says, you need not lose precious ground time while in the air. What a horrible idea indeed!

Time is our enemy: its beginning marks our end. Time must be fought, time must be managed, time must be resisted; it must be overcome, it must be twisted into convenient useful shapes for us. "Have you got the time?" comes the naive question. "No," comes the cynical and truthful answer. Countdowns and lift-offs, digital clocks that show only the time passing, not the time being nor the time coming. No wonder so many people don't have the time; they can't tell time, they can just read numbers passing before their eyes. And so our impatience is at odds with our instincts. For our instincts from ancient times onward have told us that anything worth having is worth waiting for. Your instincts and your mothers told you that. Our impatience tells us we want it now or not at all; or worse, if we don't have it now it is not worth waiting for. Thus, for those whose only doctrine and creed is relevance, they are required always to live for the moment, and to demand that life be lived as experience and not expectation, and experience that somehow "counts," that makes sense, that makes a difference, that does it: here and now, in terms that I can see and understand and put either on my bumper or my breast. Can this in some measure explain why so many of our undergraduates here take courses in Social Analysis 10, formerly Economics 10? More undergraduates here enroll in Economics 10 than in any other course, more people in economics than, say, in Latin poetry. Could it be that they and their advisers, not to mention their parents, are under the impression that somehow the study of economics is "relevant" to our daily lives or their daily lives and poetry is not? I won't make the case for poetry here today, but pity those poor fools who actually think that the study of economics has anything at all to do with the economy: that is like studying meteorology and thinking you know and understand when, how, and why it rains when it is supposed to shine.

The impatient demand, rampant in our culture, that we make our experience count for something here and now makes it almost impossible for us to take seriously a tradition in which waiting is a virtue, expectation a requirement, and the future a place that comes to us when it is ready and on its own terms, not ours. This, you see, is what Advent is all about, and this, you see, is why you and I and so many of us are impatient and confused and slightly annoyed by its muted themes. You and I, impatient, relevant, experience-centered Protestants that we are, find Advent a tiresome season. Confess it, I know it's true, it's all right. Yet tiresome or not, it is perhaps the Church's most precious season, for it reminds us that the gift of time, for that is what it is, is the means by which we embrace a future that is fully and finally meant to be good. Now how is that from a down-and-out Calvinist such as myself? A future that is meant finally and fully to be good. A future that is good because it is God's. Time helps us achieve that future. Time helps us embrace that future, and Advent is that special, precious time in which we consider how we get from here to there by looking forward and not backward, by anticipating rather than regretting, by watchful expectation rather than simple sentiment and nostalgia or satisfaction. Now there is what we can call the double glance of Advent: the look forward toward that backward look. And that is what we mean when in the first instance of Advent we talk about it, looking forward to the feast of the nativity, looking forward to that backward glance: the manger, the glory and the joy of our Christmas cast in the lighted glow of that first Christmas. We look ahead, in these weeks, in order to better look back, and the candles we light do illumine that way back, and rightly so. Would that we could in some small measure recapture not only that first Christmas, but those Christmases of our youth, those Christmases when so much seemed so possible, when the world was brighter and cheerier, and when we were quicker and sharper. So it is not just toward Bethlehem that we look back, but on all of those Christmases from Bethlehem to now. So we look ahead in order to look back, and the candles light the way. But Advent has a second meaning, a much more substantial meaning, dare I suggest. For Advent, rather than Christmas, reminds us that we look ahead, that the future is the place in which God's chief revelation is to be found. God is not to be found in some reconstructed manger, or even in some reconstructed piety, or some rediscovered theological or ethical tricks, trying to capture something that is lost because it never was: but rather, Advent reminds us insistently, relentlessly, that God is ahead of us, out there, watching even as we watch, waiting even as we wait, not some captive of a long-dead imagination, but rather summoning us to a future time that will, in justice, mercy, and peace, set all things to rights. Advent is the feast of the future, a future in which the proximity between creature and creator gets closer and closer, and we move toward it even as it moves toward us. That is the paradox, that is the insistent promise of Advent, and that is where we find ourselves right now.

The prophets understood this paradox of the nearness and the distance of God. Isaiah tells us on the one hand to seek the Lord while he may be found, call upon him while he is near, suggesting some kind of proximity, some kind of nearness of which we ought to take advantage while the taking is good; and yet in the very same passage, and on the other hand, he says that "For as the heavens are higher than the earth, so are my ways higher than yours and my thoughts than your thoughts. For my thoughts are not your thoughts and my ways are not your ways." That is not proximity at all but a sort of distance that is far removed from our world and the world which is God's, our expectations and the experience which is God's. The season of Advent is meant to remind us that the Lord is near, the time of coming is at hand. We rehearse that, and we remember this from the last time of his proximity, that strange night, and that even stranger life, where God in man walked and talked among us as Jesus Christ, teaching and preaching, living and dying, and living again in our midst. We look forward to recalling that all over again and again at this time of the year. That is the proximity of the past; we know it, we need it, we cherish it. But time is the means to the proximity of the future, and the blessed season of Advent, more than any other, requires that we take that proximity and that future seriously. We look back only that we may look ahead, and do so with confidence, for Advent tells us that what God did once with the infant Jesus, a long time ago and very far away, he will do again with the resurrected Christ, and there, in that time that is to be, we will see the fulfillment of all creation, the visions for which we labor and live will finally and fully come to pass. Advent is the season of that expectation. Advent is the season in which we affirm the second coming.

It is to this time, this time that is to be, and the proximity to it, that II Timothy speaks when it says, "Before God, and before Jesus Christ who is to judge men living and dead, I charge you solemnly by his coming appearance and his reign, proclaim the message, press it home on all occasions, convenient or inconvenient, use argument, reproof, appeal, with all the patience that the work of teaching requires." The power of the prophets is also the power of the evangelists and apostles: a passion not simply for now, but more important, a passion for the future in which the present promises and hopes will be fulfilled. The mission of the waiting, watching, working, expectant, and faithful church is a stewardship of the future in which what was begun at creation, displayed at Christmas, and upheld at Easter, will be fulfilled and experienced in God's complete and final revelation of himself, in, through, and with ourselves. That is the substance of the Christian faith. Not an easy relevance in the moment, and not a slavish devotion to the past, but an energy, a confident looking toward that which has not yet been. Orthodoxy, if there is any such thing, is a confidence in God's capacity to deliver the future as he said. Anything less than that is not authentic either to the prophets or to the apostles.

I have never understood the reservations and hassles so many thoughtful Christians have with this doctrine of the second coming, or the second Advent, what we call in the jargon of the Divinity School eschatology. Once upon a time, I suppose, in eighteenth-century Europe, or nineteenth-century England, or early twentieth-century America, one could afford to discount the future because all was so rosy and secure in the present; indeed, the future was to be ever so much like the present, only longer and perhaps better: superstition, slavery, ignorance, all of these things had been abolished, and comfort, rationality, and the pursuit of happiness were now natural, inevitable, and, in America, constitutional rights. Things appeared to be working according to plan.

We know the self-satisfactions of our own age and time, and against all of the seeming security and smugness and indifference, the church alone, above any and all other institutions, has always held out the notion that "now" was not "it." The church maintained a vision that said that creation, pleasurable though it appeared to be, was incomplete: there was much to be done, virtue rewarded and encouraged, vice restrained and punished, and that for which the faithful in every age have worked and prayed remains to be achieved.

How vainglorious, how egotistical, how silly, to think that all of history has been moving forward toward this moment of ultimate achievement, that we are the sum distillation of millions and millions of years of divine and human activity, and we are all there is to show for it. What a terrible and bitter taste of imperfection in every department of our lives. We know the private failures and the secret frustrations that we bear, and we know too well the corporate and the public frustrations and failures. And the result of all of this in recent times is to induce in us a fear, a terror, of the future: time is not on our side, we conclude. This is why we worship at the altar of youth and make our sacrifices to painful fulfillment of its illusions and its delusions. We dread the coming of the night, the coming of age and infirmity and death. We suspect that the future will take from us what we have worked so hard for: our money, our brains, our looks, our friends; and it will leave us with nothing. And that terrifying future, which we cannot control and dare not undertake, makes us content with what we cannot resolve in the present. It makes us selfish. It makes us hedonistic. It makes us indifferent to pain and injustice and passions, and makes us fascinated only with our futile attempt to hold back the tide of time.

Advent stands to remind us that this is wrong, that this is quite wrong. Advent at its best reminds us that the future is not a time of terror and fear: it is not the place of death and defeat. Indeed, one could argue that the future is the only thing we truly have, the only opportunity that is really ours, the only place left for God's work and ours to be done. My great teacher and colleague and a member of this congregation, Amos Wilder, once wrote a book called *Ethics and Eschatology* in which he argued, if I do justice to it, that it is only in the future that one can really see an ethical dimension at work, for it is only in worlds yet unexperienced but imagined that we can overcome the sad experiences and the lack of imagination in our efforts to deal with one another. Who wants to build a society based on any society that has ever existed in the history of the world? Name one and you will find yourselves sadly deluded. The society that we seek to build has not been built yet, and the only place it can be built is out there. The only opportunity for God's work and ours to be fulfilled is in the time that is before us. They are foolish, even ignorant, who argue that what we want and seek is in the past. There is no such place. Romantic visions of the past are always half and incomplete clichés and half-truths. There once was popular around here in the university a society called "The Society for Creative Anachronisms" (and that is not a code name for the Faculty of Arts and Sciences). It was a legitimate undergraduate and graduate group, and they were always busy trying to recreate the Middle Ages: reveling in the costumes of courtly love, they were always having joust out here on the delta in front of Memorial Hall, and great banquets and feasts with mead and ale. And interestingly enough, everybody who took a part in this recreation of medieval society was always a lord, or a lady, or a knight or a hero. There were no serfs in this medieval society. There were no half-wits, no village idiots, no starving peasants among them. That is hardly the real Old World.

And the present, is there anyone in the present moment truly content with the state of justice, mercy, and peace in the world as it is rationed out today? Is this really the best job that can be done of it? If this is it, the best that can be done, that place toward which all history and time has been moving, then the moment is the greatest case for despair that can be made: this is the terrible witness of the suicide for whom the future is even worse than the present.

Advent gives no comfort to the self-satisfied. It does not tell you that all is well and you shall be well. Advent talks about judgment. That is not an easy, willing message, but Advent does not give comfort to the professional doomsayers among us either, whose only joy is in the fulfillment of their dire predictions. No, Advent, and the church who guards and sanctions her season, bids us face a future for the sake of a God who has promised us that in it, he and we will be one. Timothy tells us, "You must keep calm and same at all times; face hardship, work to spread the gospel, and do all the duties of your calling." That is the Advent message to you: do all the duties of your calling. The clock is ticking, but who is counting? Do all the duties of your calling.

Advent calls us to the courage of great expectations, expectations not easily or quickly fulfilled, but nevertheless worth waiting for, waiting not for the time that once was, but for the time that has not yet been: and that, my friends, takes courage and imagination, qualities often in very short supply in this impatient church and time.

This then is a sermon about the future: that which you cannot see and have not yet experienced. A lady once greeted my predecessor, George Buttrick, at the door of the Madison Avenue Church in New York. Dr. Buttrick had been preaching a sermon on the Resurrection, which has something to do with the future as you might imagine, and the good lady said to him at the door, "Dr. Buttrick, after a sermon like that, no one need fear death." We know what she meant: we know the fear of the moment, it is the future to which faith beckons us. It is the future that is illumined by the lights of Advent, and as Advent Christians—realistic, cautious, and hopeful—we greet its coming with faithful joy and high anticipation.

47. Wonderful Words of Life
Donald Macleod

Go, stand, and speak in the temple to the people all the words of this life.—Acts 5:20

The words that I speak unto you, they are spirit and they are life.—John 6:63

MANY YEARS AGO, when Harry Emerson Fosdick was at the height of his influence as the senior minister of the Riverside Church, New York City, he was making a tour of Palestine and other countries of the Near and Middle East and he was invited to give an address before the American University in Beirut, Lebanon. Among the members of the student body were citizens of many countries and representatives of some sixteen different religions. Now, what could one say that would be relevant or even of interest to so mixed and varied a group? Well, this is how Fosdick began: "I do not ask any of you here to change your religion; but I do ask all of you to face up to this question: 'What is your religion doing to your character?'"

Doesn't this question lead you and me in our spiritual tradition to ask ourselves what might be regarded as a prior ques-

Donald Macleod was born in 1914 in Nova Scotia, Canada. He was educated at Dalhousie University, Pine Hill Divinity Hall, and the University of Toronto, where he received his doctorate. A Presbyterian, he was the founder and first president of the Academy of Homiletics, and until 1983 was Francis L. Patton Professor of Preaching and Worship at Princeton Theological Seminary in Princeton, New Jersey. Dr. Macleod is the author of ten books in the field of preaching and worship.

tion: In this matter of religion and character, in what ways does Christianity differ from the other great religions of the world? In these days, when all across the earth, the great and ancient religions are surging forward once again and their messages are being re-thought and re-examined, have you and I ever paused to ask: Well, what about Christianity? Now, we must grant that there are many things in Christianity that are not new; i.e., they existed in the mind of the ancient Greek and Hebrew world before Jesus was born. But among the many new things that Christianity brought (apart from the unique person of Jesus himself) was the conviction that the dynamics of one's religion must find expression in the quality of one's life.

To you and me, however, in these final decades of this twentieth century, this may sound ordinary, simplistic, and even commonplace. But when you say "religion in life" in the Christian context, you mean religion as the motive and means to real life, whereas many of the major religions are intended to be an escape from life. Christianity is the means whereby the human personality is liberated in order to *be*, and it provides the motive to become what God in Christ intended we should. To the mind of the ancient world, however, religious thinking of this kind was nothing short of revolutionary.

Take, for example, the great thinkers of the Greek world: they had labored and pored over systems of philosophy in a vain search for a formula for life that would be satisfactory, helpful, and complete. But constantly they went down to failure and grew more and more lonely in an ever-widening world, because they did not see that a formula for life could never save a person, nor satisfy the deep yearnings of their human nature. A slogan or formula can provide a structure in which to perform or supply an excitement for a day, but no matter how clever it is, it can never claim the continual commitment of a person's inner will.

Or, take the Jews at this time: they had built up an orthodox system of rules of conduct in the form of a law of life with some six hundred and thirteen separate regulations. This was the Law and he who would live rightly must fulfill every last one of its demands. But a highly religious Jew like Saint Paul discovered that being one hundred percent obedient to a set of rules could never solve the deadly problem of spiritual weakness and moral failure in his life; and when writing to the Christian community at Rome, he reflected momentarily upon what his life had been under the Law, and intimated how he used to cry out in his moral crises: "Who shall deliver me from this body which is taking me to death?"

The common fault, however, lying in both of these perspectives is that for the Greeks, religion was something *with* which to live and for the Jews, something *toward* which to strive or strain, while, for the Christian, religion is something *by* which to live. The Christian gospel came with a fresh and startling proclamation, and its focus was words, witness, spirit, and life. Religion was to be no longer a matter for abstract discussion (Greeks), nor imprisoned in a set of rules (Jews), but with the Christian faith there was the principle of surrender whereby religion would be permitted to enter the stream of our human existence and cleanse, undergird, and empower all our thinking, believing, and loving. And to the extent that your religion and mine is something by which we live, only then will it be caught and favorably judged by the outside world. For if our religion does not touch the great and exciting areas of the human mind, or come to grips with the deep emotions of the human heart, or lay hold upon the strong urgings of the human will, then what relevance does it have to the human situation at all? There are people among us who have all that this world has to offer, but because they do not bring religion into their human program they are utterly distracted and distressed by a life that has no meaning, motive, or pattern. Or, there are others who through their human efforts have reached positions of security and influence in the world of business, finance, or the professions, yet who feel terribly unfulfilled because they have not discovered how genuine religion can transform advantages into opportunities to serve. This is why the angel of the Lord said to Peter and John: "Go, stand, and speak in the temple to the people all the words of this life." Note the phrase, "all the words." These words were good news to and for all of us and they were inseparably related to life. Jesus said, "The words I speak unto you, they are spirit and they are life."

Now, when religion becomes life in the way the New Testament advocates and teaches, there are three things that happen inevitably to us and these three things are closely related.

I

Our life is marked by *a new spirit*. When the early followers of Jesus fanned out into the Mediterranean world, they brought with their Christianity something that the pagan world did not have but sorely needed. For instance, the spirit of hope and expectation had become snuffed out and a sense of defeat, meaninglessness, of there being no way out, had claimed the mood of their thinkers and philosophers. As J. Robert Seeley said: "Philosophy could explain what is right, but only Christianity could help people to do it." Whatever, therefore, may have been uncouth, ordinary, and unimpressive about those early Christians, it was always forgotten when people saw the radiant light on their faces. And no pagan philosopher had ever seen anything quite like this before: religion so identified with life that it transformed human personalities and filled their lives with new meaning, direction, and eager expectation. In one of Walter Pater's novels, entitled *Marius: The Epicurean,* he tells of a young Christian named Cornelius, who was a friend of Marius who was a pagan. And so great an impression did Cornelius make on Marius' pagan mind that the latter said about him, "With Cornelius everything about him seemed to point to some other thing far beyond him." This is why these early Christians made such a powerful impact upon the pagan world. The words they heard were spirit; it changed human lives and these changes became realitites in their common life.

II

This new spirit created attitudes *that molded and shaped human conduct.* Someone has said that despair has three heads: agnosticism, which makes one lose courage in the search for knowledge; pessimism, which makes one lose courage in the search for progress; and cynicism, which makes one lose courage in the search for virtue. And if there is any disease that is rampant in the world of our time it is the disease of cynicism. And one of its favorite questions is: What difference does it make what a person believes? And those who are so quick to ask this question fail to see that it is followed logically and inevitably by another question: Does it make any difference what a person does? And the answer you give to this second question determines the answer you give to the first.

Have you ever observed the attitude and conduct of the person who claims it doesn't make any difference what you believe? He believes it is human nature to make enemies and then destroy them; therefore, he acts as if war were always inevitable. She believes that business is business and hence it is to be expected that shabby deals and betrayals will obtain in the world of trade and commerce. They believe the aggressiveness of the rich is balanced by the envy of the poor and hence it is inevitable that one-half of our world will continue on the edge of starvation while the other half will wallow in plenty. We see, then, that for the cynic everything is relative, and the idea of love, honesty, and truth being absolute and ultimate values is sheer fiction. This is what cynics believe and their outward conduct and character are direct reproductions of its implications. They have no eternal context or moral frame of reference and their verdict in every crisis is: Whatever did you expect?

But the new spirit that Christianity brought cleanses human attitudes, lays restraints on human conduct, and shakes apart the routine patterns of human character. For example, suppose you were an engineer and you took your little boy into the great control room of one of our modern mills or manufacturing plants, and as you threw the switch, your son would see that, but comprehend little more. But as the great compressors began to turn and the wheels started to roar, you as the engineer would realize that behind them were the long electric power lines, the dynamos, the turbines, and maybe the mighty Niagara River itself, but especially the genius of the human mind in tune with the magnetic laws of God's universe.

Here are suggested two ways in which many of us encounter life. The cynic acts like the child; life appears as so many separate actions or unrelated things: our automobiles, televisions, condos, and all other gadgets and objects seemingly so indispensable to our American way of life. But for the person to whom religion is life, our daily existence has contacts with horizons beyond the here and now. Hence, for the Christian, life becomes an anvil upon which character is fashioned and shaped; life is a window through which God's light of truth comes into the world of human existence; and life is a medium by which God came to earth in the person of his Son and through him touched his human creatures in a new and living way. What a tremendous change would occur in our lives if this new attitude and spirit would allow God to work through us for his own ends and to the glory of his purpose. Religion would be life indeed and our outward conduct and character would endorse its integrity and power. This is what Ian Macpherson meant by saying, "When Jesus takes possession of the heart everything else is changed."

III

When religion becomes life as the New Testament teaches, *it provides power to realize all it promises.* The famous American editor, Horace Greeley, told of receiving a letter from a woman who wrote as follows: "Our church is in dire financial straits. We have tried everything to keep it going: a strawberry festival, an oyster supper, a donkey party, a turkey dinner, and finally a box social. Will you please tell us, Dr. Greeley, how to keep a struggling church from disbanding?" Greeley answered her in a message of two words: *try Christianity!*

And what did he really mean by that? Look at it this way: the ancient world failed to help men and women meet the problem of life because although its philosophers could teach, they had not the power to put it into practice. The Old Testament prophets could explain the law of Moses but they lacked the strength necessary to fulfill it. Then into the midst of the ages, came this man, Jesus, and before the wondering eyes of men and women he declared, "I am the way, the truth, and the life." And people saw in him a new ideal to emulate; they saw truth come alive in his amazing personality; and when his enemies did him to death upon the cross, his spirit seemed to be liberated and he was now everywhere whenever people in their need cried out to him. And in all the ages since, for all those who committed themselves to him, he has brought power over human weakness, victory over failure, and conduct and character that have made this world a better place in which to live.

One of the greatest Christian women of a past generation was Lady Aberdeen who came out of a Highland home in Inverness, Scotland. She lived long before all the fuss and feathers of "women's lib," but when she died in 1939 the record of her achievement in the world of men and women read like a scroll of honor. In 1882 she founded an orphanage for Scottish children that was dedicated by Prime Minister Gladstone; in 1893 she founded the Onward and Upward Association to help ordinary domestics to secure education and recreation beyond the drudgery of their jobs; in 1897 she founded the Victorian Order of Nurses to help sick folk along the far-flung miles of the Canadian frontier; and in 1919 she led a delegation to the Peace Conference in Geneva on behalf of the women of the world. What was the force that undergirded her life and character so that she was able for sixty years to give herself in this way for the needs of the world? Just before her death in 1939 she said: "I find my one resource is to throw myself unreservedly upon the power of the Holy Spirit. . . . I make it a practice of standing at a certain place where I can look up at the mountains and say, 'I will lift up mine eyes unto the hills' and then I add, 'I can do all things through Christ who strengthens me.' "

This is the same power that not only makes men and women *do* great things, but basically to *be* what they are; which gives quality and character to all they say and achieve. Saint Paul declared, "By the grace of God, I am what I am." And that grace and power are available still to all who accept God's claim upon their life and who stand in obedience to his will.

48. Songs in the Night
James Earl Massey

I think of God, and I moan;
I meditate, and my spirit faints.
I commune with my heart in the night;
I meditate and search my spirit.—Psalm 77:3,6

I

THE PSALMIST did not specify the difficulty that pressed him, but from the rest of what he wrote it seems rather clear that the problem also involved many of his people, perhaps all of them. He longed for God's help during a difficult, disastrous, and prolonged period of time. So prolonged was the time, and so difficult the situation, that even thinking about why God had not intervened brought a burden to the man's questioning mind: thus that awesome sentence, "I think of God, and I moan." National woes mingled with his personal burdens, and the psalmist reacted in desperation. Sleepless, his eyes red from prolonged vigil as he waited for God to answer, he passed the night communing with his own heart. Mitchell Dahood's rendering makes the rest of the text even more vivid:

James Earl Massey was born in 1930 in Ferndale, Michigan. He received degrees from Detroit Bible College (now William Tyndale College) and Oberlin Graduate School of Theology. A member of the Church of God (Anderson, Indiana), Dr. Massey currently serves as dean of the University Chapel at Tuskegee University in Tuskegee, Alabama, where he also is university professor of religion and society. He has written sixteen books and hundreds of articles, and is a frequent preacher and lecturer at colleges, universities, and seminaries throughout the United States and abroad.

"Through the night I play the lyre, with my heart I commune that my spirit might be healed."[1]

There are those times of inward struggle when music is our best release and our readiest resource. Thomas Carlyle dared to suggest that music is our deepest reality, saying, "All deep things are Song. It seems somehow the very central essence of us, Song; as if all the rest were but wrappages and hulls. See deep enough," he continued, "and you see musically."[2]

The depth of experience he shared with his trouble people prodded the psalmist to sing. An experience of trouble prodded Paul and Silas to sing while waiting in that dank, dark jail cell at Philippi. A depth encounter with trouble stirred Jesus to sing some of the *Hallel* psalms with his frightened disciples on that awesome night before the day of the cross. All humans suffer, and all humans sing—either a song of faith or the blue notes of fate. Traverse the world, taking notice of the music of the masses, and you will come back home aware that songs are often profiles of the soul in crisis, indications, like our text, of some dark experience during which some soul communed with itself.

Such is the story behind the Negro spirituals. Through the long night of enslavement here our forefathers and mothers played the lyre, communing with their hearts, anxious that their spirits might be healed. The Negro spirituals are songs from the night; they are shafts of light for those who watch and wait for the expected new day.

II

Although these songs are universally known as "spirituals," songs with a religious character, they cannot rightly be understood or regarded until we recognize many of them as *honest documents of social protest.*

The spirituals are sorrow songs; they show the yearnings and hopes of an enslaved people. The lines of these songs describe grief, distress, physical and mental anguish, unfulfilled longing, and the inexpressible pain of being *slaves*. A pres-

sured history stands compressed in these songs, and in line
after line there is an outcry of longing for a needed change.

Social protest is clearly evident in such lines as these:

> O brothers, don't get weary,
> O brothers, don't get weary,
> O brothers, don't get weary,
> We're waiting for the Lord.
> We'll land on Canaan's shore,
> We'll land on Canaan's shore,
> When we land on Canaan's shore,
> We'll meet for ever more.

Canaan meant Canada, by way of the free North, and the
expected "landing" there would be by help from the Underground Railroad system. While the slavemasters thought of
Canaan as heaven the slaves sometimes used the word as part
of a distinct code whose meanings were thus hidden from all
except those with ears trained to hear. Frederick Douglass
confessed this understanding of "Canaan" in one of the songs
that fired his longing to set out for the free North and
Canada:[3]

> O Canaan, sweet Canaan,
> I am bound for the land of Canaan.

As Douglass himself stated it, "We meant to reach the
North, and the North was our Canaan."

There are many songs of protest among the spirituals. The
black slaves both calmed their spirits and fired their zeal for
freedom by their songs. If we would rightly understand the
spirituals we must begin with the truth that many of them are
reactions against a sorry social condition, honest documents of
social protest.

Howard Thurman, astute interpreter of Negro spirituals,
left us a penetrating discussion of the song "Heaven! Heaven!"
Thurman suggested that some slave had heard his master's
minister talk about heaven as the final abode of the righteous,
but he wondered how it could be that both he and the master

would be in heaven together, since they were so socially distant on earth. The slave knew that his present horror was due to the master's callous and greedy heart. So the slave reasoned that there must be two heavens, one for the master, and another for the slaves. But then he remembered that there was only *one God*, and that one God could not divide himself eternally between two separate places. There was but one conclusion left: the slave reasoned that he was having his hell now, while the master was having his heaven now, and that after death their positions would be reversed.

So, chopping cotton the next day, having thought the matter through, the barefooted slave said to his working mate:

> I got shoes.
> You got shoes,
> All God's children got shoes.
> When we get to heaven
> We're goin' to put on our shoes
> An' shout all over God's heaven.
> Heaven! Heaven!

Then casting a knowing eye up toward the big house where the master lived, the slave quipped:

> Everybody talkin' 'bout heaven
> Ain't goin' there![4]

III

But over and beyond the social protest we hear in some of the spirituals, there is *a central spiritual witness these songs hold and convey*. In my view, the spirituals still rank as the highest and most original creative expression to date of the black American religious experience.

The persistent perspective regarding God—the life-affirming attitude despite their suffering—the spirit of hope that speaks so courageously about the best as yet to come— the profound conviction that no problems nor masters have the last word where faith reigns—the deep assurance that death is only a part of life and not the end of life—the soul-

embracing awareness that knowing Jesus means identity, courage, inward balance, and a saving companionship—all these
are explicit religious insights and authentic biblical emphases.
Thus the common designation by which we refer to these
songs as *spirituals.*

Historian Arnold J. Toynbee, deeply impressed by how
our black ancestors responded so creatively to their servitude
and suffering, wrote: "The Negro has adapted himself to his
new social environment by rediscovering in Christianity certain original meanings and values that Western Christendom
has long ignored." Then, based on that fact, Toynbee daring-
ly suggested this:

> It is possible that the Negro slave immigrants
> who have found Christianity in America may
> perform the greater miracle of raising the dead
> to life. . . . They may perhaps be capable of
> kindling the cold grey ashes of Christianity
> which have been transmitted to them by us
> until, in their hearts, the divine fire glows
> again. It is thus perhaps, if at all, that
> Christianity may conceivably become the living
> faith of a dying civilization for the second
> time.[5]

Was his suggestion prophetic? These songs do offer a heritage that can make us needed agents of spiritual renewal.

Max Bennett Thrasher, a Northern newspaper writer who
was closely associated with Tuskegee in its early years, wrote
about a certain chapel service he attended here. During the
course of the service, Thrasher heard Booker T. Washington
call out asking anyone interested among the students to voice
a new song for all the others to learn. There was a brief
wait. . . .

> Then far back in the house, some single voice
> chants, half timidly at first, the words of a
> hymn which perhaps had never been heard
> before outside the backwoods church or cabin

home where the singer learned it. The quaint,
high-pitched melody rises and falls—a voice
alone—until a dozen quick ears catch the
theme and a dozen voices are humming an
accompaniment. The second time the refrain is
reached a few voices join in boldly, a hundred
follow, and then a thousand, sending up into
the arches of the roof such a volume of sound
as one is rarely permitted to hear.[6]

The students at Tuskegee Institute were drilled in spiritual singing in those days. From its beginning, this school has maintained and passed on the beautiful and expressive black songs of faith and hope. The "Singing Windows" which adorn this chapel give their silent witness to our great heritage in song, but even in every service of worship held here, that witness is also voiced in one or more of these songs. The reason relates not only to precedent, but to purpose. The spirituals give us music from strugglers intent to encourage strugglers. This is music of courage to bless the weak, music of faith to inspire hope. This is music of searchers who found something eternal and someone immortal. These songs from the night are shafts of light for those who watch for a needed new day.

IV

In one of his books about the spirituals, Howard Thurman tells about a time when some of his generation seemed ashamed of this music, while some others recoiled from seeing these songs used by minstrels to amuse and exploited by whites to entertain. During his senior year at Morehouse College, a major incident occurred in chapel in connection with the singing of spirituals. In the interest of a small party of white visitors from an organization that strongly supported Morehouse, the black director of music asked one of the students to sing the first line of an announced spiritual, and the rest of the students were to come in on the song after that, singing the body of the text. The student began his line, as directed, but the student body did not join in afterward. The student repeated his directed line, but the student body again refused to respond. President Hope was deeply embarrassed and called for a special assembly that evening during which he soundly reprimanded the entire black student body. The response of the students to him was very simple: "We refuse to sing our songs to delight and amuse white people. The songs are ours and a part of the source of our own inspiration transmitted to us by our forefathers."[7]

There is something intimate and personal about the Negro spirituals, these songs from the night, and there is something intense and involving in them. They give us our history. They honor our heritage of hope. They witness to our faith. They nurture our self-respect. These songs echo our theology, voice our theodicy, and mirror our souls. They make something timely and timeless available to our spirits. They help us to get through our dark nights, enabling us to meet the exigencies of our lives with faith, fortitude, and essential pride.

NOTES

1. Mitchell Dahood, *The Anchor Bible* (Garden City, NY: Doubleday & Co., Inc., 1968), p. 223.

2. See his essay on "The Hero As a Poet," in *Heroes, Hero-Worship, and the Heroic in History*, ed. Archibald MacMechan (Boston: Ginn and Co., 1901), p. 95.

3. Frederick Douglass, *The Life and Times of Frederick Douglass* (Hartford, CN: 1882), p. 179.

4. See Howard Thurman, *Jesus and the Disinherited* (Nashville: Abingdon-Cokesbury Press, 1949), p. 61; see also his *Deep River: Reflections on the Religious Insights of Certain of the Negro Spirituals* (New York: Harper & Brothers, 1955), pp. 43–44.

5. Arnold J. Toynbee, *A Study of History*, abridgment of Volumes I–VI by D. C. Somervell (Oxford, 1947), p. 129.

6. Max Bennett Thrasher, *Tuskegee: Its Story and Its Work* (Freeport, NY: Books for Libraries Press, 1971 reprint of the 1900 publication), p. 84.

7. Howard Thurman, *Deep River and The Negro Spiritual Speaks of Life and Death* (Richmond, IN: Friends United Press, 1975), p. 6.

49. Polishing Old Dreams
W. Wayne Price

Scripture: Genesis 11:31–12:3

Introduction

Do you have any old dreams? Those you deem worthless, put on a shelf in the back of a closet, carry around unfulfilled in your pocket? You know the kind I mean; you described them after the words, "When I grow up," "One of these days," "When I get finished with," "Someday, I." Maybe you wanted to be a police officer, adopt a child, take a class in public speaking, be a missionary, start a group, volunteer in some helping agency. We all have those kinds of dreams, visions, plans, fantasies, and speculations. One of my own dreams developed in my early teen years. I wanted to finish high school, buy a car, and build a kind of wooden chest of drawers in the trunk, to provide orderly storage for everything I owned— very little. I wanted to set out on the road, with no special place in mind; stop along the way to earn enough to keep going, and see what life brought. But most of all, I wanted not to be encumbered, tied down, obligated. I look back on that dream and see how completely opposite my life has turned out. In fact, nothing could

---

W. *Wayne Price* is pastor of Williamsburg Baptist Church in Wiliamsburg, Virginia. He pursued his education at Lexington Theological Seminary, the University of Kentucky, Southern Baptist Theological Seminary, and Carson Newman College. Price has also pastored Baptist churches in Kentucky, is a frequent contributor to publications of the Baptist Sunday School Board, and is active in several community service agencies. He and his wife, a professional counselor, are the parents of two daughters.

now be more unpleasant to me than living in a motor home, traveling around the country. That dream belonged to me, however, and I remember it and value it even though I would not like to pursue it now. But let's return to your dreams. Have you recalled one or two? Have you recreated the images in your mind? Now, what happened to them? Have you stored them away, willingly and comfortably, so that you can recall them, talk about them, laugh about them in such a way that they create no sadness or regret? Or have you put them on the shelf, out of sight, where they gather dust and attract some occasional, private, and wistful regret? These dreams may even bring tears or pain because of their importance. Maybe you were forced to put that special dream aside because of circumstances, because another choice made it impossible. Maybe you put it aside because it was too much work, too risky. But you did not discard it completely. By keeping it barely out of sight, even though it may be dusty and tarnished by time and dormancy, you have continued to take it seriously. Your dream continues to be valuable. And if you can say this much, you can also admit that it is not perhaps as impossible as you had thought.

Another question. Where did the dreams come from? Are they God-given? Have they developed from your nobler side? Do they contain any qualities of mission, service, altruism, benevolence? Would they tend to make you a better person than you are? How would the fulfillment of your dreams contribute to other people, the community, the church, the Kingdom of God? In other words, what difference would it make to anyone if your dreams were realized? Maybe the place to begin is to get them out, polish them up, ask some good questions about them, and then decide once and for all if your dreams are useless artifacts of another age or useful beacons calling us to what we are meant to be.

An Obscure Bible Story Encourages Us in Our Dreams

Most of us know about Abraham. Few of us know about his father, Terah. Two men with the same dream. They lived in a place called Ur of the Chaldeans. Terah dreamed of going to another country, Canaan, or what was to be termed "The Promised Land." The story is conveniently sketchy; we can let our imaginations run wild. We have no idea why he wanted to go, how long he thought about it, planned for it, or what obstacles he encountered. But one day he left, with his entire extended family: his two sons and one grandson. Ur was located southeast of what is now Israel, and the journey was moderately long for nomads. About halfway between Ur and Canaan lay a city called Haran. The Bible says they went forth to Canaan, *but* . . . when they came to Haran, they settled there. Terah's dream apparently was put on the shelf. He did not realize what he set out to find. The saddest words in the story are these: "and Terah died in Haran." That was not his destination.

What happened? Did someone become ill? Did Terah decide his dream was unrealistic, unworthy, unnecessary? Did he find things quite comfortable in Haran? Did he break down under the difficulty of the trip? Did he receive strong objections from someone in his family? Did he run into financial trouble? Was he threatened by marauding Bedouins? We only know he went halfway, settled in, and died. His dream never materialized for him.

The story is sketchy, tantalizing, and magnetic. We all share in a story of a dream which is never fulfilled, even though we invested a great deal in it. In some sense, this is a story of middle-aged people. We dreamed of certain things when we were young; we adjusted those dreams in the light of our changing circumstances; we learned to accept those limitations; we then live out the balance of our lives with adjusted expectations. But in another sense, this story includes everyone who has ever watched a fire fighter slide down a fire pole, a chorus line of dancers, a sailor board a ship, or a ball player get a winning hit. We all dream: the little boy in a cowboy hat, the little girl playing dress up; a teenager singing along with the radio, and every young woman who subscribes to *Bride* magazine. We all share something with Terah and his family.

So What Do We Do with Our Dreams?

First of all, we take them seriously—our own and other people's. We need to consider them and reconsider them. We need to modify them and talk about them. We need to ask questions, measure them, evaluate and test them. But most of all, we need to take them off the shelf now and then, polish them up, and see where they fit in the present. An old fable tells about a nightingale that traded its feathers to a peddler for worms. All the peddler asked was one feather for one worm. It was a daily transaction; the bird had plenty of feathers; it took place over a long period of time. But you know what happened. The nightingale gave up so many feathers, it was no longer able to fly.[1] I suspect our dreams are the feathers on which we fly; when we trade our dreams for anything, even food to survive, our lives are terribly diminished. Take your dreams seriously!

Second, we need to test our dreams by some standards we trust. The people of God do well to ask if our goals, our visions, our hopes and plans contribute to God's Kingdom, the common good, the needs of others, or whether they simply feed our own self-interests. What if you realize your dream? Will you be better for it, or worse? Of course, even our most noble ambitions serve ourselves in some way, if only for the pride of setting out to do something good and succeeding. But the real weight ought to rest on a larger foundation than one's self. We test our dreams by standards higher than ourselves.

Third, take a risk. Invest something with the idea that you may fail. After all, as one preacher is fond of saying, "Christians are the only ones who can afford to fail." I often think the younger we are, the more likely we are to risk because the less we know about the pitfalls. What is risk for us now was no big deal twenty years ago. I'm glad we lose some of that fearlessness, but we may lose too much of it.

Sheldon Kopp, a Washington psychologist and best-selling author, tells about his first job, in a state mental hospital. He said he was so innocent, he did not know these patients could not be helped. His "yet unbattered personal commitment, naive and boundless enthusiasm, and exaggerated self-confidence" enabled him to rekindle a spark of life in those unresponsive, forgotten, catatonic men and women. He says that "only after age and experience made me more realistic did I achieve professional sanity so that I was no longer able to be of any help to those poor captive souls."[2]

Dreams can't be too realistic or they would not be dreams!

Fourth, dreams may need to be passed along. If they are kept alive, they can be inspiring to others. Not all dreams become reality in the dreamer's lifetime, or even in the exact way they were envisioned. Moses dreamed of the promised land, saw it, led his people to its edge, but never got in. Jesus dreamed of the Kingdom of God, introduced it, preached it and died for it, but it is still unfulfilled on earth. Gandhi dreamed of freedom for India but he died before it came. Martin Luther King, Jr., had a dream of a society without prejudice and violence, but he never saw it. Yet all great dreamers know that great dreams are never private, never easy.

I wonder why dreams seem to be the property of the powerless, and those with power seem so short on dreams. I suspect the reason is because those with so little power have only their dreams, while those with power have too much to lose. I wonder if Abraham's father Terah found the good life in Haran and figured that Canaan could not possibly offer him more that he had. And I wonder if we have not put old dreams on the shelf because we have become too comfortable, too secure. And I wonder if we ought not get them out, polish them up, take some risks, because we were never more alive than when we carried our dreams in our hands.

NOTES

1. Fredrick Speakman, *The Salty Tang* (Westford, NJ: Fleming H. Revell Company, 1954), p. 42.

2. Kopp, *If You Meet the Buddha on the Road, Kill Him* (New York: Bantam, 1972) p. 91.

50. Moving Through Darkness
Amy L. Bridgeman

Scripture: Luke 22:47–53

Back in February, in the depths of winter,
  some friends of mine came up to New Hampshire for a
visit.
While they were here, we took a trip over to Dunbarton to see
my friend Emily.
It was afternoon when we arrived at Emily's,
  but by the time we were ready to leave,
  darkness had fallen.
And it was *really* dark.
As we groped our way out to the car, my friend said to me,
  "I'd forgotten how dark it can get in the country."

It is true—without city lights around,
  the darkness seems to take on a life of its own—it seems to
have a shape and form,
And without the city lights to guide us,
  we were blinded for a time.

Amy L. Bridgeman is associate minister of the First Congregational Church in Manchester, New Hampshire. She is a graduate of Phillips University and received a master of divinity degree from the Boston University School of Theology in 1984. Bridgeman is currently an intern at the Pastoral Counseling Services in Manchester and is a pastoral counselor-in-training with the American Association of Pastoral Counselors.

Yet, as our eyes adjusted to the darkness,
    we saw the beauty and the wonder of that glorious night.
The stars stood out clearly—
    they were sharply defined by the black midnight sky.
The moon was a crisp globe spreading a soft glow over everything,
And the trees and shrubs seemed to have a stark beauty.
It was a solemn moment as we stood in silence,
    gazing around in awe,
    overcome by the power and beauty in the darkness.

Tonight, we come with a similar purpose.
    We come to experience the darkness that occurred so many years ago.
For it is Maundy Thursday—
    the night that we gather to remember the last supper of Christ with his disciples,
    the night that we remember the despair of Christ in the Garden of Gethsemene,
    the night that we remember the horror of his betrayal by Judas, and his denial by Peter.
It is a solemn occasion,
    as we remember those events that led up to the crucifixion.

And it is *difficult.*

Those of us accumstomed to the light feel disoriented by darkness—
    we are blinded, and feel as though we are groping.
And even when we become adjusted to the darkness,
    what we see can be frightening.

    The shapes of night seem odd and out of proportion to our eyes.
    What was once an innocent tree suddenly looms up like a monster, or demon, or some strange bogeyman ready to pounce.

Holy Week is hard.
When we allow ourselves to sit at the table with Christ,
    we experience again the betrayal that we have felt by loved
ones,
    we remember the times we have betrayed someone close to
us.
When we allow ourselves to enter the story of Christ's passion,
When we sit in the garden waiting,
    we remember all the times we have let someone down who
really needed us,
    we experience again the disappointment we feel by those
we have trusted,

When we stand by and watch Christ being carried away,
    we know once more the despair and hopelessness of seeing
a dream being shattered.

Holy Week— Maundy Thursday—seeing in the dark—

It is *hard*.

And yet, that is exactly what we must do.
We cannot go from Palm Sunday to Easter morning
    unless we pass through the darkness of Holy Week,
Just as we cannot truly experience the dawn
    unless we have known the darkness.
We must *claim* the darkness and *move* through it to the other
side.

Now, I have to tell you, before I go any further,
    that I have always been afraid of the dark.
When I was little, I left a light on in my room,
    and after I fell asleep, my father would come and turn off
the light for me.
Later, I moved up to a night-light.
And then, a few years ago,
    I had a dream that changed all that.

I dreamed that I stood at the entrance to a cave.
  Behind me was the light,
    in front of me—only darkness.
I was scared, but I walked into the cave.
  Sure, enough, there in front of me was a *huge* dragon.
I looked around for a sword to kill the dragon,
  but there was none in sight—not even a tree branch—
And I couldn't get close enough to poke out his eyes,
So I did some fast talking.

And I realized that the dragon was lonely—
  it wanted a friend.

So I made a deal: if the dragon would spare my life,
  I would be its friend.

Well, it was just a dream,
  but it made me realize that I needed to look at my fears,
I needed to walk into my own darkness
  and befriend the monsters I might find there.

We all have our own monsters,
  our secret fears and worries,
  our skeletons that we keep hidden away in closets of shame,
Yet there comes a time when we need to walk into our own darkest spots,
  and befriend the dragons we find there.
We need to befriend those dragons that we name anger, or fear, or desire, or
  depression.

In our lives and in our faith we cannot afford to skip this point.

We cannot move beyond our fear of the darkness,
  unless we face our fear,
We cannot move *through* the darkness

unless we take the first step and enter.
Just as we cannot come to Easter
    unless we enter into the passion of Christ as well.

We must walk into the darkness.

Second, we must allow our eyes to adjust to the darkness,
    to let go of our old ways of seeing,
    and to see with a different perspective.

Artists and painters know the importance of this way of seeing.
In creating a work of art,
    the artist does not draw the light,
    the artist draws the shadows.

Just as the darkness in a painting adds depth and dimension to
the canvas,
Just as the shadows define the shapes and forms within the
work of art,
So too, does darkness add depth to our faith.

As we enter the darkness of Holy Week— and especially of
Maundy Thursday—
    we must "see" our God in a new way,
    we must allow our faith to adjust to a new understanding of
God.
In the darkness of Christ's passion,
    we must let go of the images
    of the powerful God of the Old Testament,
    of the triumphant God of Palm Sunday,
    of the victorious God of Easter morning.
Tonight, in the darkness, we open our eyes to see the power-
less Christ,
    the victim Christ,

    the Christ who was betrayed, beaten, accused, mocked,
condemned to death on the cross.
And, when we allow ourselves to see in the darkness,

to experience the darkness of our faith,
Then our faith is richer, deeper, more alive.

Darkness calls us to see in a new way.

Last, I want to say that within the darkness there is creation—

Darkness is a place of growth, of change, of transformation.

I think about how a seed, planted in the dark soil,
    springs forth into life,
Or that a baby is born into the world
    after nine months in the darkness of the mother's womb.

For the seed, and the child,
    the darkness is a place of nurture, of growth.

Darkness is a place of creation.

Even the words of creation point out the importance of God's creative ability
    in the darkness.
Genesis 1 says:
    "In the beginning God created the heavens and the earth,
    The earth was without form and void, and darkness was
upon the face of the deep."

God chooses to work in and through the darkness to bring forth life.

    That is the importance of the passion story—
    It is the central point on which our faith hangs—
God took the darkness of death and brought new life.

God chooses to use those events that we remember tonight—
    the betrayal, the despair of the Garden, the arrest, the

cross—
to bring forth new life.

Tonight, we come into the darkness—
    we come to face our fears,
    we come to see our faith in a new way,
    we come to be transformed.
And always, we bear witness to the creative power of God,

Who moves with us, through the darkness.

51. Being Lifted Up
Phyllis R. Pleasants

Text: Hosea 11:1–4, NEB

IT WAS ONLY ten o'clock in the morning. I had been to only one class, but it had been a horrible day already. The tension had started mounting the minute I opened my eyes that morning. Who knows, maybe it started *before* I opened my eyes. I was so anxious, angry, feeling so alienated, actually, that I thought if I had to pass and smile at one more human being I was going to die. I just had to get away—to somewhere that was quiet, where I could be alone and try to figure out what was going on inside me.

There are two places I usually go when I need to be a hermit, where it is quiet and I can depend on not seeing anyone. I went to the first and there were people there. With mounting anxiety I went to the second and there were people there, too! I thought I would give up, but before I could leave, the other people left. With a sigh and a thank you, Lord, I sank into a chair. As the silence stole in and enveloped me like a fog I decided, "Well, I'm too upset to study. Might as well read my devotional since I didn't get around to that either this morn-

Phyllis Rodgerson Pleasants is a Ph.D. student in church history at Southern Baptist Theological Seminary in Louisville, Kentucky. She is a graduate of Mary Washington College and the University of Virginia. Pleasants has contributed book reviews to the *Baptist Peacemaker* and has been active in pastoral work in Kentucky, Virginia, and Indiana. She has also worked as a legislative/research assistant and has been a high school social studies teacher.

ing." I reached into my briefcase, yanked out the devotional book I had been using, and began reading without really paying attention to what I was reading.

Suddenly my whole being became alert as I read: "When Israel was a child I loved him and and I called my son out of Egypt. . . . I myself taught Ephraim to walk, I took them in my arms; yet they have not understood that I was the one looking after them. I was like someone who lifts an infant close against his cheek. . . ." (Hos. 11:1-4, NEB). What? Where was that in the Bible? Hosea. I knew I had read Hosea, but I didn't remember reading that before and had to read it again. "I was like someone who lifts an infant close against his cheek"and then I felt it. I literally experienced being lifted close to someone's cheek and all my anxiety and alienation melted away in that experience of being swooped up to the someone I love.

Do you remember what it's like to be small enough to be lifted up by someone you love? Remember that initial feeling of gleeful abandonment and the laughter as you begin to rise? Remember then the feeling of terror as you realize your feet have left the ground and you wonder what will happen next? Remember the feeling of trust that comes over you as you recognize the face you are being brought closer to as that of someone you love? Remember realizing those arms and hands are going to hold you, hug you, keep you safe, not let you fall? Hosea says that's what God is like, lifting us up as someone lifts an infant close against one's cheek.

Then I realized we experience these same things when we feel especially close to the Divine. The initial feeling of gleeful abandonment, laughter, then the terror as we bocome disoriented from being "swooped up," and then the trust, if we hang on to the experience long enough. When I went to my Bible to find the context for his passage, though, I realized how we, like the Israelites, too often wriggle free and drop to the ground once we experience the terror. We seldom let ourselves hang on long enough to know the trust that comes once we recognize the face of the one holding us as that of someone we love.

Hosea presents us with one of the most intimate portrayals of God ever until the self-revelation of God in Jesus Christ. Using the imagery from his own tragic love for someone who rejected him, yet whom he still loved, Hosea described what he felt had happened between Yahweh and Israel. "Seldom is the revelation of God mediated through such depth of person anguish and suffering as one finds in Hosea's agony. Only the later suffering of Jesus transcends the personal sorrow of Hosea as a medium of divine revelation."[1] Hosea felt he had a sense of how God must feel as he experienced the depths of his own pain at being rejected yet being unable to stop loving the one who had rejected him.

After using his own love relationship as an analogy for Israel's relationship with God, Hosea then recorded God's case against Israel. "Hear the word of the Lord, O Israel; for the Lord has a charge to bring against the people of the land" (Hos. 4:1, NEB). The largest section of this prophet's message is God's case against Israel for faithlessness again and again and again, regardless of what God did to show God's love for them. "I took them in my arms; yet they have not understood that I was the one looking after them."

Following this soliloquy of faithlessness on the part of God's people, Hosea tells us about the judgment of God that is a result of this faithlessness. It is in the midst of describing God's judgment, though, that Hosea uses the intimate imagery I read to illustrate God's care for God's people. Hosea reminds Israel of their being called out of Egypt by God as *children* of God. "Called" is an election verb; it means "summon into a relation." The focal event for all of Israel's history is the Exodus and here Hosea clothes the event with all the feeling and personal involvement that belong to a father's (parent's) relation to a beloved child.

In our passage, the basic notion is the helpless dependence on an adult that every child experiences. James Luther Mays says, "So far as one can tell from the Old Testament Hosea is the first to base Yahweh's relation to Israel on his [Yahweh's] love."[2] Such intimate imagery in the midst of judgment! How

God must grieve to pass judgment on God's own children! As in "the parent both mercy and discipline are present within the context of love," so Hosea shows us God's mercy and God's wrath within the context of deepest love.[3]

God had called Israel to be God's people, to depend on God with the absolute dependence of an infant on an adult. God had lifted up Israel, held them close, but again and again Israel had wriggled free and chosen to pursue other gods. Other gods seemed more real, closer, more present. You could see them and they certainly seemed to be protecting the mighty nations which surrounded Israel. Why depend on Yahweh, an unseen force, to protect them when there was Egypt or Assyria? They could see their might and force, and feel safe. Again and again Israel chose to follow the course that appeared the safest, but was a dead-end disaster from which Yahweh would rescue them. With every rescue Israel would rejoice. You can almost feel their gleeful abandonment and hear their laughter as once again they are restored to God.

However, being in close communion with God is a disorienting experience and soon the terror would set in. Demands for more tangible forms of security, and frustration with the elusive other, would lead to rebellion—seeking to experience trust and love in more tangible expressions of gods before whom they could perform their rituals in hopes of assuaging the fury of those gods. In a desperate search for intimacy and communion with God, Israel settled for gods they hoped to appease rather than the God who loved them "like someone who lifts an infant close against his cheek." In their terror they rejected the very source of that which they most desperately sought.

We are the Israelites of today. Frederick Buechner says in "Message in the Stars,"

> For what we need to know, of course, is not just
> that God exists, not just that beyond the steely
> brightness of the stars there is a cosmic
> intelligence of some kind that keeps the whole

show going, but that there is a God right here
in the thick of our day-by-day lives who may
not be writing messages about himself in the
stars but who in one way or another is trying to
get messages through our blindness as we move
around down here knee-deep in the fragrant
muck and misery and marvel of the world. It is
not objective proof of God's existence that we
want but . . . the experience of God's presence.
That is the miracle we are really after, and that
is also, I think, the miracle that we really get.[4]

I agree with Buechner. How often do we miss experiencing that miracle? How often do we, like the ancient Israelites,
insist on having our own gods who are shaped, formed, and
controlled by us? Manageable presence, available on demand
if you just know the right code, perform the right ritual. How
often do we settle for making gods of ourselves? For pushing
our ambitions, our desires, our needs down the throats of everyone within a fifty-mile radius as a mask for the desperate
need for communion, for intimacy with the God who created
us, who calls us into being? How often do we search frantically,
trying every religious or psychological fad around to experience intimacy in the hopes of being reassured that God is
"walking in the fragrant muck and misery and marvel" of our
lives? How often do we, like the Israelites of old, become disoriented when God does enter our lives, and lifts us up to hold us
securely? Because our feet have left the ground, we become
terrified, wriggle free, and search for something more tangible on which to depend. How often do we say that experiencing the very presence for which we do desperately search is not
real, and then search for another reality? How often does God
say about us, "I took them in my arms; yet they have not understood that I was the one looking after them."?

Hosea reminds us of a love that will not let us go no matter
how much we deserve to be let go. The prophet's words end
with a message or repentance, forgiveness, and restoration, a
chance once again to be in intimate communion with God.

Such love we cannot fathom, reason, or explain. We *can* experience it when we allow ourselves to be as helpless children totally dependent on an adult. We can experience such love when we hang on long enough to get past the disorienting terror of being lifted up to recognize the face of the one we are approaching as the one we love and have been searching for all along. Hosea reminds us, "God loves us not because we are lovable but because God is love."[5] God's nature is love. We need to depend on that love as the ultimate source for our life.

The woman had struggled for some time with feelings of inadequacy, fear, searching for something tangible on which she could depend. She was terrified that what she had thought was following God was once again merely following a god of self-justification, trying to prove to herself that she was worthwhile. In the depths of the struggle this prayer poured out: Oh God! I'm so scared. I want to be a star! I want to be somebody! I want to be recognized and admired. I want to be an expert in something! I want to achieve and accomplish and be rewarded with respect and admiration for it. I want to be a star!

Why? Is my self-image so low that I'm afraid no one, not even you, will know I'm around unless I *do* something extraordinary? I don't want to do just anything—I want to be extraordinary! Buechner talks about how we're all afraid of the shadows because we don't want to be one. We strive for the sunlight—to be seen, recognized, admired—because no one wants to be a shadow.

> I want to be a star! I want to be the exception to
> everything! Not out of arrogance but because
> I'm afraid. Afraid to be ordinary. Afraid to be
> me. Afraid that no matter who or what I am, it
> will never be good enough for anyone or
> anything on this earth, never mind for you.
> But that's the point, isn't it? We're never
> good enough for you. And in my fear of not
> being good enough, I miss the glory of
> knowing you love me anyway, with a love that is
> more than I will ever conceptualize or fully

understand in this life. Thank you. How I praise you for your faithfulness even when mine wavers.

Amen.

NOTES

1. "Hosea," *The Broadman Bible Commentary*, Roy L. Honeycutt, Jr., Vol. 7 (Nashville: Broadman Press, 1978), p. 1.

2. "Hosea," *The Old Testament Library*, James Luther Mays (Philadelphia: The Westminster Press, 1979), p. 153.

3. Fred M. Wood, *Hosea: Prophet of Reconciliation* (Nashville: Convention Press, 1975), p. 97.

4. "Message in the Stars," *The Magnificent Defeat*, Frederick Buechner (New York: The Seabury Press, 1966), p. 47.

5. "Hosea," *The Interpreter's Bible*, John Manchline, Harold Cooke Phillips (Nashville: Abingdon, 1956), p. 681.

52. Go Ahead and Grow
Edward Paul Cohn

MY DEAR FRIENDS and gentle hearts;

You know it and I know it, that legend that our people have recounted for at least two thousand years, and it invariably comes to mind on this holy night of the New Year.

It's one of those tales that we often first hear as young children, and though we may mature and grow in sophistication and awareness, its unforgettable imagery impresses our deepest subconscious, only to be revived each and every year at this season.

Rav Jochanon, scholar and sage of the first century of the Common Era, tells us that three great books are opened in heaven on the Rosh Hashanah evening. The first for the thoroughly righteous, and another volume for the unrelievedly wicked, and then the third: an enormous book for those of us who are the in-between, by no means saints, but surely not devils either.

The thoroughly righteous are immediately inscribed into

Edward Paul Cohn is senior rabbi of Congregation Temple Sinai in New Orleans, Louisiana. He graduated from the University of Cincinnati, Hebrew Union College–Jewish Institute of Religion, and St. Paul School of Theology. Cohn is a contributing editor of *Pulpit Digest* and is a contributor to the *Journal of Religion and Aging*. He has also been rabbi of congregations in Georgia, Missouri, and Pennsylvania. This sermon was preached on Rosh Hashanah Eve 5747 (October 3, 1986).

the book of life for the New Year. The unrelievedly wicked are forthwith inscribed into the book of death for the New Year. But ah, the fate of the in-between! Their future is left in suspension, under advisement, from Rosh Hashanah until the final blast of the shofar at the close of Yom Kippur.

Now it is during this ten-day period, according to our legend, that the divine all-seeing eye and all-perceptive judge will deliberate each one's verdict from heaven. "Let's see—Chaim Yonkle—the book of life or the book of death?" And I ask you, dear friends, is there any wonder that this temple is filled tonight? We want life! I want it. You want it. And when we consider our future, our fate, our continuance, our life, even a legend becomes a matter of no little consequence, doesn't it?

Speaking of life, I happened upon this whimsical fancy, the product of an anonymous author, and I think it raises a rather intriguing notion: that you and I really should live our lives *backward*. Yes, that's right, *backward*. Listen to this:

> Life is tough. It takes up a lot of your time, all your weekends, and what do you get in the end of it? . . . I think that the life cycle is all backward. You should die first, get it out of the way. Then you live twenty years in an old-age home. You get kicked out when you're too young. You get a gold watch, you go to work. You work forty years until you're young enough to enjoy your retirement. You go to college; you party until you're ready for high school; you go to grade school; you become a little kid; you play. You have no responsibilities.
>
> You become a little baby; you go back into the womb; you spend your last nine months floating; and you finish up as a gleam in somebody's eye.

Well, that sounds great, but that's not how it works. John Lennon once said that "Life is what happens while you are making plans," and I am here tonight to tell each and every one of you that Judaism is what can happen all the while Jews live life. And there isn't a single instant along life's continuum, from womb to tomb, about which our Judaism doesn't have something to teach, to impart, to sanctify, and yes, to celebrate and affirm.

Frankly, too often I meet folks who have come to think that our tradition is little more than a dusty, old collection of lingering "Thou shalt nots." Some even assume that its teachings are so designed as to limit our participation in and enjoyment of life. And I don't believe *that* for an instant, that such ever was ever the purpose of dynamic Jewish law and discipline. Had it been no more that *that*, we Jews, intelligent people that we are, would have given up on Judaism long age. History records no such defections.

Judaism is predicated upon joyous, ethical, and positive living. It's faith which, I believe, realistically surveys the world and those who walk around in it and that honestly acknowledges our moral frailties and challenges, but also endeavors to lift up and exalt the human spirit. There is no intent to confine us from dreaming or to hold us ransom to gloom or despair because of anyone's sin—original or otherwise.

Such is the hope-filled, liberating message of a thirty-five-hundred-year-old faith which has a profound statement to make to us in this day and at this time. Now I speak to you as a rabbi who proudly chose to be a Reform Jew. Traditional law, halakah, has a vote but certainly not a veto in my assessment of God, Israel, and Torah. I stand before you this evening as an unrepentant religious liberal who passionately believes that there lives a God, that we Jews have a mission to maintain our covenant with that God, and, moreover, that God wants us to go ahead!

I labor to interpret our tradition with reverence and conscience, in an earnest desire to make of it far more than a mere religion of convenience. And as I have come to know our Judaism, and continue to study and love it, there has dawned the wondrous realization that God wants us to go ahead and grow!

And that's it in a nutshell, what Cohn has to say to you on this holy night: go ahead and grow!

A burglar stole into a house in the dark of night. But as he entered one of the rooms, there was a parrot in a cage which quickly spotted him. "Burglar, burglar," the parrot cried out. "Burglar, burglar!" And with that, unnoticed by the thief, two of the meanest Dobermans you've ever imagined walked silently through a side door and into the room.

Well, the parrot continued, "Burglar, burglar" and the thief, in sheer disgust, looked up at the parrot and said, "You dumb bird, is that the only word you know?" To which the parrot replied, "No, I also know Sic 'em! Sic 'em!"

Well, dear friends, I am a one-word, one-issue man, and for me the word is growth. Our God-given potential for growth stands as the entire impetus of my theology. Thomas Scott concluded that growth "is the only evidence of life," and I'll agree with that!

By growth, I mean the construction of character: the capacity to improve, to attain understanding, to live better, to do better, to *be* better.

By growth, I speak of that process by which we take blocks of time and , with the mortar of our moral and religious ideals, labor to build a structure before the end of our days in which we may live with dignity. That's growth! And it incorporates such ingredients as dreams and hopes, perseverance and sacrifice, courage and goodness, self-esteem, and the ability to befriend both others and ourselves.

Norman Mailer remarks:

> Every moment of one's existence, one is growing into more or retreating into less. One is always living a little more or dying a little bit. . . .

Our tradition bids us go ahead and live a little more. Go ahead and grow. And here's how to grow.

I. Grow Out, But Don't Grow In

During World War II, a name was coined by French doctors for a disease that made its appearance in prison camps. They called it "barbed-wire sickness." One of its symptoms was an appalling sense of futility and meaninglessness of existence. No matter what camp activities were organized, nothing, it seemed, could banish from their minds the awareness of that barbed wire. As much as to the barbed wire and the guards in the towers, these prisoners, you see, were captives to their own despair. And I think that some of us have become afflicted by this self-same disease: barbed-wire sickness!

Grow out of your self-absorption! We need to free ourselves from those self-erected barbed-wire fences, don't we? Author Leo Buscaglia has written a fine new book, *Bus Nine to Paradise,* and by way of explaining its unusual title, he writes:

> One peaceful Sunday I found myself wandering
> in one of Melbourne's distant suburbs. I came
> upon a bus stop that had a large sign. My eye
> was struck by a designation that read "Bus
> Nine to Paradise." How wonderful it sounded
> . . . . Wouldn't it be wonderful if we could
> settle back on a bus destined for Paradise? It
> seldom occurs to us that Paradise is within us
> and of our own making. . . . Nothing is ever
> enough until *we* are enough.

I was intrigued by the cartoon depicting a modern jet liner that had just crashed and was sinking into the ocean depth. Two or three lifeboats were making their uncertain way filled with survivors and, in one of these boats, a woman turned to her husband to ask, "Alfred, are we still in first class?"

Now, by "growing out" I'm not talking about becoming the richest person in town, or the most prominent for that matter. I'm talking about selflessness, empathy, that insight into life that is essential for setting priorities.

Not long ago I received a letter from a man who is way up in his seventies, who wrote to fill me in on his activities. This fellow had been sick, very sick, and forced to resign his position as the comptroller of a snack-food company in another city and state. The job was just too much pressure for one in his condition, so he was resigning. And then he wrote, in the very next paragraph:

> I am now doing volunteer work at the hospital
> two afternoons per week. Also, I am active in
> my Masonic Lodge. Also, I am active in my
> AARP chapter.

There's a man who could teach us all about growth—outward and not inward. It was Lord Chesterfield who said, "Some live and die with all their greatness within them." And I say, "What a waste!" So, grow out, but not in!

II. Grow Up—But Don't Grow Old!

Second, we have to be sure that as we grow up, we don't grow old! Many of you know of Rabbi Dr. Abraham Twersky. Twersky is a Chassid, a rabbi, and he is a well-respected psychiatrist in our city. His great-grandfather was one of the grand rebbes of Europe. Once, while he was sitting with his Chassidim, the decision was made to celebrate the completion of the study of a talmudic tractate with a L'chayim. One of the group offered to pay for the refreshments, but there was no one who volunteered to go make the purchase.

According to Twersky, in his book *Generation to Generation*, his great-grandfather, the grand rebbe, said, "Just hand me the money, I have a young boy who will be glad to go." After a rather extended period, their teacher finally returned with the refreshments, and it became obvious to them all that the rebbe himself, their own teacher, had gone and performed the errand.

Noticing their discomfort, the rabbi explained:

I didn't mislead you at all. You see, many
people outgrow their youth and become old
men. I have never let the spirit of my youth
depart. And as I grew older, I always took
along with me that "young boy" I had been. It
was that young boy in me that did the errand.

You see, dear friends, there is no need to allow our growth
capacities to weaken as we age. Cast our complacency. Refuse
to become sedate and inert. To be forever striving for knowledge, for new insights, for fresh perspectives, that is the way,
Dr. Twersky reminds us, that we can all take youth along with
us far into old age. I've always been an Erma Bombeck fan.
She writes the following in a column titled, "If I Had My Life
to Live Over." Listen to this:

> I would have invited friends over to dinner even
> if the carpet was stained and the sofa faded.
> I would have sat on the lawn with my children
> and not worried about grass stains.
> I would never have bought anything just because
> it was practical, wouldn't show soil or was
> guaranteed to last a lifetime.
> When my child kissed me impetuously, I would
> never have said, "Later. Now get washed up for
> dinner."

"There would have been," Erma concludes, "more I love
yous, more I'm sorrys, but mostly, given another shot at life, I
would seize every minute, look at it and really see it, live it, and
never give it back."

Those of us in our middle years (you know, they claim that
there are three stages to life; youth, middle age and "gee you
look good"); those of us in our middle years hear carefully this
challenge of Erik Erikson. Ours is now "to choose between
generativity and stagnation, between continuing to have an
impact, or sitting around waiting to die."

III. Grow Strong, But Don't Grow Bitter

Go ahead and grow *out,* but don't grow in!

Go ahead and grow *up,* but take along that little child within you.

And, next, go ahead and grow strong, but don't grow bitter. Comedian Charlie Chaplin once said that the greatest gift that his mother gave to him was the large view of life. When his mother was eighteen, she eloped with a middle-aged man and they went to live in Africa.

The marriage was a failure, so she returned to London and married a struggling artist who fathered Charlie, but then died at thirty-seven. Chaplin's mother, once a singer, lost her voice; she lived on the edge of poverty, but nevertheless entrusted to her son a precious gift. Said Chaplin: "Mother was always able to stand outside her environment." We can grow to persevere through the ruts and disappointments of life without allowing ourselves to become embittered.

IV. Go Ahead and Grow In Faith

And finally, go ahead and grow in faith. The poet writes:

Oh, for a faith that will not shrink,
Though pressed by every foe.
That will not tremble at the brink
Of any earthly woe.
A faith that shines more bright and clear
When troubles rage about.
A faith in the time of pain
Keeps heart and knows no doubt.[1]

That's our goal, yours and mine, to find our way and to grow to such a faith. God intended each one of us to grow. Growth is built into life and we ought never to sit back with our hands folded in self-satisfaction. There are always, within each one of us, far greater possibilities for growth, but only *you* can or should be the final judge of that growth. Only you! And that's your responsibility.

A restaurant owner came to these shores from the old country. He kept his accounts payable in a cigar box, accounts due on a spindle, and cash in his register. "I don't know how you can run your business this way," chided his son, the accountant. "How do you know what your profits are?"

"Well, son," the father replied, "when I got off the boat, I had nothing but the pants I was wearing. Today your brother is a doctor. Your sister is an art teacher. You're an accountant. Your mother and I have a nice car, a city house and a good business. So you add all that together, subtract the pants, and there's the profit."

And so it is that this New Year's Eve, each of us knows best just how to honestly survey our lives, to examine our growth and to figure out the amount of our truest, most enduring profit.

A friend from my Georgia days—a preacher—was sitting in the departure lounge waiting for his plane. A young man sat next to him, looking at the minister as if he desired to talk. My friend had a lecture that he had to prepare and so he kept his head down, nose in a book. But the young fellow was undeterred. "What do *you* do?" the stranger asked. Not exactly sure how to answer, the reverend thought for a second, but the young man persisted: "What *are* you?"

The preacher surprised even himself when he quickly replied: "I'm a pilgrim." "What the heck is that?" "Surely you know what a pilgrim is!" "Yeah, but I thought they were all dead!"

"I'm another kind of pilgrim," the minister admitted. "I'm trying to find the way from birth to life!"

"Don't you mean from birth to death?"

"No," my friend said. He assured the young man that he meant just what he had said.

This night, dear friends, we are all of us pilgrims trying to find our way from birth to life; from what is to what may yet be!

So, go ahead and grow!

Go ahead and grow out, but don't grow in!

Go ahead and grow up, but don't grow old—take along that little child within you.

Go ahead and grow strong, but don't grow bitter.

Go ahead and grow in faith.

And perhaps thereby succeed in writing your own name into that legendary book. You know the one I mean, of course? The one for life!

NOTE

1. From a printed sermon by Robert Schuller. Printed in 1986.

Index of Contributors

Index of Sermon Titles

Index of Scriptural Texts